THE
SOVIET
TRIANGLE

THE SOVIET TRIANGLE

*Russia's Relations with China and
the West in the 1980s*

Donald R. Shanor

ST. MARTIN'S PRESS
New York

To Constance

Copyright © 1980 by Donald R. Shanor

All rights reserved. For information, write:
St. Martin's Press
175 Fifth Avenue
New York, N.Y. 10010

Manufactured in the United States of America

Library of Congress Catalog Card Number:

Library of Congress Cataloging in Publication Data

Shanor, Donald R
  The Soviet triangle.
    Includes index.
    1. World politics—1975-1985. 2. United States—
Foreign relations—Russia. 3. Russia—Foreign
relations-United States. I. Title.
D849.S44   327'.09048   80-240
ISBN 0-312-74906-6

Acknowledgments

BESIDES CONSTANCE, other Shanors, Katherine, Rick, Rebecca, and Lisa, helped in other ways. Columbia University deserves thanks for giving me time off for research and writing. The officials and diplomats, governments and institutions of the United States, the USSR, Great Britain, France, East and West Germany, Denmark, Sweden, Poland, Hungary, Italy, and Yugoslavia, as well as the North Atlantic Treaty Organization, cooperated in varying degrees. Particular thanks are due the Osteuropa Institut and Radio Free Europe/Radio Liberty, both in Munich; the Swedish Institute of International Affairs in Stockholm; Danmarks Journalisthøjskole in Aarhus, Denmark; the Universities of Edinburgh and Glasgow; the United States and Canada Institute of the Academy of Sciences of the USSR; the Federal Institute for Eastern and International Studies in Cologne, West Germany, and the Lehman and Journalism libraries of Columbia University.

Thanks are also due these individuals: Elie Abel, Erik Andersen, Jim Anderson, Maribel Bahia, Al Balk, Jonathan Beard, Charles and Mary Bierbauer, James F. Brown, Keith

Bush, Kevin Devlin, Martin Dewhirst, Wade Doares, Søren Dyssegaard, Arne Ejbye-Ernst, Osborne Elliott, John Erickson, Dr. Vilem Fuchs, June Gordon, Zdenek Hejzlar, Eva Hemmer-Hansen, Barbara Herne, Arthur and Donnelle Higbee, Alec Issigonis and the Morris Minor, Robert and Christine Korengold, Marilyn Lake, Dan Larsen, Ethel Leith-Ross, William and Elisabeth Mahoney, Hertha Mertens, Charles and Laurana Mitchelmore, Aline Mosby, Barrows and Dagmar Mussey, Samuel and Annette Rachlin, Edward Mayhew, Alec Nove, Bernard and Joan Redmont, Erik Reske-Nielsen, Leona Sargasta, George Sibera, Elizabeth Scheetz, Theresia Schramm, Gerd Smistrup, Dr. Theo Sommer, Karol Thaler, George Urban, Pat Van Gelder, Dr. Heinrich Vogel, Ralph Walter, Dr. Gerhard Wettig, Dottie Wood, Frederick T.C. Yu, and Mai Zetterling.

I cannot list the many other men and women in Eastern Europe who would not be helped by publication of their names, but without whom the book could not have been written.

Thanks, finally, to my editor, Barbara Anderson, who managed the difficult task of keeping a book project going at distances as great as those between New York and the Soviet Union.

Needless to say, none of the individuals or institutions that helped in preparation of the book can be held responsible for its imperfections, content, or findings, which remain my sole responsibility.

St. Jeannet, France, September, 1979, and
Chappaquiddick Island, Mass., January, 1980.

Contents

Part I

THE SOVIET UNION AND THE WORLD

1

Introduction

RUSSIA, CHINA, AND THE WEST. A new, triangular pattern is emerging in the world, a system that includes elements of both alliance and rivalry in the relations among the nations it encompasses. The triangle, with the Soviet Union and its camp on one side, China and sometimes Japan on another, and the United States and Western Europe on the third, came about because of the shifting of the old power blocs. But its relationships are much different from those of the classic postwar structures of power. The contemporary world is far too complicated a place to permit the movement of China from the Soviet to the American orbit and, because of this complexity, the new triangle can serve only as a rough chart to help predict political behavior, not as the table of organization of any new bloc arrangement.

The triangle was altered but not basically changed by the Soviet invasion of Afghanistan in the closing days of the decade of the seventies and the retaliatory measures taken by the United States in the opening days of the eighties.

Soviet-American relations were cooled, not broken, and Chinese-American relations were warmed, but not converted

3

into an alliance. Room for maneuvering was left on all sides.

The unusually large number of nations condemning the Soviet Union in the United Nations showed that Russia's move into Afghanistan belonged in a different class than previous Russian adventures in the Third World, the main difference being the use of divisions of Soviet combat troops rather than Soviet advisers.

But when the initial outcry subsided, and American officials began to admit privately just how hard it would be to persuade other nations to cooperate in U.S. embargo measures, the new diversity of international relations became clear once again. No nation—neither the United States, with its condemnations, nor the Soviet Union, with its growing willingness to use force to settle scores with other countries— has the strength any longer to have more than limited impact on the rest of the world.

This new complex world came about through many different processes in the years since the end of the Second World War. Nationalism, the independence of former colonies, religion, the struggle for oil and other raw materials, the expansion of Communism and the development of its ideological schisms, the American defeat in Vietnam and subsequent domestic crises, and the economic recovery of Western Europe and Japan were the main ones.

It is only necessary to recall the early postwar world to measure the extent of the change. In the fifties, the United Nations was half its present size, with sixty-seven members. A tiny minority voted with the Soviet Union and the rest more or less automatically supported the United States, so much so that the United States was proud of never having to use its Security Council veto. Only when India and Yugoslavia began the trend to nonalignment was there ever much need for diplomatic maneuvering. If North Africa presented a problem, France would handle it. Britain took care of much of the rest of Africa, and Latin America was no worry to the United States. If the question of China came up, it could be referred to Moscow, or perhaps to Washington.

That old system began to come apart when Britain and France freed their colonies and withdrew most of their armies from Africa and Asia, when Russia freed its technology and politics from the constraints of Stalin and began the push for space, military strength, and diplomatic initiatives under Khrushchev, and when minorities from Alabama to Cyprus began to assert their rights, with surprising success, against powerful adversaries. The collapse of the system accelerated in the sixties, as young Americans took to the streets to protest their government's support of unpopular regimes abroad, and as the Soviet Union turned allies into enemies by its misplaced zeal in forcing a particular kind of Communist behavior on the weak Czechs and Slovaks and the powerful Chinese.

All these disparate events and developments (and dozens more that cannot be catalogued so easily) converged in the seventies to create a world much more interesting, much more promising, but much more difficult for any single bloc or nation to try to keep under control. Africa's independence brought upheaval instead of peace in the countries remaining under colonialism and in those countries not satisfied with the system their own rulers had created. The former colonial powers competed with the United States, China, and Russia for influence; local governments competed with liberation movements. The process in colonial Asia took a different form, far more violent and tragic. Russia's industrial development and diplomatic activity landed it squarely in the middle of these situations. Russia could offer the emerging nations weapons and technology, in competition with the Americans and West Europeans. Concrete evidence of this capability could be seen as Soviet transport planes, advisers, and delegations spread out all over the world, exercising boldness or caution in direct relationship to their distance from the United States.

As the Russians (and the Chinese, for a time) entered a new imperialist phase, the United States was drawing back, bloodied and divided, from its own imperialism—a decade or so too late for the retreat to have been made as gracefully as the British had made theirs. But the mistiming on the part of the United States was not nearly so serious as the Russians' mistiming in their imperialist phase. The Russians were trying to found a colonial empire at least a century too late.

The fact that the Russians expanded as the Americans contracted has given rise to a great deal of preaching about a change in the world's balance of forces. There has been a change, but it is hard to argue convincingly that it is in favor of the USSR at the expense of the United States. It is, rather, in favor of diversity and against client and dependent relationships. The West was the first to recognize the new phenomenon and to change policies. Russia has refused to recognize it at all; far from relaxing its grip on its dependencies in Eastern Europe, it is trying to acquire other dependencies in Africa, Asia, and the Middle East. The same centrifugal forces that made the West yield, however, must work eventually for the East.

The United States gave up unwillingly in Vietnam but did not give up unwillingly in postwar Japan or Western Europe. No nation has ever done so much to promote the independence and prosperity of its potential rivals. The rewards were ample, it is true, and came in the form of trade ties and defense links. By contrast, the Soviet Union considers it necessary to keep occupation troops in its part of Europe and Asia, on the territory of its former allies as well as that of its former enemies.

The argument about a basic shift in power relationships comes mostly from Moscow (and from Western critics of détente). The Soviet Union has many reasons to argue that the "correlation of forces," as it calls it, has turned in its favor, whether or not its leaders believe this to be true. One reason is the bandwagon effect, intended to persuade the small states and liberation movements to join the winner, either in UN votes or in the acceptance of arms and advisers. A second reason is the pressure of Russia's military-industrial complex to keep ahead of the United States, justified by its claims of success in the race to date but perhaps concealing the need to catch up. A third reason would be the continuation, in other terms, of the "we will bury you" line of the late Premier Nikita Khrushchev. The old boasts of catching up with the capitalists in specific fields like meat production were quietly dropped, along with Khrushchev, and the dates set for catching up passed without the goals' having been achieved. Russia's present leadership finds it easier to use vague terms such as the balance of forces to present the same message: the inevitable victory of Communism.

Russia's claim of having a superior power position is more believable if one has first constructed an image of an immensely powerful United States, once able to have its way without opposition from anyone in the world, but now much weakened. The Russians never took this line in the first three postwar decades, of course; all one heard about was their great power. Much of the historical image of American power, it can be demonstrated, is larger than it ever was in life.

The best place to check the validity of Russia's claim is in the Soviet sphere of influence. It is true that American votes could overwhelm the Russians in the UN, but, when tough military decisions had to be made in the first years of the nuclear age, the United States either avoided those decisions entirely or watered them down. Would an all-powerful United States have permitted the six nations of Eastern Europe to become Communist? Would it have let the Communists win in China, or would it have had to resort to an airlift to break the Berlin blockade? What the United States was able to do in the world in those days was nearly the same as what it can do now: provide limited help through economic aid and encouragement of democratic trends. Where such methods have a fair chance of succeeding, which means in countries with a reasonably sound economic base—and geography far enough from the Soviet Union—then it does provide such help. Where they do not, there is criticism over loss of American "power" from enemies of the United States, and over loss of American "resolve" from its friends.

Those who consider factors other than rockets and throw weights still argue about an American moral weakness that cripples the West in its rivalry with the East. They base their arguments on the multiple crises of the Vietnam defeat, the Watergate affair, the revelations about the CIA and the FBI, and the changes in living patterns and the economy imposed by the oil shortage.

Other nations' ability to withstand similar crises is never measured, because they do not permit such crises to be talked about. The Soviet Union did not lose an Asian war; it did much worse, from its standpoint: it lost an Asian ally in China, the world's most populous nation, and then it drove that former ally into the arms of the United States and Japan. As of this writing, the Soviet leadership crisis is yet to come, but come it will, since there has never been an orderly change of power in Soviet history. Russia's CIA and FBI do not stand accused of any misdeeds, at least not at home; they are far too powerful to permit the first timid criticism. And Russia can appear to solve its energy problems simply by raising the price of gas by 50 percent and ordering citizens to write letters of praise.

A final factor in the examination of United States power in the world is to see who has gained by the new relationships.

The United States has not abdicated its position to another power, in the classic sense of Spain's loss of power to England in the sixteenth century. Instead, the United States is being overtaken by many smaller powers in a variety of ways, political and economic, as a result of their arrival on or return to the world stage. If this is happening to the United States, it is happening to the Soviet Union, too, in parts of the world where smaller powers can have their say and, more and more, even in parts of Eastern Europe.

This new world is a rather discouraging place for the ideologists, because ancient ties and enmities seem to count for more than modern theories, whether of Marxism or democracy. Countries such as Angola and Mozambique proclaim something called Afrocommunism but then water it down so that the old element, the Afro, outweighs the new, Communism. The same process can be seen working in the Eurocommunist parties of Italy, and Spain, as they become increasingly critical of Moscow and hence more Euro.

It is a discouraging place, too, for the power advocates. The United States despairs over the independent actions of the nations it helped to their feet in postwar Europe. Such countries devalue the dollar and lecture Americans on saving oil. They take their troops out of NATO and they side with the enemy on issues like the neutron bomb. But the Americans do not invade France and do not force the neutron bomb on the Dutch or NATO. They accept the fact that Europe thinks less of the dollar than it once did, with the consolation that the dollar did much to put Europe in that position. All this is often derided as weakness. But is temporarily winning arguments with armed force a sign of strength?

The problem for the Soviet Union, and for the nations that must follow its policies at home and abroad, is that it hasn't recognized the world's diversity. It is still trying to keep its part of the world in line, on the old basis of Marxism-Leninism, and to add to its domain, on the even older basis of European overseas adventurism. The repeated lessons learned from countries like Egypt, Somalia, and Iraq (countries that find Soviet advisers more harmful than helpful) seem to be forgotten.

China provided the main lesson about the changing world when it removed itself from Soviet ideological tutelage in the sixties and then went on to challenge the Russians in every area of the world: at the United Nations, on the Ussuri river, and finally in competition for the technology and friendship of the United States, Japan, and Western Europe.

China could do this (and Poland could not) because it is powerful, and East and West both pay attention to power. Although the United States formally advocates democracy and independence for Latin America and actively for Africa, where it has fewer business and political ties, it devotes far more genuine concern to the stronger partners like Germany and Japan, in summits and consultations, pacts and promises, because those countries are more able to make life unpleasant if they are neglected.

China was strong enough to be the deciding factor in the new triangular power relationship. With a China dependent on Moscow, it is obvious there could be no scope for the West and Japan to try to play off Russia and China against each other; this was the case for two decades. If China had remained in the isolation it chose after the break with Moscow, it could not have been used as a lever, either, because a lever must have movement.

It seems perilous to try to impose the clean, straight lines of a triangle on such untidy conditions as the contemporary world presents, and such a figure, of course, must leave out many factors. Nevertheless, it is one of the few discernible patterns. Moscow's relations with the more than 150 nations of the world are many-sided—as are those of the United States. But Moscow's special relationships with some nations, allowing among other things its right to intervene in the internal affairs of Eastern Europe and Afghanistan, is a little different from the special relationships the United States has with its closest allies.

The main lines of the Soviet Union's relationships look something like this: enmity toward China, with the door to negotiation left open a crack; equivocacy toward Japan, with some worry about its ties with the West and China but with eagerness for its trade and developmental help; competition with the United States in arms, in the Third World, in ideology (with spells of tempering behavior when technology and arms limitations are at stake), and in policies toward Western Europe; encouragement of France in its nationalism; discouragement of Germany in *its* nationalism; support for quarrels among other European countries and between such countries and the United States; and finally, because of the Germans, worry about what would happen if the United States did pull out of Europe.

There is diversity, too, in the line that links Eastern Europe with Moscow. Poles and Romanians are warned that the Chinese attack on Vietnam was the ultimate folly of nationalism and are told to dampen their own. The Poles nevertheless manage to keep polemics with the Chinese at a low level, and the Romanians continue to receive Chinese delegations.

Czechoslovakia, with little nationalism left, receives confidence-building measures, as does East Germany. They range from token withdrawals of Soviet troops to more consumer goods to buy in the stores. The Bulgarians are praised for their usual policy of not rocking the boat and serve as a useful example to hold up against the troublesome Romanians on their borders. The Hungarians manage to hold on to their marketplace economy, the best-functioning economy of its kind in the area, but are told to keep hands off in foreign affairs.

With the United States, frequent changes of the line are necessary. The Soviets say this is so because the United States changes its course so frequently between true détente and confrontation. And this, in turn, is caused by the rise and fall of the influence of "certain circles," not always identical with the government but always suspicious of Soviet intentions and unwilling to be reasonable. Things always improve with the return to ascendancy of the "realists," but the permanence of good relations can never be counted on.

The one reason that might be used to explain these shifts more satisfactorily—the actions of the Soviet Union—is never used. The Soviet Union considers that its policy, based as it must be on the principles of scientific socialism, is never wrong, although sometimes when new leaderships come along, it is admitted to have been wrong in the past. This makes the Soviet Union difficult to deal with, unless one pays less attention to what Moscow says and more to what it does.

What Moscow does is to talk peace but launch a massive military buildup on its Western provinces and along the Chinese border, cross other borders with troops to conquer Afghanistan, build up its navy into an attack force, engage in proxy wars in Southeast Asia, and spread out into other parts of the Third World.

All this has been accompanied by a great many assurances that Russia's only interest is peace. If Russian technicians and Cuban troops are observed in Ethiopia, helping to fight the Eritrean separatists whom the Cubans once backed, it is because they have been invited there by the government for peaceful construction and defense.

An invitation is also blandly cited for the invasion of one

of Russia's last independent neighbors, Afghanistan, although Afghans would be hard put to understand how their late President Amin would invite himself to be killed in the process. Consistency and the telling of the truth are not hallmarks of recent Soviet policy. Consider President Leonid Brezhnev's 1978 pledge in a West German interview that the Soviet navy had no aircraft carriers and did not plan to build any, and the 1979 disclosure that at least one Russian nuclear attack carrier was being built and probably had been under construction at the time of the Brezhnev interview.

Whether the sum of this activity adds up to the danger of World War III, a Soviet stranglehold on Western oil supply lines from the Middle East, or a plan to dominate the world is something that will be discussed at length in the pages that follow.

What is important for international relations in the short term, and for the Soviet Union in the longer term, is that much of the rest of the world calls these adventures warlike, not peaceful, and worries about them and, because of them, distrusts the Russians.

The Soviet Union has had some of its greatest international successes in the true pursuit of peace instead of war. It is easy to wage war, particularly in distant undeveloped countries with someone else's young men. Waging peace is much more difficult, particularly the kind of peace that brings no territorial gains and does not advance ideology. And yet waging peace is the highest calling a nation can aspire to. Russia apparently thought so when it called the Tashkent meeting in 1966 to end the Indo-Pakistani war—without territorial or ideological gain—or when it more clumsily tried to team with the United States to stop the British and French invasion of Suez in 1956. These achievements make the world admire the Soviet Union far more than do

Red Square parades of missiles and bellicose statements by marshals, and they gain for the Soviets the great power status they seek the world to recognize.

But most of the time the Russians only *talk* of peace. The *action* too often consists of thinly disguised movements in exactly the opposite direction.

It is possible that the Russians will learn by themselves that if the United States cannot function as the world's *gendarme,* then neither can they, and that they will try instead to emulate the United States' cautious emergence as world conciliator. Or will they have to experience, at first hand, the heavy costs in money, the neglect of domestic needs, the resistance at home, and the ingratitude of those presumably helped, as the United States did? It may be that Russia will not be able to skip this stage of development. Responsibility in the world arena may be something that must be learned by repeated failures of other policies, and perhaps there have not yet been enough failures. Assuming responsibility also must come from a deep conviction that such a course is desirable, and there are many indications that Soviet leadership has no such deep conviction at all, despite its constant professions of peaceful intent.

There may, however, be another way to convince the Soviet Union of the wisdom of more responsible and predictable behavior in world affairs. That is the leverage and the opportunity provided by the Soviet triangle.

Leverage can be applied, broadly, in two ways: by force and by persuasion. Full force consists of arming China; forming a military alliance among Beijing (Peking), Washington, Japan, and Western Europe; confronting Russia with this overwhelming show of power, as the Chinese say they would like to do; and simply telling Russia to behave. The Soviet reaction to this tactic cannot be predicted, but surely a preventive strike against the weakest member of this super-NATO (North Atlantic Treaty Organization) would be an option seriously considered. Even if Russia could peacefully accept its newly shrunken role in the world, the domestic repercussions would be enormous, and the trend would not be in the direction of liberalization.

Or the triangle could be used only for quiet pressure, to make it clear to the Soviet Union that when all the other powerful nations in the world are loosely, not formally, aligned against it, it might be a good time for some accommodation. The methods would be persuasion and encouragement, the means would be internal liberalization, and the goal would be a safer world. It should be added that the same kind of encouragement, and the same justification, should be given to liberal trends in China. The Soviet response to this second course is equally hard to predict. Moscow has managed to be quite resistant to previous attempts to liberalize it from the outside. But there has never been an alignment like the triangle for Moscow to have to deal with.

The United States must play a key role in the diplomacy to come, not only because it is the most powerful actor in the triangle, or because it is accustomed to leading Japan and Western Europe in foreign policy initiatives, but also because it matches the Soviet Union in strategic nuclear armaments and, despite the setback to SALT caused by the invasion of Afghanistan, is concerned about limiting them for mutual benefit.

The Strategic Arms Limitation Treaty talks remain in a very real sense hostages to Soviet behavior. Delay and distrust are part of the history of SALT, but throughout the ups and downs of U.S. Senate debate, Soviet invasions, and events in other parts of the world, the important thing is that the negotiators have always returned to the conference table.

Both sides dismiss linkage of SALT to other foreign policy actions, and both give the same reason: the chance to avert or limit the prospect of nuclear war is too important to waste by tying it in with other less permanent issues in world affairs.

Both sides practice linkage, however, despite their disavowals, whether the issue for Americans is a Soviet brigade in Cuba, the invasion of Afghanistan, or simply unrest in a third country such as Iran.

But both sides also eventually get back to talking. As one observer in Moscow put it, the situation is the same as that of two rival European powers of the nineteenth century, who, as long as their generals talked away from the field of battle, no matter how unproductive the meetings, knew that they were safe from war.

The necessity of the arms negotiations means that Soviet as well as American actions in other fields, now and in the future, cannot remain out of the considerations of the negotiating nations. Both sides may argue that putting a cap on the production and deployment of weapons of mass destruction is too important an endeavor to threaten with linkage of human rights or Third World wars. But it can be argued with equal force that the United States Senate, the ultimate arbiter of the treaties, does not consider these issues extraneous.

Quiet Soviet removal of the issues that block the SALT agreements of the future, along with commensurate reasonableness on the United States side, could thus have an effect on the prospects for a more stable world. There would be fewer areas of tension in international affairs, and there would be fewer weapons and better controls to help keep the remaining ones from leading to nuclear war.

2

Soviet Foreign Policy

IS THE SOVIET UNION an expansionist power determined to
spread revolution or acquire colonies in the Third World,
to seize control of the oil tanker routes of the Western industrial nations and Japan, to dominate governments through
Eurocommunists, Afrocommunists, or its own kind of Communists? Or is it a large and powerful, but inefficient and
underdeveloped, nation that considers itself encircled by
capitalist and Communist power alike, with strong enemies
west, east, and south and no allies of any consequence to
turn to for help?

The first view is dominant in the West, and it is by no
means the product of hawkish imaginations. Over the years,
the Soviet Union has been trying to push its influence far
beyond its borders and the borders of its dependencies,
through naval bases and a blue-water navy, through Communist regimes and liberation movements, through wars
fought by a Cuban expeditionary force and aid missions
staffed by East Germans as well as Russians, through invasions by Vietnamese and coups by Afghans, followed by invasions by Russians. Sometimes the effort to expand fails

17

and the Soviet advisers are forced to pack their bags, leaving
the expensive row of MIG fighter bombers on the airstrips of
the former partner.

But Soviet assertions of a worldwide role, which used to be
dismissed as bluster, now are listened to more closely. We
are now strong enough, the line from officials in Moscow
runs, "to exert tremendous and ever-growing influence on
the whole world; we are capable of influencing modern international relations in their entirety, the general direction of
their development." As these officials explain, this means
that Russia's voice, once only a factor in the Communist
world, is now a voice in the world at large.

From the standpoint of history, ideology, and perceived
strategic needs, there are many reasons for the Soviet Union
to seek such an expansionist role. Access to warm-water
ports and safe passage through straits have been a constant
in Soviet planning, as they were in czarist planning. The extension of Communism to other countries and continents is
believed not only to provide those places with benefits, but
also to benefit the exporting country as well. The nations that
have become Communist since the Second World War may
not seem to offer much advantage to the Soviet Union, but,
in Soviet eyes, the situation is far better than its prewar position of isolation.

There is also a missionary factor to be considered: The
Russians claim that they want to help the world's downtrod-
den, although the regimes they set up never seem to be much
better than the original oppressors.

The Soviet Union seeks expansion for some very important negative reasons, too: to remove movements, countries,
areas, and continents from the opposing powers, whether
Western or Chinese, and to reduce the size of opposing
powers' spheres of influence while at the same time extending their own.

With all these convincing rationalizations for pushing out-ward, there are many others, internal and external, that make it far more likely that the Soviet Union will be looking inward, for the most part, in the decade ahead, with occasional thrusts into other territory that will alarm and alert the rest of the world.

Some of the reasons for Soviet caution are the result of choice; most are the result of necessity. Conservatism is as traditional to the Soviet leadership as the search for ice-free ports and distant satellites; because the first exists, the second is often abandoned as too risky.

The problems of governing so large and uncertain an empire as the Soviet Union make it less feasible to try to extend it. A monolithic Party and a powerful military impede expansion every bit as much as they encourage it. The nation lacks the flexibility to deal with a whole range of problems it shares with the rest of the world—slowing rates of economic growth, energy bottlenecks, inflation—and those problems that trouble authoritarian governments—human rights and dissidents, dissatisfaction among religious and national minorities, and the problem of making an orderly change to the next generation of leadership.

This is why the classic Russian siege mentality and expansionist ambitions can exist side by side, but also why the attraction of the old and safe fortress Russia is likely to dominate.

The red-brick Kremlin walls, 13 to 16 feet thick, 26 to 55 feet high, and a mile and a quarter around, are such an obvious symbol of the Russian siege mentality that care must be taken not to oversimplify. Since the twelfth century the hilltop fortress has dominated Moscow, but it was not until 1958 that the public was permitted to enter parts of it. About 150 years before that, Europe's other cities had torn down their remaining walls and forts, creating the pleasant parks and ring boulevards their people enjoy today. Russia, of course, had its modern capital of St. Petersburg for a time, but the Bolsheviks saw fit to return to governing from behind the walls.

In an office overlooking one of the Kremlin towers, on a day when *Pravda*, the Party daily and authoritative voice of the leadership, has simultaneously attacked the foreign policies of Japan, China, West Germany, the European Community, and the United States, two Soviet officials * held a wide-ranging briefing on foreign policy. What went in was a thorough and carefully reasoned justification for Russia's actions in Africa, Asia, and the Middle East, and a confident rejection of any idea that the shifts of China and the United States into a new alignment left the USSR uncomfortably isolated in the middle. What came out, in this and dozens of other conversations and interviews in the Soviet Union, was a feeling of uncertainty and concern not far below the surface, and between the lines of the confident and even arrogant phrases.

The talk was of tropical Asia, Central America, and Africa, but outside, the 20-below-zero temperatures sent clouds of steam from subway entrances and formed frost patterns on the Kremlin masonry. Heat seeped through the cracks in the old doors along the street, and where it met the sharp cold, frost outlined the cracks, softening the squared corners and curving with the decorations on the panels.

Editorial attacks made that day on all the other major powers of the world could not be interpreted as an expression of Soviet isolation or encirclement, I was told. There is no encirclement in the age of nuclear rockets. The Soviet

---

* Under ground rules agreed to with my Soviet hosts, names, titles, and even organizations of the men and women I interviewed may not be used, hence the somewhat wearisome repetition of "officials" in the pages that follow.

Union may be surrounded by powers not presently friendly to it, and it may be encircled by their rockets (Chinese shortcomings in weaponry were emphasized in passing), but Russia also encircles its adversaries with its own enormous and universally respected missile force. Thus encirclement is outmoded as a way of looking at things.

Or is it? "Of course we feel encircled," the senior of the two officials, interrupting the practiced routine of the briefing, said. "But that is nothing new. What is new is that you feel this, too, since the age of the intercontinental missile. The United States lived for nearly two centuries in absolute security from attack. We have never known that security, from the interventions of the Allies after World War I, to the Russian Civil War, to World War II, and—even with more friendly governments on our borders since the second war—with the encirclement of United States missiles on our other borders."

As the briefing returned to its regular course, the weaknesses of Russia's adversaries and the great strengths of the Soviet Union were stressed. The Soviet Union is a world military power, and all its citizens know that. As individuals they are not afraid. But perhaps the citizens of other countries ought to be. China, in fact, seems to fear Russia, and with good reason: The Soviet military created the Chinese army, and the Chinese respect Soviet strength. Japan has no foreign policy independent of the United States' wishes; Germany has realistically accepted the loss of its eastern territories and showed that "even with hatreds we can have good relations."

The United States criticizes the Soviet Union for domestic and foreign policies it has long practiced itself, denying human rights to minorities at home and dominating small governments abroad. The United States supports dictators in Latin America and then attacks Russia for supposedly supporting them in places like Ethiopia. It is true that there is violence in Ethiopia, just as there has been in Nicaragua, and it is true that Soviet advisers are very much involved in Ethiopian affairs. But there are differences. The Russians, it is stressed in a ghostly echo of Washington briefings during the Vietnam war, are in Ethiopia because the lawful government there has invited them to come, as they have invited the Cubans. Another difference is the ultimate goal of the bloodshed. Where the United States is involved, bloodshed is rationalized as a means to preserve privileged and even feudal regimes. Where the Russians are involved, bloodshed is seen as assisting the inevitable progress of world revolution, of more progressive classes replacing those deemed less progressive. Violence may be necessary; it is, as Engels said, the midwife of revolution.

"Ethiopian soldiers are killing feudal remnants. In Latin America, American-supported soldiers are trying to maintain feudal rule. That is the difference: yes, Ethiopia kills, but Ethiopia wants to make people happy."

That rationalization was an extremely hard act to follow, but two other important sets of Soviet official opinions on the questions of foreign adventures and encirclement ought to be appended to make the record more complete.

In another interview, it was stressed that Latin American and Asian dictators must choose the United States to help them because of their level of historical development, and that revolutionary leaders of the same countries must turn to the Soviet Union because they represent a higher level, as does the USSR. All this is inevitable and set down in the writings of Marx and Lenin. It does not seem to explain Soviet help for someone like former Ugandan leader Idi Amin, but it does serve to quiet doubts about colonialism.

Thoughts on encirclement were offered in an on-the-record interview granted to West Germany's *Spiegel* magazine by Georgii Arbatov, head of the U.S.A. and Canada Institute of the Soviet Academy of Sciences, adviser to the Politburo, and America expert: "Imagine," said Arbatov, "if America had the armies of the Warsaw Pact to its north, instead of Canada, its ally, and that instead of Mexico to the south it had a state that demanded, let's say, New Mexico and some additional territory, and besides had a population of 850 million and a noticeable and growing nuclear potential; and in addition, it had, instead of two oceans, Germany and Japan—then the United States would probably acquire a much stronger conventional defense force."

Arbatov's conclusion was that the Soviet Union had two choices: to seek a security arrangement with the West, or to tighten belts and build a defense force that would be able to prevent another attack like Hitler's in 1941.

The Russians, in fact, seem to have decided to follow both these policies, in tandem with a third one of hitting out at targets of opportunity in that belt of unrest, poverty, and violence that circles the world on both sides of the equator.

Building up an arsenal is fully consistent with a siege mentality, and diplomats in Moscow who have followed the path of Soviet intervention in the Third World consider that, too, to be just as consistent. It is natural to try to break out of the encirclement, even though the ring of distant missiles and bases is less of a physical presence than the armies of neighboring kings of a century ago. Soviet support for the 1978 Communist coup in Afghanistan is a good example. It was designed to add a reliable ally as well as to establish a corridor to Pakistan and Iran. That it failed to work out that way was a surprise to Soviet officials, because they do not ordinarily advise moving into a situation without plentiful assurances of victory. They chide Americans for backing lost causes, and they assess each new coup and appeal for arms from all aspects to make sure that Russia always backs the winning side. Others can be ignored or allowed to maneuver and battle in obscurity or be crushed. When their chances in war improve, so do their chances of help from Moscow.

Afghanistan was an exception, because no one had gauged the power of Islam and the resistance to Communism in the country, and no one had predicted the speedy victory of the Islamic revolution in neighboring Iran and the spread of its appeal beyond Iran's borders, an appeal that caused serious concern about the future behavior of the Soviet Union's large Moslem population.

Nationalism, religion, conservatism, human rights, the economy, problems of the military and the Party leadership, the challenge posed by the other nations of the triangle: all are better keys to understanding possible Soviet behavior in world affairs than are attempts to understand the Russian soul or convenient symbols like old men making secret decisions behind the medieval Kremlin walls. Each will be examined in turn.

The conservatism of Soviet leadership is a thread running through Soviet governments from the beginning, teamed at first with radical slogans and a few revolutionary proposals like the publishing of secret czarist treaties and the ceding of vast territories to put an end to the First World War on the Eastern front. Soon the People's Commissars became ministers again, and the Soviet Union became the most conservative major power in the world. It has learned through internal and external threats to preserve what it has and to take as few risks as possible to do so.

Conservatism does not rule out the occasional venture on other continents, but, until the special situation of Afghanistan, it did dictate a protocol of using other nations, as well as domestic forces, in the front-line positions, so that if the venture failed it could be blamed on the Cubans or the South Yemenis, not on the Russians.

Conservatism also means that the pluses and minuses will be carefully weighed, but always with more weight on the side of caution. This provides guidelines for Western analysts trying to figure out Soviet intentions. They know that if they come down on the conservative side, they are usually right.

A radical Russia would have set up an independent republic inside Iran in the early days of the Islamic revolution; a radical Russia would have established an airlift for Cuban troops to help overthrow the Somoza dictatorship in Nicaragua. Conservatism does not mean giving up hopes of power or influence in such areas, but waiting until time and circumstances are more opportune, success more certain, and the reaction of adversaries less likely.

The sobering effect of nationalist stirrings inside the vast Soviet empire makes caution outside its borders more likely. But any regime ill-advised enough to abolish a national language from a new constitution, as the Russians did with their Georgian republic, at a time when language and ethnic demands are being granted and fought for all over the rest of the world, does not show much political sensitivity. The Georgians angrily took to the streets and got their ancient language recognized once again as the equal of Russian. But as a citizen of the neighboring republic of Armenia described conditions in the trans-Caucasus in a series of Moscow conversations, Russia's avowed aim is integration and absorption of all fourteen Union republics into the great Russian one, whatever the Soviet Constitution's claim that "a Union Republic is a sovereign Soviet socialist state that has united with other Soviet Republics in the Union of Soviet Socialist Republics." It could also be noted that the republics are guaranteed constitutions "with the specific features of the Republic being taken into account."

The republics are the Soviet restructuring of the old czarist empire, which splintered when the Bolsheviks took power and had to be brought back together by force of arms in the first years of the Soviet state. Georgia, Armenia, and Azerbaizhan, across the Caucasus mountains on the Empire's rim, were among the longest holdouts. Their history since then, according to the Armenian in Moscow, has been one of resistance, against the odds, toward the Sovietization and Russification process. Every time a factory is built, he said, it is hailed by the local press as progress, but the Russians provide the technicians and most of the work force as well. These modern carpetbaggers stay and intermarry; Armenia has a new factory but has lost some more of its identity. The ancient Armenian church has served as a bulwark but has suffered, as churches have in other societies, from the same modernization and industrialization that are undermining Armenian traditions in other ways; people simply don't go to church as much as they used to.

The Armenians don't want to hold back progress and are proud of their relative prosperity, but they wonder whether it could not be accomplished without the destruction of their culture.

The opposite viewpoint was argued in conversations with a citizen of a republic no less ancient and traditional, Uzbekistan. As with the Armenian, the conversations were held in settings that put no damper on frankness. The Uzbek was a middle- or high-level manager in one of the state enterprises. Intensely nationalist, he was nevertheless far more positive about the contribution of the Soviet state to the Uzbek people. All the Asians in the USSR, he said, were brought into the twentieth century by Moscow, and although the system they live under is by no means perfect, most appreciate the strides made in 60 years. People whose parents could not read or write and who rise to relatively high posts in their society might be expected to be grateful, but his view transcended such narrow limits. And, in contrast to the official propaganda, he stressed how very much alive the Islamic faith was in the republics of Central Asia. A devout and practicing believer himself, he saw no conflict with his Communist Party membership, but he did mention wryly that the Moscow Communists underestimated the power of Islam, considering it an outmoded way of life that would soon disappear, and as a result granted it far more concessions—including religious weddings and the other family rites—than were permitted the Russian Orthodox Church, which was perceived as the real danger.

The Uzbekistan citizen departed from the official line as well in his admiration for the achievements of China, the nation across Uzbekistan's border, and thought that American help might succeed in developing China's backward regions just as Soviet help had done in Central Asia.

Two voices from the 140 or 150 million non-Russian Soviet citizens do not even constitute a sampling of a sampling. But the issues raised by both are not new. These issues have been debated in the press and in the trials of dissidents, brought up in protest demonstrations, and made capital of by China and other nations.

These "centers of falsehood abroad" must be combated with more energy, the Communist party secretary of the Soviet Turkmen republic, Mukhamadnadzar Gapurov, said in a long 1979 white paper on the difficulty of stamping out the influence of Islam in his republic, which borders both Iran and Afghanistan. "They direct unrestrained propaganda for nationalism, for pan-Turkism, and pan-Islamism," he said. The report went on to complain about the domestic manifestations of Islam, including the growing influence of holy men and the fact that even good Party members continue to take an active part in religious rites.

These troublesome republics are getting relatively bigger, and European Russia relatively smaller. Ethnic Russians constituted 53.4 percent of the population of the Soviet Union in 1970. The 1979 census figures did not state the proportion as clearly, but analysts believe the ethnic Russians are at 50 percent or less. The Soviet population, which totaled 262 million in the 1979 count, had grown by an average of only 0.9 percent a year in that decade. The lowest total rates of growth were the 6 percent figures registered in the Slavic republics: the Russian, the Byelorussian, and the Ukrainian. The highest were in the Moslem republics of Central Asia, and they ranged from 28 to 31 percent.

Hélène Carrère d'Encausse,* the French authority on the Soviet nationalities, notes that the statistics are heavily weighted by the increasing urbanization and higher education in European Russia, where family size ranges from an average of 1.77 to 2.08 children, depending on income. Families in the Moslem republics average from 3.88 to 4.22 children.

The Moslems are not only growing at a much faster rate, she says, but also they are making use of their religion to get around the domination of the Communist Party and the Great Russians sent to run their republics, usually as behind-the-scenes second secretaries of the republic party, not as top men. They do this by playing down their religious differences, as between the Shiite and Sunni Moslems, and emphasizing Islam as a community. Every Moslem, practicing or non-practicing, can feel a part of this cultural tie. Moslem leaders in these republics say that socialism is acceptable to their followers, since both systems have identical goals. They have adroitly sidestepped or revised the religious duties of a good Moslem, such as fasting, praying, and making pilgrimages, to conform to the demands of modern Soviet life. Unlike other religious groups, the Moslems encourage their children to join the Young Pioneers, Komsomol, and the Communist Party. The parallels with the attitudes and prac-

---

* In her book *L'empire éclaté,* Flammarion, Paris, 1978.

tices of Polish Roman Catholicism toward a Communist leadership are striking.

The Poles will never outnumber the Russians, but there is every likelihood that the non-Russians inside the Soviet Union, from the Caucasus to Central Asia, already do or soon will.

All the net increase in the Soviet labor force and one in three new military recruits will come from non-European Russia in the eighties. The new workers will not want to move to the industrial centers of old Russia—not to mention to Siberia, where the most pressing manpower needs are—and many of the new soldiers will not be able to speak Russian.

At the minimum, these trends put the republics in conflict with Moscow over the allocation of resources. At the maximum, they push the Soviet Union toward the point at which empires historically have proved to be impossible to govern, when the colonial population too heavily outweighs the home population.

But even in the European homeland, most prominently in the Ukraine, there is a dissident movement seeking decentralization, or at least a stop to the systematic Russification. Human rights will be discussed in detail later, but suffice it to say that dissidents seeking greater autonomy for nations long under Soviet domination may pose some hindrance to Soviet plans to dominate others.

Economic problems, however, are more of a factor than the still-weak voice of dissent, and it is clear that the immunity the Soviet Union long enjoyed from worldwide trends, whether real or the result of juggling of figures, is past. Between the lines of the Five Year Plan are labor shortages in some areas and disguised unemployment in others, inflation concealed by an increasingly heavy burden of state subsidies for basic commodities and not compensated for by adequate pay raises, and apparently insoluble shortages of meat and a wide variety of consumer goods. Standing in line is a way of life in the Soviet Union; there seems no way for the chronic shortages to be solved, after decades of tinkering, decentralization, recentralization, and firing and hiring of those supposedly responsible.

The one exception to the shortages had always been energy; Soviet consumers and industry long enjoyed cheap oil, as well as electric power and other fuel. Because of the great resources of the nation, particularly in Siberia, much of it really was cheap, and where it was not, the prices could be kept low by the bureaucracy. In the early eighties, however, the prospect arose that energy lines, for individuals and factories, would form in the Soviet Union as well.

As long as the Plan ruled, the market did not matter. But markets elsewhere began to rise after the Organization of Petroleum Exporting Countries' (OPEC) 1973 blockade, and the Soviet Union, although not an OPEC member, found that it could get four times the earlier prices when it sold oil abroad and be paid in dollars besides. The world price surge in oil happily coincided with the massive retooling of Soviet industry with Western technology, and with the need for hard currency to pay for it. The days when oil and gas were treated like water were over. Domestic prices went up, too, and domestic supplies began to be limited.

Then came the controversial forecasts of Western analysts that sometime in the eighties the Soviet Union would become a net importer, rather than an exporter, of oil. Soviet officials deny the accuracy of such forecasts. But their figures do show a decline in the rate of growth of oil production in recent years, if not an actual production drop.

There is less heat in the denials of the more general Western forecasts of a decrease in overall growth rates. Soviet officials say the economy has expanded at such a high rate for many years that some contraction is natural, and they point out that Western nations, too, are experiencing such decreases. But the Soviet economy has other long-range problems the West does not: not enough hard currency earnings to continue the modernization program for industry at the needed pace, a continuing need for expensive grain purchases to make up for the inefficiency of state and collective farming as well as the vagaries of the climate, and such marginal increases in living standards that few incentives are provided for the improvement of productivity.

Could these economic ills become a reason to argue for expansionist policies rather than the more sensible ones of concentrating resources on needs at home? History is full of such examples, but the pattern of Soviet expansion to date is reassuring. The only nations Russia has been able to penetrate have been those that are without many resources and hence poor and desperate enough to accept a Soviet presence. Thus the first years of the new colonialism have clearly been a drain on resources rather than a means of supplementing them; Moscow may well wonder what it is doing wrong that the British did so right.

A weak but oil-soaked nation would be a tempting new target, but the international risks that such an attempt would call into play would be too high, given the conservative stance Moscow has exhibited thus far.

Such caution is to be expected now more than ever because of the inevitable task that lies ahead: that of installing a new generation of leaders.

Three statements can be made about Soviet leadership changes: they are infrequent, they are accomplished by palace revolts (since there is no other mechanism for them), and they require a long time for the final results to become settled.

The backstage coup that brought Leonid Brezhnev to power in October 1964 was only the fourth change since the founding of the Soviet state. The United States managed to change presidents eleven times between the Lenin and Brezhnev eras; all the Russians needed was Stalin, a short spell of his successor, Georgi Malenkov, and Khrushchev in between.

The Party statutes provide for Party congresses every 4 years to elect the Central Committee. The committee in turn chooses a fifteen-member Politburo from whose ranks the top man is selected by democratic vote. The actual process is somewhat different, as shown by the occasional glimpses afforded by former participants (above all Khrushchev in his memoirs). What is important, however, is the uncertainty, the lack of institutions, and the impossibility of successors' being groomed successfully (Malenkov was the only successor so designated, and he was quickly scuttled by his colleagues not long after his mentor, Stalin, was in his grave).

It took 4 years for Stalin to come to terms with all his rivals in the first change of power in the twenties, after Lenin's death. Indeed, it could be said that the struggle did not really end until the Alpinist's pick crashed into the exiled Lev Trotsky's skull in 1940 in Mexico.

Stalin's successors also needed 4 years to eliminate the various anti-Party groups, beginning with the execution of Lavrenti Beria, the secret police chief, and continuing through Malenkov's dismissal and that of V. M. Molotov, the former foreign minister, and his cabal, and the elimination of Prime Minister Nikolai Bulganin and the war hero Marshal Georgi Zhukov.

Brezhnev's coup d'état against Khrushchev, only 7 years after the latter had emerged as sole leader, was tidier; only minor adjustments like the sudden removal of a figurehead president were needed to tighten the leadership team.

In the past, during these long interregnum periods, Moscow's foreign policy did not go through any radical changes. The energies of those remaining on top had to be directed at consolidating power in Party bodies. The only exception was the short-lived Beria plan to grant broad concessions to East Germany, and it was aborted with Beria's removal and execution. Khrushchev tinkered with foreign policy in his first years, before the leadership question was finally settled, but his innovations were peace offensives, not acts of war or conquest. Brezhnev had been expected to attempt to heal the breach with Mao Zedong after ousting Khrushchev, chief target of Chinese criticism. But Brezhnev offered no real departure from the former line and thus lost the opportunity for Chinese rapprochement. If future behavior can be predicted on the basis of a long and consistent record in the past, the leadership changes in prospect, first round or second, will not bring sudden explosions of foreign activity.

Leadership transition will also not bring about very great differences in leadership style or policy, in the view of those who follow the rise and fall of Politburo fortunes. Not until the year 2000, former Moscow correspondent Robert Korengold has determined, will anyone be ready for the top post who has not had his education or early experience in the bureaucracy under Stalin, with all the implications that has for narrowness of outlook. Diplomats serving in Moscow during what they felt was the end of the Brezhnev era looked in vain, in the biographies and statements of anyone remotely considered a successor candidate, for any new departures.

The world had a telling example of the results of the Soviet practice of selecting and replacing leaders during the Vienna summit meeting to sign SALT II. Television images of Presidents Brezhnev and Carter were startlingly effective in contrasting the fumbling old man and the vigorous middle-aged one; Carter seemed positively bouncy by comparison. There are plenty of bouncy potential presidents in the Soviet Union, but there is no system that would bring them to the top in the way that Carter, the unknown from Georgia, managed to rise. An ambitious native of Soviet Georgia might reach the republic leadership, but if he were very innovative or questioning of the central leadership, he would go down instead of up. These are the qualities that attract attention in both systems. In the American, they often lead to advancement; in the Soviet, they almost always lead in the other direction. Carter represented a successful opposition candidate who chose to attain power outside the regular Washington hierarchy. Both opposition to the incumbent and maneuvers outside the hierarchy are foreign to the Soviet system, where the rules are: get in line, win promotion by loyalty to those above, do not question their policies very much, and stay healthy, because when they die you may be chosen to replace them.

To the Soviet Union, the Western system of selecting leaders is arbitrary. uncertain, and a sign of weakness rather than strength. Real strength, Soviet officials say, lies in permanence of arrangements, not pandering to public opinion, and if the Soviets nevertheless stress the democratic nature of the Soviet system, it is in terms of the people's confirming and approving the decisions of the leaders, not of their making those decisions themselves.

Thus the characteristics of the Soviet system are not dynamism and change but solid anchors of security: territorial, military, and ideological.

The size of the Soviet Union, and of the Russian empire before it, and the mere fact of its having so many neighbors, have led it historically to try to dominate the territory around it and to seek alliances, both with the aim of enhancing its security.

World War II, fought and won at such terrible cost to the Soviet people, left the USSR with a double ring of dominated nations on its Western side, and one vast one, China, to the south and east. The ring begins with the Union republics, from the Baltic to the Caucasus. It is made up of nations that were once independent or would have liked independence; all escaped the Empire for a time, but all were brought back under Stalin's formula: "Proletarian in content, national in form." This meant that each nationality had the right to choose its own course, as long as that course was socialist. And being socialist meant being subordinated to the Great Russian majority, despite paper guarantees of the right of secession.

The second ring is made up of nations still nominally independent. It was added to by conquest or coup after the Second World War and comprises Eastern Europe and, less securely, Afghanistan. Of the great bulwark on the other side of the world, only Outer Mongolia remains.

The loss of China shows the high price that attempting to enforce relations of friendship and cooperation exacts. It is expensive to keep troops and armies of loyalty inspectors in neighboring countries, but the truly great cost is the loss of trust and reputation that such policies lead to.

The Soviet Union has every right to be concerned with the policies of Poland, Afghanistan, and its other neighbors, and to wish to influence them through diplomacy and aid. It has a total of thirteen neighboring countries, sixteen if one counts the annexed Baltic nations, from Norway in the northwest to Japan in the Far East. But the Soviet Union has not trusted the normal kind of relations to provide it the security it feels it needs against threats from abroad. Hence the constant striving for "safer" allies, the kind whose policies are certain to please Moscow since they are made, or at least frequently checked for approval, in Moscow.

But this kind of security is not popular with the nations that can get away with rejecting it. No neighbors have been able to join China and Yugoslavia in this course, but no other country, near or far, has shown the slightest indication to enter into any kind of binding alliance. And thus the super-safe policy of foolproof alliances has left the Soviet Union with no real alliances at all. Czarist Russia was able to make partnerships with and against France, Germany, Poland, England, and Austria, changing allies to suit its security needs. Soviet Russia has been unable to play this classic European power game. Its last major continental alliance, the Hitler-Stalin pact, resulted only in the German invasion.

A nation in relative isolation, which considers itself still threatened by the outside interventions it has experienced so many times in the past, will typically choose the safe and the sure for its internal system. In the Soviet Union, the safe and the sure is the Communist Party. The Party may be unwieldy, and it may be costly to the nation in terms of morale and living standards as well as in the stifling of new ideas, but it has managed to run the state—after a fashion. Party officials are well aware of its shortcomings; nevertheless, the decisions made three-quarters of a century ago by Lenin are confirmed again and again by each successive leadership team. Power will not be shared by the Party, whatever the cost, and the Party will direct every facet of society, from the permitted shapes of modern sculpture to deciding whether the Jews are a religious community or a nationality.

The solid bulwark of the Party is backed up by the equally solid military. The average Russian is never allowed to forget the part the military played in winning power in the civil war and against foreign intervention. Power won in the twenties was power preserved in the forties, when the Red Army turned back the Wehrmacht. The blunders that nearly caused defeat—the purges of generals as war clouds were gathering, Stalin's refusal to heed warnings of the impending German attack—are not mentioned too loudly. Revisionist historians can find no work in the Soviet Union, and the retelling of the tale in its countless versions does not vary much from the straight brand of patriotic history that used to be the fashion in the West. Those who fought are honored citizens, with civilian suits weighted down with medals. There is a kind of small-town-American-Legion simplicity about it all: The men who fought in those distant days saved the country, and now they are respected and rewarded. The men who were too young feel very much left out, although their need for medals can be supplied by Party decorations for economic heroism. A military career, real or invented, is as much a political asset as it is in the United States (where every postwar president except Lyndon Johnson was propelled into politics by military service).

It was worth standing in line at the Tretyakov Gallery in Moscow to see the iconlike portrait of Brezhnev as a young officer—actually, he was a political commissar—and to watch its effect on the men and women filing by. In full Socialist realism, it shows Brezhnev at Novorossiisk, on the shore of the Black Sea, surrounded by an appropriately representative group of soldiers and sailors. There is no actual halo, but there is a suggestion of one. The painting is hung in a part of the gallery devoted to scenes of factory and farm, Party meetings, muscular workers, and the other staples of the realistic school, and thus it takes visitors by surprise. This first reaction is followed by a faint smile of recognition, then a quick look around to see whether anyone noticed, then a return to the original look of indifference.

The American Legion doesn't have much of a role in American society anymore, but there has been no diminution of the Russian Legion's role in the Soviet Union. Until there is a Soviet Vietnam—a major defeat in some Third World conflict—the military will not lose any of its importance. And thus, although economic growth may slow to the 3 percent annual rate predicted for the eighties, there will be no slowdown in military expenditures, which will continue to grow at the rate of 4 to 5 percent a year and continue to constitute 11 to 13 percent of the gross national product of a country too poor to afford such a vast outlay.

Even in the periods when generals do not sit directly on the Politburo, the military has been able to maintain its strong role in decision making and resource allocation. The state industrial bureaucracy, facing manpower shortages because of the slowing birthrate, cannot get the military to give up its claim on the nation's young men; a continuation of the present draft rate, projections show, would draw in eight of ten 18-year-olds coming of age in the mid-1980s.

Because of its power to have first call on resources and manpower, the military is one of the few branches of the Soviet system that really works. Western analysts are sometimes critical of the lack of flexibility displayed by individual commanders during maneuvers, but in discipline, supply, and, in particular, arms and equipment, the Soviet army, navy, and air force are given high marks by those who make a study of them. In fact, in contrast to their usual run of export offerings, Soviet arms are very much sought after. Design innovations in tanks, warplanes, and small arms result from the high priority that military research and development has in the Soviet Union. Much sought after and much sold abroad: arms sales are estimated to be running at an annual rate of $21 billion. (The Soviet sales figure is about half the American, because the Russians give away as much as they sell.)

Along with the arms exports these days, however, go ideological exports, as could only be expected from a society that pays so much attention to the correct interpretation of Marxism-Leninism. This particular export of ideology is less Messianic and more precautionary. The Russians were tired of experiencing a series of events in the Third World that went like this: a radical government makes overtures for friendship, advisers, and aid; weapons are shipped in; and the government is either overthrown or decides on its own to remove the Russians but keep the arms.

Now Soviet arms salesmen are accompanied by Soviet ideological salesmen whose job it is to couple the delivery of weapons with certain basic agreements in point of view. If possible, the recipient should organize his followers into a Party of the Marxist-Leninist type, although it need not be called Communist, and in most cases ought not to be. Such conditions are difficult to swallow for someone who has come to power in a guerrilla war or domestic upheaval, or for someone who is still trying to come to power. It is not a question of learning the niceties of the doctrine, but of accepting its basic tenet, the one East Europeans smart under: the primacy of the wants and needs of Moscow. It also often means handing important posts in the movement or government to locals who have been trained in Moscow, who then compete with those who came up through the ranks during the days of struggle. Finally, it means that solutions to the nation's problems will be put forward on the basis of wholly irrelevant Soviet experience. Ethiopia's decision to establish collective farming was defended as a step forward from a feudal land relationship, which it certainly was. But the fact that it was introduced by Soviet advisers in a year when their own rich agricultural country bought a record one-tenth of its grain needs from the West, partly due to weather problems but also partly due to inefficiency, makes one wonder how much advice like this the Ethiopians need.

But from the Soviet viewpoint, the export of ideology makes good sense. Central planning, the militarylike organization of the Party, the impossibility of organized opposition, censorship, and a strong security arm to ward off counter-revolution: all can be found in Lenin's interpretations of how Marx would have organized a Communist society, and all have proved successful in the gaining and holding of power. The costs, both human and economic, are not counted, because Lenin also teaches that there have to be a few broken eggs in a successful revolution.

A victorious ideology leads quite naturally to certain feelings of superiority on the part of those who hold the keys to progress. These feelings come out in conversations, and, only a little below the surface, in official statements. "They truly believe that they are superior, that their system, and their people, are of a higher order," a European diplomat in Moscow said. "Furthermore, with their professed belief that history is on their side, they will someday be able to show this superiority to the whole world."

Others familiar with the phenomenon interpret it as evidence of a massive national inferiority complex. The experience of a Hungarian intellectual supported this view and also showed that superiority is not linked with being Communist, but with being a Soviet citizen. He had tried to get a book published in the Soviet Union with a rather innocuous theme of the need for world peace for all nations. He found that Soviet editors refused to accept his thesis that all the peoples of the world are alike in their basic striving for peace. All the peoples of the world are *not* alike, he was told. There are Soviet people, and there are the others. Only the Soviet people were purified by the revolutionary struggle; only they have created true, real socialism. The writer went away with two lessons learned: he had better revise his book, and he had better stop thinking that even members of other Communist parties, citizens of other Communist states, like himself, had reached the Soviet stage of development.

It would be hard to remain indifferent to the temptations of asserting superiority in a society so steeped in a doctrine of predestination. Like its religious precursors, Soviet doctrine emphasizes postponing real happiness until the next world, useful solace when standing in line for pork chops or theater tickets in the Siberian cold of Russia. Soviet doctrine further resembles religion in insisting that the movement may not *want* to control the world, but that objective laws say that someday it *must*. The future thus sketched out is of grateful people in all parts of the world joyfully seizing the doctrine and making it their own, not having it forced on them.

But as with the other inevitable movements of history, it doesn't hurt to help the cause along a little. Rendering this help in such a way as to avoid scuttling the whole project in a nuclear war will be the main impulse of Soviet foreign and military policy in the years ahead.

The method, as shown to date in Russia's record in the Third World, will be to start with the weak links in the world system and, if successful in these areas, to use that success and these new allies as resources for extending the plan.

The Soviet Union is not strong enough to challenge the systems of government in the West and Japan, and both sides know this. Despite all their talk about unemployment and inflation in the democracies, the Russians know that these societies are never going to try to solve their problems with such a totally unsuited kind of remedy as Soviet-brand Communism. They are even less likely since the Soviet economy has begun to contract its own ills.

The Soviet Union may turn to Italy, France, or Portugal, to name some weaker links, to support local Communists in the hope of a sudden overturn of middle-road parties. But this policy carries with it all sorts of risks: in retaliation from the West, in trade, in arms buildups, or in a cooling of détente—most of all, in the uncertain nature of the policies a popularly elected Communist Party would follow. To stay in power, such a party would have to continue to be critical of Moscow (the Portuguese might manage one without the other), and this attitude would be difficult for the parties of Eastern Europe to deal with.

Thus, despite the clear attractions to Russia of Communist governments in NATO countries, better opportunities are afforded by countries offering less risk. There are a number of conditions that candidate countries must fulfill.

First, the situation must be so desperate that help from Moscow seems to be an improvement. A good example would be a nation in which one military clique has just overthrown another. There is no question in these cases of returning to pluralism or democracy; it never existed, and the new rulers are just as anxious as the Soviet advisers that there be no counterrevolution, which means no free press or legal political opposition. The main rule of a Communist takeover has always been to change the rules to make the takeover irreversible as soon as you have the power to do so. In places such as South Yemen and Ethiopia, this tactic presents no great philosophical or ethical problem. Staying in power is often reduced to a matter of watching the younger officers.

The second condition is a great need for national reconstruction, which is to say that the economy must be in as disastrous a state as the political life, so that promises of Soviet aid can be coupled with promises and deliveries of Russian arms. It is no coincidence that the six nations where Soviet influence has grown the most in recent years—South Yemen, Vietnam, Cambodia, Ethiopia, Laos, and Afghanistan—are at the bottom of World Bank tables for income and most other economic indicators. They are also out of other nations' normal spheres of influence—the Southeast Asian nations after considerable struggle, with Cambodia perhaps reluctant to leave China's sphere of influence—and isolation is the third condition. The Soviet Union makes fun of the Monroe Doctrine but by and large observes it. Africa does not pose the challenge to American hegemony that an expedition into Latin America would, and this is why the Cubans have been fighting so far from home.

But the fourth condition is that the country in question cannot be so isolated and unimportant as to cause no harm by coming under Communist influence. It must afford its new allies the chance to come down on the side of right and humanity (although the record here is not very consistent) and at the same time to cause pain to the Soviet Union's adversaries by its new allegiance.

Southern Africa fits most of these categories, particularly if the point of view is that of the black guerrilla, not the white ruler; it is not surprising that it has begun to emerge as the main new theater of action in this probing of the weak links. Western diplomacy in the region shows that the United States and its allies place equal importance on future developments in Namibia, Zimbabwe, and South Africa itself. Does this mean that battle lines are drawn, and that there will be airlifts of troops from both sides? It need not, because the Soviet Union's adversaries have many other ways of dealing with the outward push of Soviet influence.

These adversaries can begin by disputing the premises: Nothing in Marx can remotely justify the airlifting of Soviet or Cuban battalions to settle accounts in the developing world, and if the Soviet Union insists that all these actions are inevitable, no attention need be paid to such claims. Russia's opponents can continue by trying to alleviate the conditions that make people want to turn to such a system as a lesser evil.

Through diplomacy and embargoes of grain and technology, through freezing cultural exchanges and suspending the other advantages of détente, they can make the Soviet Union consider more carefully the effect that future foreign adventures would have, both for the state of the Soviet economy and of world peace. But embargoes and freezes are often difficult to maintain, as the Carter administration learned in the very first days of its Afghanistan retaliations. Even if they can be kept up, they often have the opposite of the political effect intended.

The new element in the equation is China. Trade, exchanges, scientific cooperation, even what Secretary of Defense Harold Brown, on a visit to China a few days after the Afghanistan invasion, called "complementary" defense action—all can be established, or expanded, between the United States and China. Besides being desirable in itself, such a course demonstrates to the Soviet Union that real cooperation is possible between the United States and a Communist power, if only the Communist power is willing to behave in the international arena.

But if the triangle is to work, it is not enough simply to transfer these relationships from the Russians to the Chinese. It should not be either/or. The United States may wish to move China into the position the Soviet Union had as the main beneficiary of détente, but it should not make China the sole beneficiary. That would leave the West with no leverage with the Russians—nothing to embargo, suspend, or chill as a deterrent to future invasions—and, as a result, would make the world an even more unstable place.

3

Russia and China

IN THE SPRING OF 1969, the first year of the Soviet occupation of Czechoslovakia, a dusty convoy of Soviet army trucks moved down a back road in the middle of the country bearing an astonishing message. Since the previous summer, the "Russians go home" signs had faded from the cities and the highways, but here, written in the dust on the tailgates of the huge trucks, were other statements from occupied to occupier: "To the Ussuri," "Go occupy China," and other variants to make the same point. There was fighting on the Chinese-Soviet border, and instead of a powerful ally in Asia, the Soviet Union now had a powerful enemy.

The clashes on the Ussuri river frontier in March 1969 and the failure of the final meeting between Premiers Alexei Kosygin and Chou En-lai 6 months later meant that for as long as anyone could reasonably predict, the differences between the two great Communist powers had become irreconcilable. The most important shift in international relations since the immediate post-World War II period had taken place.

This new stage in East-West relations had implications far

beyond those of the loss of a satellite, even such a huge one, by Russia. The Sino-Soviet break was a decisive factor in a whole series of changes between East and West—in détente, arms limitation, trade, and freedom of movement for some Communist parties. It led, by circuitous routes, to the human rights controversy, and to the reconciliation of China and Japan for the first time in 40 years. Some of these changes were initiated by the Soviet Union as a result of the break, some were mutual, and some came about, against Soviet wishes, through the opportunities afforded by the break.

For the Czechs and Slovaks, the Chinese border fighting meant a brief flareup of hope, some more slogan writing, and then disappointment as the chill of the occupation continued. It proved not only possible but also quite easy for a military machine the size of the Soviet Union's to police two sets of borders at once.

Czechoslovakia's and China's situations were related in many ways, despite the 2,400 miles that separated them. Both had begun as allies of the Soviet Union and had ended up being dominated by their partner. Both had changed Communism from the standard Moscow form, and both had been punished for it. The differences between Czechoslovakia and China mattered more, however. It was easy for the Soviets to impose obedience on a small country, and very difficult to impose it on a big one.

What happened to the little country in 1968 had an important effect on the big country. The invasion of Czechoslovakia showed the Chinese leadership how far the Soviet Union was prepared to go to prevent deviation from the path it dictated for the socialist camp.

The Chinese had approved the invasion of Hungary, a dozen years earlier, because to them it meant the crushing of a counterrevolution that would have thrown the Communists out and returned Hungary to the Western side. But the use of armor and troops in Prague was wholly unjustified, in the

Chinese view, since the Czech and Slovak reformers wanted to keep Communism and make it work. If Czechoslovakia could be crushed, who would be next? China's interpretation of the doctrine enraged the Soviet ideological arbiters as much as the Prague version had; only the difficulty of a punitive expedition against China seemed to stand in the way. But after Prague, the Chinese did not rule out such an invasion. As a Chinese diplomat in a Western capital put it, the Prague invasion "had the real sense of showing us the true face of social imperialism. We had known in the previous ten and twenty years what the Soviet Union was like in its relations with other states, even Communist states. Our planning after that took this possibility into active consideration."

There is no direct link between the use of force in 1968 in Eastern Europe and its use less than a year later in the Far East. No one has been able to figure out for certain how the border fighting on the Ussuri started, but clearly it was nothing on the scale of a Soviet punitive expedition against Maoist heresy, and it is just as likely to have been caused by a Chinese attack.

But just as the Prague events had driven home to the Chinese leadership the seriousness of Soviet intentions, the river battles and the other clashes that followed elsewhere on the border between China's Sinkiang province and Soviet Central Asia that summer of 1969 showed Russia the force of Chinese enmity.

Russia reacted with unusual flexibility. Within half a year of the shots fired on the Ussuri, Soviet diplomacy had changed course 180 degrees, and a new Soviet course, opening to the West, was being pushed with great energy in the capitals of Europe and the United States.

These openings followed with remarkable speed the final closing of the door to China. Kosygin and Chou had their final, futile meeting in Beijing on September 11, 1969. On the very next day, the German chargé d'affaires in Moscow received an answer to a note that had been ignored for weeks. In their reply, the Russians agreed to a German proposal for non-aggression pact talks. At the same time, it was announced in London that the Soviet government had accepted the suggestion of the three Western powers for a new round of talks on Berlin. Within 2 months, Soviet and American negotiators were meeting in Helsinki for the first round of SALT. All these ventures were proceeding under a new definition of Soviet Westpolitik, put forward by foreign minister Andrei Gromyko that July. The new definition conceded, for the first time, that good relations between Moscow and the West might be possible on a broad, general front, not limited—as they had been previously—to playing one Western partner off against the other.

The stage was set for that interlocking structure of treaties with the West that secured Russia's Western approaches, brought the Russians the benefits of Western technology and trade, and limited strategic arsenals, freeing some Soviet resources and research capability for the conventional and medium-range weapons for China, the more likely target on the other side of the world.

Other factors helped shape this new East-West relationship, of course; France and Britain had laid the groundwork for it in the earlier sixties, and the United States had made probes that were mostly abandoned as the United States became more involved in Vietnam. Russia sought trade and technology because its experts had finally convinced its leadership of the need for modernization throughout industry. But the growing apprehension about China's threat pushed the Soviets further than they would have gone otherwise.

This China factor made the Soviets agree to lift some of the legendary Russian secrecy about armaments in the SALT negotiations and give up much of their ability to make Berlin and its access routes a source of tension. It led them, at the Helsinki conference on European Security and Cooperation, to accept unpalatable Western provisions on human rights in exchange for guarantees of secure borders and the renunciation of claims to the old German territories in the East.

It forced them, too, to grant freedom to disagree with the Moscow line to the Communist Parties of the West and even to one of the East (Romania). All could have been expelled from the world Communist movement, which they, in any case, said had ceased to exist. But the de facto expulsion of China had not proved salutary.

Did China really cause all this? Soviet officials insist it did not; they contend that all the changes in Westpolitik came about because Soviet strength grew to the point at which the West finally had to recognize it and begin a new relationship on the basis of equality.

Nevertheless, when the day comes for a future generation of Soviet leaders to calculate the cost of the policies of the sixties, someone will have to answer the question of who lost China. It might be argued that Chinese intransigence played as great or greater a part as Russian intransigence did in the split, or that it was a blessing in disguise to Moscow because of all the Western benefits that resulted. But Russia is a nation that takes its internationalism very seriously, and the loss to its camp of nearly a billion people is a disaster compared to which the earlier American loss of China seems mild indeed. In the forties, America backed the wrong leaders and ended up with an annoying adversary in Asia that later turned to it for help. Russia, a nation in far greater need of allies, lost the most powerful ally it could ever have hoped to have.

A second loss of almost as much importance is that the break between Russia and China showed not only differences in the way Communist societies should be run, but the fact that such differences are possible. No single version of the doctrine is universally acceptable. Perfectly respectable revolutionaries, men who won wars and who manage vast economies, can differ with the hallowed writings and practices. Moscow may denounce the Chinese as members of a clique (what must surely be the largest clique in the world) but their credentials are accepted by others looking for social blueprints. And finally, the Communist differences caused large numbers of people to question both conflicting versions of ideology, as well as most others. The continuing weakness of both Moscow line and Chinese model Parties in the West—where members have a choice—is witness to the cost of this squabbling over doctrine.

For Russia and China, the seventies ended in warfare and unabated hostility. Direct clashes were infrequent and minor, like the brief flareup on the Sinkiang border in 1979, just as low-level talks on the conflict were to resume between Soviet and Chinese negotiators in Moscow. Neither the talks nor the clash brought any basic change to the border situation.

Both powers fought more seriously in proxy wars—China's against Vietnam, the Soviet Union's ally, and Russia's against Afghanistan, a campaign that threatened the security of China's ally Pakistan.

At the start of the eighties, it was possible to draw up a Sino-Soviet balance sheet that took all those ideological, political, and military factors into account.

For the Russians, China still represented a dependent that got away while still immature, a former friend and ally now an enemy on the battlefield, in the Communist movement, and in the power relationships of the world. Chinese soldiers have killed Soviet soldiers and become the first enemy to do so since the hated Germans were driven away in 1945. The two sides patrol the longest (4,200 miles) and most potentially explosive border in the world.

In Party affairs, the Soviets have never forgiven the Chinese for questioning Moscow's position as leader and arbiter, all the more so since their criticism of the bourgeois tendencies of Soviet Communism and their own ascetic practices under Mao had such an effect on the true believer. As they became more prosperous, the Russians really were neglecting their basic, egalitarian doctrines.

"The Russians have never even forgiven the Yugoslavs for their mild heresy thirty years ago," a former European ambassador to Moscow said. "They cannot admit that the Soviet Party is wrong and any other Party is right. They cannot come to terms with another Party's right to be different. They do not and cannot recognize that such a right exists."

Ascetic Communism—rather than Soviet Communism— had more initial appeal in the Third World, but the far greater ability of the Russians to deliver the arms and the advisers paid off in the end. And thus China remains a rival in the developing world, but a much weaker one than it had been. China's new pragmatism tips the balance even more in Soviet favor: Beijing can no longer preach purity and egalitarian aims, since it has abandoned them at home, and it can no longer afford the costs of the ambitious Third World aid programs it once sponsored.

"If we have a dollar to spend abroad or at home, what proportion of it should go to helping our own needs first?" a Chinese diplomat asked. "More and more we must answer that our home development needs come first. But that doesn't mean that we have given up our revolutionary mission, what you would call spreading Communism. We cannot do this as long as there is a single oppressed nation, even a single oppressed person, in need of help in the world."

The new Chinese course in foreign policy, too, means that Third World activity must be subordinated to the needs of getting along with the West. The Chinese cannot condemn Soviet adventures in Africa and Asia while simultaneously conducting their own, although in the Indochina fighting of 1978–1979 they managed to do so. The Americans could look the other way when China attacked Vietnam, since that was a conflict within a region already lost to them, but they could not ignore some new incursion elsewhere. As long as the Chinese place such high value on their Western ties, such considerations ought to dampen their ambitions in the Third World as much as their limited resources do.

For the Chinese, Russia has long represented Big Brother, first in the favorable and then in the unfavorable sense of the term. The Soviet Union supplied much of the arms and advisers that enabled Mao to defeat Chiang, although the Chinese now contend that Soviet help was of no decisive importance. Russia also supplied the ideology—but this, too, is disputed.

In any case, when the quarrel became serious, Russia withdrew both its technicians and its approval of the way Chinese society was being run, and this was perhaps worse than not having helped at all. It is widely believed in the Soviet Union that Russia wasted $2 billion in aid and investments in China. The Chinese contend that Soviet help came in the form of loans, not grants, and that all were paid back. What rankles them most is that the development programs never really got a chance to get started before they were terminated. China might have done as well in its early modernization if it had tried development solely on the basis of its own resources.

Russia also represents the Czars, the power that took territory from China when it was weak. Bolshevik Russia promised to return the territory, but at that time there was no revolutionary government in China, and by the time there was one, Russia somehow never got around to keeping its promise.

Russia, in short, represents strength and a constant reminder of China's weakness. The Chinese have failed in every previous attempt to redress the balance. They tried to outflank Moscow in the world Communist movement but found no real allies. In the West, even the admirers of Mao now turn to Albania as the only remaining model of revolutionary purity. China's tests of strength on the Soviet border turned out to be further displays of Chinese weakness, and even the attack on the outnumbered Vietnamese failed to convince the world of China's military power.

This disparity in power, in the view of a Chinese analyst now in the West, is the key to the enmity between Russia and China, and all the other reasons—ideological, territorial, and political—are subordinate to it. If the disparity had been greater, as it is between the Soviet Union and countries like Poland and Hungary, then even the most ambitious Chinese politician would have had to agree to a subordinate role without hope of challenge. But as it was, the powers were close enough, at least in potential, to make the challenge worthwhile.

According to this analyst's view, the real beginning of the split came about in 1949, when the Soviet Union took the first step to subordinate Chinese wants and needs to its own, and when the first Chinese challenge was defeated. It was the time of the Korean war, when Russia decided to play its China card to force the United States off the Asian mainland.

China was as concerned about the American presence in Korea as were the Russians but did not want to fight them, particularly not at that time. Mao had promised the Chinese people that their war of liberation would be their last war. The Chinese economy was in deep trouble and in no way suited to the demands of war. All the nation's energies were needed, instead, to recover from the civil war and to make Communism seem an attractive alternative to the decades of fighting and want. But Mao argued these points in vain in his two months of Moscow talks with Stalin and other leaders in 1949. The first set of proxy troops, the North Koreans, were not considered enough, and the Chinese, despite their objections, were forced to agree to join in the fighting.

Chinese officials do not accept this version of events in Korea. They contend that their nation had no hesitation about coming to the aid of the North Koreans, particularly when the war reached their borders. Having succeeded, in the seventies, in winning North Korea away from Soviet influence, the Chinese would have little to gain by being depicted, 30 years later, as a reluctant wartime ally.

How and why Russia made use of this first playing of the China card will be fully explained only when Communist history becomes considerably franker. Until it does, one line of argument may have to serve: that under the conditions of the Soviet-Chinese relations of the period, it would have been impossible for the Chinese to have acted the way they did in Korea without the approval of the Soviets, or against their wishes, just as it was a generation later for the Cubans.

The power to seize and defend territory is another aspect of the problem, and the Russians have had this power for more than a century, through changes of government systems on both sides. Chinese propaganda about the "new Czars" is more than a clever turn of phrase. The czarist treaties of Aigun, in 1858, and Peking, in 1860, ceded the area east of the Ussuri to Russia. It was a period when the rest of the world was also carving off chunks of the Manchu Empire: the French in Indochina, the British in the Himalayas, the Japanese in Formosa, and the Russians in other sections of the borderlands.

Mao told Edgar Snow in 1936 that he wanted to get these lands back. And in the fifties, the Chinese began to publish their famous maps, showing what areas had been lost to the various imperialists between 1814 and 1919. The total area in dispute is enormous: as large as France, West Germany, Great Britain, and the Benelux nations combined. The Russians contend that there is nothing to argue about, and that raising claims at this late date is nothing other than naked expansionism. Even when the two sides agreed to discuss the issue in 1962, the way each described the talks showed how far apart they were: China called them "discussions about corrections of the borders," and Russia, "explorations for confirmation of the borders."

"Russia didn't take territory from the Chinese; it took it from local tribes," a Soviet official said. "China used to be defined by what was behind the Great Wall. What was outside that, in the days of czarist expansion eastward, wasn't China—and it was up for grabs. They have no claim to those territories. It is as though Mexico demanded Texas and New Mexico from you, or we demanded Alaska and part of California, which after all we used to own. There must be an end to this, and that is what we have achieved in Europe. Even the African states, with borders left by the colonists, insist on the inviolability of those borders. There is no other reasonable way of proceeding in international relations."

What the official referred to as local tribes is one of the two immediate causes of the border fighting, especially along the Soviet Central Asian-Sinkiang frontier, where non-Chinese Asian nationalities live on both sides of the border. When Chinese repression got too bad in the early sixties, many of these nomadic peoples began drifting over into the Soviet Union. There were incidents with police and troops on both sides of the frontier, the apparent basis for Peking's charge in 1963 that there had been 5,000 such reports of trouble in the previous year alone.

Neither side can point with very much pride to its record of treatment of the minorities along the frontiers. A member of the small group of Mongolian intellectuals, in a conversation in a city outside Moscow, told the story of his own people in terms devoid of propaganda effects. "We are treated like blacks by the government of South Africa," he said of his 1.4 million fellow citizens of Outer Mongolia, the Soviet puppet state that serves as a buffer against China.

"But that is nothing to the way our Mongolian kinfolk are

treated across the border in China," he continued. "There it is a simple matter of national survival, and the Chinese are determined we will not survive as a people. Mongolian youth, men and women, are moved into the cities of the interior, with offers of jobs or education. They do not often come back, or if they do, it is after marrying Chinese. At the same time, Chinese people are sent to Mongolia to take their places, and they, too, intermarry.

"Soviet policy is difficult for our nation. There is far too much Sovietization, Russification, in Outer Mongolia. But for all their excesses, we do not feel they are trying to destroy us, only to dominate us. That cannot be said of the Chinese."

The other immediate cause of the border fighting is the shifting channels of the frontier rivers, the Amur and Ussuri, in the Soviet Far East. Border forces of both sides use the changes as excuses for claiming bits of sand that did not exist on one side or the other in previous years. That was the basis for the dispute over Damansky Island, the enlarged sandbar that the Chinese call Cheo Pan, in 1969.

The first clash was company-sized. Ten days later it resumed, with regiments armed with mortars, tanks, and artillery thrown into battle from both sides. The Chinese lost "hundreds" in dead and wounded, the Soviet Union said; Russian losses were put at thirty-one killed.

Territorial claims, shifting channels, claims on the loyalties of peoples on both sides of the frontiers: both sides admit privately that some settlement could be found for all these issues if agreement could be reached at the top on the basic differences that keep Russia and China apart. Both Moscow and Peking have the authority, and the lack of opposition, to sweep aside unpopular details when they feel there are larger stakes. Otherwise there would be no British Crown colony of Hong Kong and no agreement permitting Soviet citizens of German origin to emigrate freely.

But there is no sign of any wish for agreement at the top. Chinese diplomats, asked if the new pragmatism in Peking would not logically encompass an effort to reduce tensions with Russia, said there is no connection between the two.

Soviet officials concede that the border clashes are a symptom, not the basic illness, but it seems difficult for them to frame any kind of overall agreement to cure both without insisting on a full retreat on the part of the Chinese.

With this seeming impasse along the lines where their interests directly clash, China and the Soviet Union have moved their rivalry to other theaters. Militarily, they have engaged in proxy wars in Southeast and Southwest Asia. Diplomatically, they have fought a curious contest for the grace and favor of their old enemies, the United States and Japan.

The Chinese know that even if their wildest hopes of territorial concessions were ever granted, the Soviet Union would remain an immense Asian power, with its might spread across seven time zones from the Urals to the Amur river border with China, over the tops of Iran, Afghanistan, Pakistan, India, China, and Japan.

This represents Soviet strength and Chinese weakness, and both sides know it. When the two economies are compared, the gap is even more apparent. Russia, with a quarter of the population of China, has more than double the gross national product. Per capita, the 1978 World Bank figures were $3,010 for the Soviet Union, $410 for China. China is rich in people and undeveloped natural resources, yet Russia is better off in both respects. It could use more settlers in Siberia and the far north, it is true, but it is not saddled with the task of feeding such a huge populace, and its resources, to date, seem to be greater than China's.

Nowhere was this difference in strength more evident than in the two Asian wars of 1978–1979, when Vietnam, with

Soviet backing in materiel and advisers, overran China's ally Cambodia and then put up a spirited fight against the Chinese punitive invasion.

Russia ended Vietnam's carefully balanced neutrality in the Sino-Soviet dispute in November 1978, forcing the Vietnamese to sign a treaty of friendship and alliance as a counter to China's newly concluded treaty with Japan. Soon afterward the veteran Vietnamese units began to move into Cambodia. They were supposed to be Cambodian opponents of the Khmer Rouge, organized in exile by the cooperative Vietnamese, but the attempt at deception was so transparent as to appear deliberate. Soviet officials made only weak attempts to deny suggestions that the liberation force was a Vietnamese army. "They raised a dozen divisions in ten days," a Chinese diplomat said. "It was as though they were telling the world that the liberation movement was a farce and, in the process, challenging us (Chinese)."

If the quick victory in Cambodia showed the world China's weakness in defending its allies, China's retaliation, although intended to show strength and resolve, did little to promote China's image, militarily or morally. It is hard to sort out the truth when two Communist nations are fighting and making conflicting claims, but some objective evidence, such as the 3-to-1 ratio of prisoners taken, does support Chinese claims of a victory over its much smaller neighbor. There are indications, however, that the victory was bitter.

In the first place, it did great harm to the image of the new China that Mao's successors had worked so hard to promote in the West and Japan. Although the Chinese made it clear from the start that they did not intend to conquer territory, the news of Chinese units crossing international frontiers brought back memories of Tibet and India and the specter of an expansionist power.

"A blunder, really," was the way a British diplomat and China expert put it. "It showed that they are unreliable, everything that the Russians say. The smaller nations in ASEAN (The Association of Southeast Asian Nations) were shaken by the invasion. They will be reluctant to join with China in any plan for an Asian security zone."

The United States felt the shock of the attack most of all, because its timing at the end of Deng Xiaoping's visit to the United States to seal the new relationship gave the appearance of collusion against Vietnam.

"America didn't play the China card; China played the America card," a Soviet diplomat in a Western capital said. "It used the Deng trip to plumb the depths of anti-Soviet feeling in United States government leadership circles. Then it used this knowledge to launch its attack on Vietnam."

This view is a little more sophisticated than the line taken by *Pravda,* which charged Chinese-American collusion. But whatever the real thinking in Moscow, it is clear that China was able to force the United States into a position of at least appearing to be hitting out at Vietnam again, this time through proxy armies. Such a position was good neither for the United States' image in the world nor for its relations with Soviet Union.

But the main effect of the Vietnam affair was felt by China. "By talking about the possibility of teaching Vietnam a second lesson," the British diplomat said, "they show how much the first failed. No one thought they were all that great militarily before Vietnam, but now we are certain."

Officially, the Chinese cannot be expected to agree with such assessments of weakness. But what emerges in conversations with Chinese diplomats is the feeling that the lesson that was supposed to have been taught the Vietnamese was one for the Chinese instead.

It is a lesson of Chinese weakness and Vietnamese and Soviet strength, although no hint of this appears in the official statements. In the first place, the Chinese armed forces' performance showed the Beijing leadership how much the national problem of backwardness is reflected in its weaponry, logistics, communications, and organization. In the second, Vietnam's reputation for fighting was enhanced, and the threat posed by the "Cubans of Asia" made more real. Chinese officials do not use the term "containing the Vietnamese," but that, in effect, is the situation they face on their southern flank in the years ahead. And finally, the war showed the firepower advantage the Soviet Army enjoys. Chinese officials admit to being impressed by the number and performance of the Soviet weapons used in Vietnam. And the Russians can be assumed to be saving their really impressive weaponry for the defense of the homeland.

All this added up to a more sober Chinese attitude toward the resumption of talks with the Soviet Union on the border dispute, particularly when the coincidental slowdown of the Chinese modernization program is taken into account. The demands of Chinese farmers and consumers for a larger slice of the pie mean that the technological advances that would have been passed on to the military will come much more slowly.

The Russians, too, probably had second thoughts about the entire series of events in Southeast Asia touched off by their treaty with Vietnam. They finally succeeded in making Vietnam decide for them and against China. They found the Vietnamese very useful in pushing over China's ally, Cambodia. But they also helped Vietnamese ambitions in the area by these two actions and ultimately may learn, as did the French, Americans, and Chinese, how difficult it is to control them.

But the main loser was China. And the more its weaknesses and deficiencies are revealed by such events, the more one wonders what the Soviet Union is so worried about. By any standard—production, national income, development of science and technology, even government stability and predictability—the Soviet Union is in a leading position, and there is no indication that any closing of the gap can take place very soon. Despite its inefficiency, mismanagement, and widespread discontent, the USSR will reach the magic year 2000 many strides ahead of China.

And yet, even before the falling-out of the sixties, there was a China fixation in Russia, and since then it has increased sharply. The East always seems to become the main topic of conversation when foreigners meet Soviet officials or ordinary Russians. "We talk about the weather for a few minutes, and then a little about their business," a Western trade official said about receiving Soviet delegations. "And then they start asking me about China." The East means Siberia as well as China (actually, mostly to the south of the USSR), but the two are linked. The Soviet leadership had looked to Japanese and American capital and technology to develop Siberia but now is worried that the developing will be done instead in China. And this, in turn, gives rise to fears of a strengthened and aggressive China, one more able to close the gap.

Russia's is a defensive reaction, threatening but essentially inward looking, brashly confident but often somewhat doubtful: The concerns expressed publicly and privately are those of a nation that again feels itself threatened by encirclement.

How genuine the feeling is becomes difficult to measure. But it does seem safe to say that in the decade after the border fighting China became the single greatest problem for the Soviet Union in areas of decision making, ranging from missile modernization to concessions to the West. That was China alone. When China's treaty with Japan was added, followed by the normalization of its relations with the United States a few months later, the threat from China was seen in a different light: It was not what China was, but what it might become.

Events have been moving too fast for the conservative Soviet leadership to cope with. These old men are used to slow deliberation. They consider time, along with territory, the traditional defenses of Russia. Thus Soviet negotiators took their time—more than two decades' worth—in their peace treaty talks with Japan. They refused to surrender the four southernmost Kurile Islands or island groups annexed during the 9-day Soviet participation in hostilities against Japan in the closing days of World War II, or even to split the difference at two islands apiece. Giving back territory might be seen as a reversal of history's irreversible direction. And it might give other nations ideas.

The islands total only 4,244 square miles. They stretch to the north of Japan's main northern island, Hokkaido, with the closest, Habomai and Kunashiri, nestling within 70 miles of Hokkaido. There are other Kuriles and other islands in the Northern Pacific, including Sakhalin, a large island important for gas and other raw materials, that have changed hands between Russia and Japan, but neither side is disputing ownership.

The Japanese contend that the four islands in question— Habomai, an island group, counts as one, and Shikotan and Iturup are the others—were not part of the Japanese conquests of the thirties or World War II, as were Sakhalin, Manchuria, and other territories surrendered by the Japanese. The South Kuriles were peacefully acquired by treaty or purchase from Russia. The Soviet Union will have none of this: "To demand the return of the South Kuriles," a Soviet official said, "is simply to attempt to revise the results of World War II." Soviet statements on the issue have an air of finality about them: "There is no territorial problem in Japanese-Soviet relations." The Russian position is based on Japan's unconditional surrender and Allied agreements at Yalta. Japan contends that the USSR was not a party to the first, and that the second dealt only with territory illegally occupied by force of arms.

But legalities seem less important than the effect of the dispute on Russia's relations with Japan. If that relationship is deemed important, along with the prevention of Japanese-Chinese rapprochement, diplomacy ought to be able to find a way through the legal barriers. When the record is examined from the standpoint of what would have been good politics, Soviet behavior seems puzzlng indeed.

Immediately after the war, hostility to Japan did constitute good politics. Condemning the Japanese imperialists went over well with their chief victim, China, and strengthened the new Soviet-Chinese alliance. Japan, in fact, was made the main target of the Sino-Soviet friendship treaty of 1950. At a time of Korean war tension in Asia, the Soviet Union built up its military presence on the islands, and any discussion of their return was clearly out of the question.

In 1956, however, the Soviet Union decided to try to improve relations with Japan. Talks on a proper peace treaty broke down over the territorial question, but Japan did come away with an agreement to end the state of war and establish diplomatic relations. Most important was the Soviet position on the islands: The two northernmost ones, it was agreed, would not be returned, but it was possible that the other two might be, with the signing of a peace treaty.

From this point, however, things began to go downhill for the Japanese, a process all the more mystifying since it coincided with the serious worsening of Russia's relations with China. In 1960, the Japanese were informed that the return of the two southern islands would not be possible until every United States soldier was withdrawn from Japan, and every American base closed.

At the same time, the Russians increased their own military activity, using the islands as staging areas for maneuvers off the Japanese coast and waging a war of harassment against Japanese fishermen who crossed what the Japanese considered arbitrarily drawn territorial limits. Transgression was more than a matter of fines and confiscated catches; Soviet jails in the South Kuriles were filled with Japanese fishermen serving terms of several years, and boats were frequently seized and kept.

Japanese compromise proposals found no favor at the negotiating sessions. One would have declared the islands open territory under the Hague convention of 1907 and would have barred their use for military purposes by Japan and its American allies. Another would have returned the islands to Japanese sovereignty, then leased them back to the Russians for 100 years. But the Soviet position hardened. Foreign Minister Andrei Gromyko said on his 1966 visit to Tokyo that the issue was "already settled." A dozen years later, after the United States had returned Okinawa to Japan, and at a time when China and Japan were nearing agreement on their treaty, Japanese and Soviet negotiators in Moscow did not even find it possible to issue a communiqué. The Japanese wanted to refer to talks about the future of the islands. But Russia refused to agree to any reference to unresolved territorial problems, because it said such problems simply did not exist.

And so, instead, the Japanese went ahead with their historic opening to China, putting an end to a generation of warfare and enmity and making possible the wedding of Japanese technology with the vast potential of the Chinese market. Russia kept the islands.

It did so, as far as can be determined, because it considered the precedent that would be set by returning territory far more dangerous than the prospect of Japan's new alignment with China. Three different nations—Germany, Poland, and China—have been put forward by Soviet officials and diplomats in Moscow as likely to raise territorial claims if such a precedent were established. But China is clearly the main worry.

During an official briefing in Moscow on U.S.-Soviet relations, a Soviet official made a rare private admission that his government had been wrong in pressing the Japanese too hard: "It might have been a good idea to conclude a peace treaty with Japan to prevent this alliance of an aggressive, dynamic technology and a vast field for its development in China. We don't always make all the right moves in foreign policy—not only you [the Americans] make mistakes. But that agreement would have opened up another, more serious question, and that is the inviolability of the World War II frontiers. Someone else would certainly have brought it up, and that might prove to be as serious a cause of tension as the situation we face now."

It could be argued that none of the territorial claims has any realistic chance of fulfillment in the present balance of forces in the world. China's claims are rejected out of hand. Germany's claims are signed away in a bundle of treaties with Poland, the Soviet Union, and East Germany. Poland's loss on the East has been compensated for by gains on the West.

But perhaps the cautious decision makers in the Kremlin do not want to create claims for the future, in case the balance starts to change. In any case, they appear to be following an entirely different line of reasoning: Because of Japan's trading needs, and the attractiveness of the Soviet market, Japanese-Soviet relations can prosper without a peace treaty. Trade statistics and plans for the further joint development of Siberia show, in fact, that this is so.

Despite political coolness, naval shows of force, arrests of fishermen, and the central refusal to give back the islands, Soviet trade with Japan has soared since commercial relations were established a decade after the end of the war. Volume increased tenfold between 1956 and 1964, for example, and doubled again in the succeeding 6 years, to 600 million rubles both ways. Japan is far closer to the coal, gas, and oil of Eastern Siberia than are the Soviet industrial centers of Europe; Japanese equipment and skills are a natural complement to the Soviet stores of untapped raw materials. Project after project was launched in the 1970s, sometimes to compete with Western Europe or the United States, sometimes to act as their partners, as in the case of the giant gas project in Yakutia. At the end of the seventies, Japan had at least $4 billion involved in Siberian projects, and half a dozen or more 10- and 25-year plans on the books or in operation. The Soviet Union seemed to have worked out a way to have its cake and eat it, too.

It did so by suspending one of its rules of international conduct, that of linking politics and trade. It refused to give up an inch of island territory but nevertheless got the benefit of Japan's developing its resources and paying in hard currency or goods.

But did Russia really get the full benefit of possible relations with Japan? The Japanese argue that business involvement with Russia is only a fraction of what it might be, if a real basis of political trust were established between the two Pacific neighbors. As long as Soviet intentions seem to signal exactly the opposite, Japan is going to be reluctant to commit too much of its capital, its processes, and its technicians. Japan worries above all about becoming dependent on the Russians for supplies of certain raw materials—natural gas for one—that could be cut off if politics dictated.

The treaty with China permits Japan to trade with both Russia and China. It gives Japan leverage with both. By any reasonable measurement, it is a good thing for Japan, and not a good thing for Russia. But reasonableness seems out of place in a situation where some remote specks of real estate in the Pacific count for more than the rapprochement of Asia's old enemies on a basis that clearly challenges Russia's position in the region.

In the vast territory of the Soviet Union, the argument over the Kuriles seems sillier than ever; surely the Russians, with a sixth of the world's territory, have no need for more land. The morning train from Moscow's Yaroslavl station, the *Rossiya,* clears the yards and the wooden houses of the suburbs and begins to move into the space of Russia. Long before the Urals, the kind of density of settlement familiar in Western Europe has ended. Only a thousand miles from Moscow and the *Rossiya* is in Asia, in Siberia. It is 22° F below zero, and the snow is so deep on the branches of the firs that birds must perch on the top, like Christmas tree ornaments. The snow transforms the architecture of the log hut villages, giving them thick roofs and lower walls. The wood smoke rises straight up from each chimney, turning into white vapor, and during the short, clear days, the sun projects a kind of frost rainbow against the cloudless skies.

The landscape is forest or steppe until, at infrequent intervals, red and yellow Party banners introduce an industrial area. Then come the factories, with more slogans ("Long Live the Great Soviet People! Our Strength: the 25th Party Congress"); half-completed buildings and cluttered equipment yards; trucks and tractors on snowy roads; rows of little garages with private cars snugged in for the winter; plain apartment boxes; and finally the station, with people trudging along with bags and boxes, and an occasional horse-drawn sleigh to pick up freight.

Compared to these small cities and towns, Novosibirsk, the Soviet Union's fourth city and Siberia's unofficial capital, with a population of a million and a half, seems grand indeed. The city grew with the Trans-Siberian railway, starting at the turn of the century, when the tracks reached the broad Ob river, but got its real impetus during the Second World War. At great cost, the Soviet Union moved its factories east of the Urals, safe from the advancing German army and out of the range of German bombers. With this head start, Novosibirsk has never looked back at its European Russian rivals and has managed to attract ballet dancers, college students, and some of the nation's top scientists.

There is a good view of the city from the ninth-floor editorial offices of *Soviet Siberia,* the regional newspaper. The editors are fond of calling their city the Soviet Chicago, and they talk more of local affairs (in good booster language) than of international ones. The exception is China, 600 miles to the south, a third of the distance to Moscow.

One editor pointed with pride to a crayon drawing his granddaughter had provided as office decoration. In Siberia or Chicago, children's art themes seem to be standard: a sun with prominent rays, green grass, blue sky, brown trees, large birds.

"But lately, she's been drawing another, disturbing kind of picture," he said. "It shows warplanes and rockets, bombs falling, people getting killed. Where does she get such ideas? Of course, she sees the parades here on our holidays, sees the planes flying over. But it all shows a fear. We are worried that there are forces that want war. And some of those forces are in your country."

To the editor, the problem could be easily solved if the American people would seize control of the United States arms industry from monopolists and not make arms any-more. Such an action wouldn't be necessary in the Soviet Union, since Soviet arms don't threaten anyone. But what about China? Certainly the monopolists are not in control of the arms industry there? China, it is explained, behaves as it does, despite the lack of monopolists, because it has bad leaders, and because of the undeveloped nature of the masses. In time, with industrialization, the character of the masses will change, they will choose new leaders, and then it will be possible to live in peace with China. Should the West then help China industrialize? Trucks can be used for military purposes, tanks can be made from tractors. Does this mean China must be relegated to permanent underdevelopment? No nation should be able to dictate to another. Yet it is important not to arm an aggressive China. Certainly, the editor concluded, the problem is complex.

In Novosibirsk's bookstores, stacks of greeting cards display the ubiquitous space motifs or the classic Palekh lacquer painting patterns. A bigger stack contains the military and patriotic themes. One shows two Soviet soldiers being offered the traditional welcoming gift of bread by an attractive babushka-clad blonde. A child proffers a bouquet, and a war veteran, his medals showing, looks on approvingly. In the background of the greeting card are Soviet factories, set against a sunny landscape, and soaring missiles and warplanes, set against a threatening sky. Other themes include teenage boys and girls in junior military uniforms, with real soldiers going into attack behind a red banner in the distance.

At the Novosibirsk memorial to the city's 30,000 war dead, boys and girls aged 14 and 15 stand guard, dressed in the beige sheepskin coats and red-starred fur hats of the regular army. It is considered an honor to be chosen for the guard in this and other Soviet cities. The watch changes every 15 minutes in good weather and every 10 minutes in bad. A windy day of −6° F is considered good weather. The children, carrying carbines a little too large for them, marched smartly back and forth from their barracks to the monument, stamping their felt *valyenki* boots in the snow.

Down the street, sitting contentedly on a sled, was a soldier of even smaller scale. A 2-year old boy, waiting for his mother to do her shopping, was kept warm in a miniature uniform, cap, sheepskin coat, boots, and belt, with the starred brass buckle—regulation size—dominating the ensemble.

These conversations and impressions made it easier to understand Sasha, a slim young blond with the close-cropped hair of the military, who had been on the train from Moscow. He had left his compartment frequently to talk to the foreigners clustered around the little coal stove at the end of the car that served as bathroom water heater and samovar for tea. As his story proceeded, it seemed to depart more and more from reality. He had been a paramedic, he said, in action on the Chinese border, and had been captured by the Chinese and forced to perform surgery with a flick knife, a fierce-looking weapon he waved, opened, for emphasis. The Chinese were savage fighters and cruel captors, but he had survived, had been exchanged, and was now on his way back to the border for another tour of duty.

Soviet television shows propaganda films as lurid as Sasha's story, using devices like scenes from the cultural revolution, Mao applauding his own speech, and then an execution sequence. Chinese soldiers are portrayed as fanatics who can swarm antlike over walls and break bricks with a blow of a bare hand. The Chinese threat. The message is reinforced with editorials and commentaries, and, beginning in 1978, with the first anti-Chinese cartoons. The caricatures showed the Chinese as fat, grinning, and looking quite a bit like the top-hatted Wall Street figures Soviet readers are so familiar with.

This campaign, and particularly the quasi-documentaries on the television, has a strange effect on sophisticated Russians, according to conversations in Moscow. One group of intellectuals, people who have been in the West and know it well enough both to praise and to criticize conditions—and who certainly know their own system well enough for both—confessed they were unable to sleep after one such program brought home to them the gravity of the Chinese threat.

A diplomat who had seen many of the programs thought that the intellectuals' reaction might have two causes. The first was that intellectuals might have been used as part of an official effort to convince Westerners just how dangerous the China card could be. In such campaigns, even cocktail party chatter is considered useful. The second was that they were truly worried about China because of their ignorance, based on 15 years of misinformation or no information: "They can handle propaganda about the West and their own domestic propaganda," he said, "but they just don't know China on their own and have no independent basis to evaluate it."

Moscow, of course, has its China experts, who analyze for Party and government and publish in the newspapers and specialized journals. In interviews, they seem more concerned with keeping within the ideological boundaries than with seeking fresh information or providing insights. Their caution and narrowness contrasts with the flexibility of the analysts who follow events in the United States and are quite sophisticated about interpreting and understanding them.

The China watchers see the Sino-Soviet dispute as a problem both political and ideological. The political differences focus on territory, but they are really based on Chinese fears of Soviet domination, which, of course, are entirely unfounded. The Helsinki agreement of 1975 put an end to European attempts to revise borders, and there must be an end in Asia.

In ideology, the Chinese claim that they have the only true version of Marxism, and this is something the Soviet Union will never accept. Lenin, in effect, invented modern Communism, and the Russians don't think it can be improved by a bunch of Chinese peasant upstarts who came along 30 years later. If this sounds arrogant, they say, a certain pride in Soviet achievements is justified, and reminding China of how far it has strayed does not mean Moscow is trying to dominate it.

Soviet citizens have no opportunity to hear the other side of the story. There used to be hundreds of books on the achievements of Maoism in libraries and bookstores, but they vanished long ago. So did the Chinese population of Siberian cities like Irkutsk, once a center of the China trade, and Khabarovsk, located in the Soviet Far East, beyond Siberia, on the Amur-Ussuri border with China. The Maoists summoned all the Chinese back when the trouble started,

Khabarovsk residents say, although many ethnic Chinese of Soviet citizenship remain.

Khabarovsk looks like European Russia: yellow and white stucco buildings, boulevards, parks, and many views of the Amur, the broad river the Chinese call the Black Dragon. The actual border is a security zone barred to foreigners and Soviet citizens alike. Khabarovsk has its hillside slums, log hut settlements where women bearing wooden yokes haul water home from the ice-covered neighborhood pumps. But the downtown cafés, the new theater for operettas and an occasional guest appearance from the Yiddish troupe of the neighboring Jewish Autonomous Region, the bookstores, the squares and department stores: all these give the city, 5,300 miles from Moscow, a European feeling.

But Khabarovsk is in Asia and is built, in fact, on territory the Chinese say was wrongfully taken from them. Yerofei Khabarov, who led a band of Siberian settlers to the area in 1649, fought Russia's first battle on the Amur and won it. Now Khabarov's statue stands in an inconspicuous part of town, overlooking the traffic, civilian and military, of the border city.

The military predominates. Lots of soldiers are not unusual in any Soviet city, but Khabarovsk clearly has more than its share, and if Western reports that the Russians have a quarter of their 3.6-million-man armed forces on the Chinese border are correct, the number in Khabarovsk isn't surprising. The need to find homes for officers' families worsened Khabarovsk's already considerable housing shortage, local residents say, and army personnel are put ahead of locals on housing waiting lists. All this is reported in a patriotic way, which is to say that much mention is made of the sacrifices the army is making to guard the border.

From the huge troop-transporting helicopters under camouflage nets on the edge of the city to the rows of clipped soldier heads at the operetta, the army is everywhere. Soldiers patrol the grounds of the barracks and military hospitals on the hills above the Amur, crunching through the snow past posters showing other soldiers fighting along a river border. Young men in sheepskins and fatigues work to extend a barracks in −20° F weather, using the Siberian burn-and-dig method. Since construction can't be confined to the short frost-free period of the year, a way must be found to dig through the frost. The soldiers and other construction workers heap coal on the ground, then put planks and scrap lumber atop the coal as kindling. They ignite the pile and allow it to burn down. Then they shovel the coal aside and attack the thawed ground with picks and shovels, until another layer of frost is reached, and another layer of coal added.

Siberians and Far Easterners keep warm with vodka, of course, despite frequent antialcohol campaigns, but they keep both warm and comfortable with tea. The samovar heats the tea water, but it also keeps up the level of humidity. It may be 40 below outside, but the air can be as dry as it would be in a desert, and there is often the same thirst and discomfort. Samovar steam in homes and offices helps. The samovar is also a sign of hospitality offered visitors by officials, a signal that the talk may be expected to be friendlier and more open. Dark Georgian tea and a little hot water go into a china pot, and then clear hot water is added from the samovar—these days, more likely to be chrome than brass and electrified rather than charcoal-heated.

In such a talk in Khabarovsk, an official with close and frequent contacts with Party, military, and industrial leaders of the region recalled the hopes the Far East had had when President Ford and President Brezhnev met in Vladivostok, their city, in 1974. There had been promises of expanded trade and better political relations, and the Russians in the area foresaw a pleasant future of cooperation with American technologists and engineers in exploiting the oil and other raw materials of the region. But instead they got the Carter administration, which replaced what seemed to them a perfectly good set of Republicans by means of an electoral process they do not fully understand.

Carter, the official continued, began by grossly interfering in the internal affairs of the Soviet Union when he brought up the human rights issue. This meant trade declined rather than flourished. Then the United States encouraged Japan, Khabarovsk's neighbor and natural partner, to sign a very bad treaty with China and followed it up with its own China card. The United States will regret these actions, since it does not understand the true nature of the Chinese, and it will find itself betrayed by them, just as the Russians did after decades of selfless help. In the course of the discussion, it becomes plain that the Soviets consider the Americans nearly as volatile and unpredictable as the Chinese. More in pity than in anger, the arguments for and against American help in modernizing Chinese industry are summed up: "You don't give a gun to a baby." And, in contrast to the polite and vague disapproval expressed in Moscow over the normalization of relationships between Peking and Washington, this blunt judgment: "We don't like it."

As long as China slept or remained under Soviet control, it was not a real threat, only a convenient one, sometimes, for propaganda use.

The Chinese 1978 changed that. In that year of breathtaking change, a decade after the Czechoslovak 1968, China came to life under its new leaders, introducing sweeping reforms in the economy and society, and sending hundreds of missions around the world (160 came to West Germany alone in that year) to arrange for modernization orders totaling $40 billion. In international relations, China concluded agreements with Japan and the United States that reversed decades-old patterns of hostility and created what Moscow immediately called the Pacific Triangle.

The invasion of China's ally Cambodia at the end of that eventful year was, in a sense, the Soviet Union's retaliation, but in contrast to the punishment of Prague for its reform efforts 10 years earlier, the retaliation could not be inflicted directly on China, and it could not and did not result in a change of leadership or policy in China, as it did in Czechoslovakia. Moscow does not have this power.

Instead, Moscow must watch from the sidelines as the giant awakens, no longer a participant and now aware that the United States will have the dominant outside influence on China's course.

This represents two missed chances for the Soviet Union: the chance to remain on friendly terms with its Asian neighbor China, and the chance to offer the United States enough benefit from détente to keep it from turning to the Chinese. It is unlikely that the first mistake can be righted, but despite the chill that followed Afghanistan, there is still time and scope for better Soviet-American relations.

4

Russia and America

I<small>N</small> <small>THE ENTIRE COMPLEX WORLD</small> of international relations, the Soviet-American relationship stands alone. It is the only one that affects the relations, and the futures, of all the other nations in the world, because it is the only one that could produce full-scale nuclear war, an unprecedented kind of conflagration that could not be contained within the national boundaries of the Soviet Union and the United States.

For this reason, when the United States and the Soviet Union agreed to a policy of détente at the beginning of the seventies, most of the rest of the world believed the words of their leaders about a new era of peace, one in which cooperation would replace the rivalry of the Cold War.

Only the first part of the promise—the absence of direct war between the two great powers—has been fulfilled. Instead of cooperation, however, the United States and Russia are engaged in a rivalry as great as ever in most areas, with only a few exchanges, some cautious arms limitation agreements, and a somewhat higher level of trade to distinguish the era of peace from that of cold war.

These gains should not be disparaged, but the hopes were

far higher—too high, in fact, in different ways, in both East and West. Some in the Western world expected to see détente lead to something like the Western-Soviet alliance against the Nazis of the Second World War when, despite differences in their systems, the two sides joined to defeat a common enemy. The Eastern leadership saw détente as a means of retaining all the benefits of its old policies with greater gains and fewer risks. It could continue to clamp down on its old empire and seek to add to it. It could enjoy the boost of Western trade and technology and the savings of arms control, and the only thing it had to worry about was avoiding too direct a challenge to the interests of the United States and its partners.

The Western high hopes failed because there was no common enemy or threat that would unite the two opposing societies for their mutual benefit, or perhaps because each saw the other as that enemy. The Eastern high hopes were more completely fulfilled, but they were disappointed to some extent by a Western reluctance to push exchanges and trade very hard as long as there were such great stresses on the relationship elsewhere, and by a Western insistence on bringing up human rights, perhaps as a counterirritant.

A complete examination of what happened to détente must include both Eastern and Western views, as well as a review of the main milestones of the process. And since both the past and the future of détente are of such concern to the other nations of the world, the standpoints of those nations must also be considered.

No matter how great the potential of China for world influence, or how powerful the economies of Germany and Japan, or how independent the policies of France or Romania, all must ultimately subordinate a part of their national aims and tailor a part of their national policymaking to allow for this great power relationship that exists outside their control.

Some of those nations can influence the policies of one or the other great power, and some can influence both. China's actions, in particular, would seem the most capable of pushing the Russians and the Americans toward conflict, or of pulling them away from it, but the world is full of other examples—in the Middle East, in Southeast Asia, and along the frontier of divided Europe, where a divided but powerful Germany still constitutes a menace to the wary Soviet Union.

With the exception of the volatile states of the Middle East, the agreement of the great powers to relax the tensions in their relations and create the policy, or situation, of détente has found general favor. Even in Southeast Asia, in conditions of continuing guerrilla warfare, the chief power, Vietnam, wants better relations and aid from the United States to match the relations and aid it gets from the Soviet Union.

Western Europe's leaders benefit in their own little policies of détente when the umbrella relationship of the big powers is in a satisfactory state. They may be able to make short-term gains when it is not, but in the long run, their trade and political ties are dependent on the general atmosphere of East-West relations.

Eastern Europe benefits most of all from East-West cordiality. Its small nations, like others all over the world, do not want to see the world enveloped in war. Unlike most of the others, however, they see their region as the probable battlefield. Détente helps under conditions of peace, too. One of the few things uniting dissidents and officials in Eastern Europe is the hope that both groups place on the continuation of détente and the avoidance of a return to the Cold War.

Both dissidents and Communist leaders in Eastern Europe have a role in détente, too, although they admit it is marginal. Officials in Eastern Europe believe they can act as intermediaries between East and West. Poland and Hungary, the two most liberal nations, are valued by Western diplomats, at least, for this function. The reasoning is that the Poles and Hungarians are closer to the American way of thinking than the Soviet Union may be and are better at catching nuances and interpreting American standpoints. They are then able to present these views to the Russians in a way that draws on their ample experience in Communist thinking and diplomacy. If this intermediary function proves of even marginal help to détente, officials say, it is considered well worth the effort and the cost of sometimes being misinterpreted by the Soviet Union or the United States.

Eastern Europeans are far too familiar with the effects of the Cold War on their societies—the shrinking of freedoms, not only for the individual, but also for the leadership—not to realize what an end to détente would mean for them. And here, dissidents agree with the leaderships. It is only the relatively relaxed atmosphere between East and West that permits the relatively relaxed atmosphere in Eastern Europe and the Soviet Union, they believe. For this reason they support measures that seem to have nothing to do with human rights, such as Most Favored Nation status for the Soviet Union in its trade with the United States, because of their liberalizing effect. The more contacts between East and West at any level or in any field, they say, the better. The dilemma for the dissidents, as will be discussed later, is that their very existence and continued activity can be seen as a threat to détente.

The Soviet Union's public position on détente underwent surprisingly little change as the direct result of the Afghan events. At a time when American commentators and politicians were mourning—or cheering—the death of détente, their Soviet counterparts were not. Détente was excepted from the tough propaganda language that poured from Moscow in response to the American embargoes. If Soviet officials mentioned it at all, it was to blame the United States for endangering détente, and, in background conversations, other Communist diplomats expressed the hope that a change of American leadership might restore it.

Western Europe's leaders saw détente as endangered, but not dead, and the same views were privately expressed in the Carter administration, as a quiet counterpoint to the election-year attacks on the Russians.

And thus, despite Afghanistan, the circle of world opinion remained complete: Nations, big and small, involved directly or peripherally, those that condemned the Russians and those that thought the United States overreacted, even leaderships and some of those who would like to overthrow them are in favor of this policy that has so much potential for peace.

Why then is the world such a place of upheaval, war, revolution, invasion, expansionist plans and counterexpansionist plans, arms buildups and exports? To use the definition of détente, why has not tension been relaxed?

There are many reasons, but the main one is that détente has done nothing to change the fierce rivalry between the Soviet Union and the United States. It may have channeled some of the rivalry into less dangerous forms, but the basic relationship remains as it was.

The few acts of amity that emerged during what the Russians call the golden age of détente, the Nixon years, were more showmanship than friendship. Scientific and technical exchanges (of immense benefit to the Russians and of marginal benefit to the Americans), scholarly and educational exchanges (impeded by Soviet restrictions on research), and increased travel (largely limited to delegations in the east-to-west direction)—all were improvements over the Cold War, but not great steps forward. The much-publicized joint space venture was probably the best symbol for the general lack of substance.

And yet all these ventures are stressed by Soviet officials, along with the profits of trade, as examples of how beneficial détente can be—if the Americans would only follow the rules. Both nations are, in fact, following the rules of détente as they see them. But since their interpretations grow out of different systems of government and different needs, there are bound to be conflicts, and the world order being what it is, no one to judge them but the disputants.

The only policy on which both agree, in their actions if not their statements, is the exploitation of the weakness of the society and sphere of influence of the other. Détente does not stop this; it only defines the furthest limits to which exploitation ought prudently to go. The Americans say the Soviets had been getting very close to that limit in Africa and Asia, while the American side had been holding back. If that is a strength, as the Americans think it is, in the view of the Soviet Union it may be a weakness, one that encourages more exploitation rather than equal reticence. The Soviet invasion of Afghanistan went beyond that limit, in the United States' view, and the American retaliation, in the Soviet view, was just as much a violation of the unwritten rules of détente.

How the two sides look at each other in detail, and what the weaknesses are that each seeks to exploit, will be examined in the pages that follow.

Any short history of détente will show a steady progression downward from initial hopes for cooperation to the bare elements of mutual survival. The two SALT summits, the Nixon-Brezhnev meeting of 1972 and the Carter-Brezhnev conference of 1979, show this contrast most clearly. The first was hailed as the start of a new era, variously described as one of peace, negotiation, and cooperation, all to be achieved on the basic foundation of détente. The second produced only talk about disagreement, except for the doggedly negotiated SALT document, and even that faced an uncertain future in the United States Senate.

Nixon brought an impressive bundle of agreements home from Moscow in May 1972. There were eight, with the last one containing a further twelve "basic principles of mutual relations." Nothing much has been heard of these since.

The others were promises to work toward what became the Helsinki agreement of 1975, toward reduction of conventional forces in Europe, toward expanding joint efforts in science and technology, toward cooperation in space—which meant the Soviet-American linkup in orbit—toward laying the groundwork for a comprehensive trade agreement, toward reducing the chances of dangerous incidents between the two nations at sea and in the air, and toward further limitations in offensive and defensive nuclear weapons— SALT I and its accompanying interim agreement.

The Soviet Union agreed with the president that the visit had been "of genuine historical importance." More important was its stressing of both the passive aspects of détente— to reduce the threat of war—and the active ones of future cooperation, cultural and scientific—in the twin space shot and in trade.

It was significant, in light of later developments, that the two sides discussed but did not produce an agreement on the areas of the world where Soviet and United States interests were in conflict. And those who paid attention to the commentaries directed toward Party members and Soviet allies in Eastern Europe noted, too, the stress on the continuance of the ideological struggle under conditions of détente, the emphasis that the new set of agreements did not mean a retreat from "class or internationalist positions."

That was for the East. For the West, there were more summits and a growing list of new agreements and exchanges. Brezhnev came to the United States in 1973; Nixon returned to Moscow in the final weeks of his presidency the following year, and his successor, Gerald Ford, met Brezhnev at the end of 1974 in the Soviet Pacific port of Vladivostok to negotiate the guidelines for extending the SALT I agreement Nixon had concluded.

The Soviet Union noted with satisfaction that despite the dislocations of Watergate, more agreements had been concluded between the two countries in the Nixon-Ford years than had been shown in the entire previous record of Soviet-American relations.

But even before Jimmy Carter entered the White House, the hopes many Americans had placed on détente were being shattered. One of the first instances was the way in which Soviet traders took advantage of the capitalist grain market to drive up the price of wheat in 1972. Soviet support for OPEC's oil price increases the following year added to the conviction that the Russians were somehow responsible for American inflation. The retreat from Vietnam and the apparent success, by contrast, of Soviet-backed guerrillas in Angola projected this domestic uneasiness onto the world stage. Congress retaliated with the Jackson-Vanik and Stevenson amendments to the trade agreement Nixon and Brezhnev had worked out, making it dependent on more liberal emigration policies from the Soviet Union. Russia scrapped the agreement as a result.

When Carter took office, press coverage in the Soviet Union was more admiring than critical. Moscow liked the anti-Washington tone Carter had set during the campaign; it liked a man who walked down Pennsylvania Avenue and eschewed a top hat at his inauguration. It was also engaging in the traditional honeymoon period it accords each new president, partly from caution and lack of understanding, partly from hope. The honeymoon did not last out Carter's first month. Human rights, already a sore point because of Jackson-Vanik, became the symbol of Soviet-American relations under the new administration, and it was clearly a symbol of confrontation.

Andrei Sakharov, the conscience of the Soviet human

rights movement, started the controversy by writing Carter a letter dated January 21, the day after the inauguration, asking his help in securing the release of fifteen political prisoners and urging him to speak out "to defend those who suffer because of their non-violent struggle for justice."

The new administration did speak out, and the Russians responded with charges that an anti-Soviet campaign was underway in Washington, helped by "the renegade A. Sakharov," and "certain bodies which organize ideological subversive activities." They were careful, however, not to attack the president personally.

The White House view was that Carter had campaigned on a platform of human rights, among other things, and this concern reflected fundamental human values held by all Americans and guaranteed, in fact, by the signatories of the Helsinki agreement, the Soviet Union among them. And although the administration denied that it was seeking to link the human rights issue with progress in the SALT negotiations, it made it clear from the start that the Senate might decide to do so when it came time to ratify the treaty.

A certain linkage became apparent for correspondents in Moscow in the following weeks. They had to put up with tire slashing and other harassment; George Krimsky, an Associated Press reporter, was expelled. Back in Washington, Carter received Vladimir Bukovsky in the White House, and when the new Secretary of State, Cyrus Vance, made his first visit to Moscow in April, he was warned by Brezhnev that normal development of relations would be impossible unless such gestures were halted.

Vance also brought sweeping new proposals for arms reduction as well as limitation, proposals the Soviets rejected as "inequitable." They called for the reduction of both missile launchers and multiple warheads below the levels agreed to at Vladivostok, a halt to the deployment of all new weapons systems, and a freeze on American Minutemen and the

Soviet SS-17s, S-11s, and S-19s at then-current levels of about 550. The proposals, it was generally agreed, were too much of a departure from the accepted pace of SALT for the Soviet Union to consider, and it was this reason, not irritation over human rights, that caused their rejection.

The administration shifted to general talk of human rights rather than specific cases in the months that followed, but even this softening of the challenge did not placate the Russians. In the first half-year of the Carter administration, the Soviet Union decided to try the Jewish dissident activist Anatoly Shcharansky for treason, to decrease the number of Jews permitted exit visas, to increase jamming of foreign broadcasts, and to refuse television time to United States Ambassador Malcolm Toon to deliver a Fourth of July speech, a newly instituted practice, because the text contained the passage, "Americans will continue to state publicly their belief in human rights and their hope that violations of these rights, wherever they may occur, will end."

Soviet and Cuban involvement in a new area of Africa, Ethiopia, dominated relations in 1978, reviving talk of linkage to SALT. Carter touched on another aspect of the relationship, all but forgotten, in a tough speech at Wake Forest College in North Carolina at the start of his second year in office. That was cooperation. "We are prepared to cooperate with the Soviet Union toward common social science and economic goals," he said. "But," he continued, as if predicting the events in Afghanistan, "if they fail to demonstrate restraint in missile programs and other force levels, and in the projection of Soviet or proxy forces into other lands and continents, then popular support in the United States for such cooperation will erode."

But the United States had, in fact, extended the term of the joint commission for cooperation for science and technology for another 5 years that previous July, when the mutual irritation over human rights was at one of its periodic peaks. Until Afghanistan froze the exchange, hundreds of scientists traveled in each direction each year to work on joint projects ranging from microbiology to the application of computer techniques to management.

This kind of cooperation continued, then, but other forms were hard to find in Carter's turbulent second year. Americans hammered hard at the human rights issue in the Belgrade conference called to review the Helsinki agreements, and the Russians hammered hard at the Americans in Moscow: putting two correspondents on trial for slander, arresting an American businessman on trumped-up currency charges, and brushing aside United States representations to convict Shcharansky as a CIA spy.

The Russians lamented the unpredictability of American behavior under Carter, "as changeable as the weather," as the Soviet *New Times* put it. They also continued what seemed to the United States to be unnecessary and threatening support for the war against Eritrean rebels in Ethiopia and for coups and plots in South Yemen, areas far from the Soviet Union but uncomfortably close to the oil routes from the Middle East.

Partly as a result, the Americans began to pay more attention to bringing the earlier opening to China into the forefront. China's burst of activity on all fronts in 1978 gave the Americans their opportunity. If the world was surprised to learn of the national security adviser's joining his Chinese hosts in taunting the Russians in May 1978 in an outing on the Great Wall, more was in store: the announcement that December of the normalization of relations starting January 1, 1979.

Carter thus went into the Vienna summit with Brezhnev that June with a stronger China card than the one Nixon had brought to Moscow in 1972. In the first summit, four months after the Nixon visit to Peking, United States-China relations had been in a much more tentative stage.

Why, then, did the first summit produce so much, and the second so little? The answer depends on who got much, and who got little. An analysis of the first important complex of Soviet-American agreements shows Russia to be the main beneficiary of the 1972 summit. The agreement to go to Helsinki was thought of at the time as a clear Russian victory, because Russia's purpose in staging the Conference on European Security and Cooperation was to seal the postwar division of Europe and to win Western approval for its gains in Eastern Europe. For this reason, the West had dragged its feet for years. The Soviet Union could not know in 1972 that in exchange for the border pledge, it would have to make concessions on the far more explosive issue of human rights. The agreement on mutual troop and conventional arms cuts was an agreement to go to Vienna and negotiate; it gave away nothing and took nothing. On scientific and technological exchanges, the Soviet Union stood to benefit far more than the United States, and the same was true to a lesser degree for expanded trade. The space shot was of more value to the Russians in putting forward another claim to equality with the United States in technology; certainly the Soviet Union publicized it far more than the Americans did.

The two agreements on reducing dangerous incidents, and, of course, SALT, were of mutual benefit, the rock-bottom kind of thing that is likely to survive all but the worst plunge in relations. The final one, the twelve points of mutual relations, was so vague as to be meaningless.

At the time of the Nixon visit, the Russians did not know what the effect of the relationship with China might be, and they moved as fast and as far as they could to take advantage of their improved relationship with the Americans before the latter could do more with Peking.

At the time of the Carter-Brezhnev talks in Vienna, the new emphasis the United States was putting on ties with Peking made the Russians pessimistic about the chances of further cooperation. With the issue of American interference in Soviet internal affairs (as the Soviets put it), or in human rights (as the Americans put it) unresolved, there was no incentive for the Soviet Union to produce a package of promises for the press. More important, it already had the really valuable agreements locked up for another 5 years, because of the 1977 renewal of the 1972 summit arrangements for exchanges of scientists and technologists.

The Americans, too, might have produced some token agreements for signature, but this would have indicated approval of current Soviet policies at home and abroad, an attitude the administration did not wish to assume.

As a result, the Vienna summit, like the Moscow summit, produced agreement on one basic issue, the limitation of the strategic nuclear arsenals of the two sides, an important enough reason for such meetings. And although much of the world's press left Vienna convinced that Carter had gone home otherwise empty-handed, it could be argued equally that it was Brezhnev who had done so.

If the Americans secured no promises of reduced Soviet influence in the Third World, this represented no dashing of hopes. And the agreement to continue SALT negotiations, as will be discussed later, probably offers more leverage on future Soviet behavior overseas than any number of principles distributed to summit meeting pressrooms.

But does the United States have any right to be concerned about questions that are not within the limits of direct Soviet-American relations? Is the Soviet Union's taking over neighboring countries, its sale or gift of arms to Third World governments and liberation movements not really the business of those two parties? And is not its treatment of its citizens entirely its own business?

The United States view is that in the first case, the expansion of influence into new areas of the world may indeed be a matter for the Soviet Union and its partners, puppets, or dependents in those countries to decide on, but it is equally up to the United States to decide just how closely it wants to cooperate with a nation that seems bent on expansion.

In the second case, it is argued, human rights questions transcend national boundaries, not only because Western nations say they do, but because the Soviet Union, in signing the Helsinki agreement as well as previous international documents, concurs. (It should be added that by not yet ratifying some of those same documents, the United States considerably weakens its human rights arguments.)

There is no question that a vast gap separates Soviet and Western ideas about individual rights, and this means not only in practice, where the gap is greatest, but also in the official view of what constitutes rights. The new Soviet constitution balances the paper rights it allows citizens with a formidable list of duties to the state—the way of earning the rights, which thus become privileges. The concept of inalienable rights granted as part of the natural order of mankind's social arrangements is alien in the Soviet Union. Rights are more or less reluctant concessions by the State to keep things running smoothly, now as in the centuries of czardom.

The Helsinki conference (most of which was conducted in Geneva) thus ran into difficulties, to put it mildly, trying to reconcile Western and Eastern concepts of individual rights. That it succeeded in producing such a strong statement as that contained in Provision VII of the Final Act is astonishing; that the Soviet Union chose systematically to ignore and violate the provision, to the extent of rounding up and imprisoning for long and severe terms almost every one of the brave little group that sought to monitor its compliance, is less so. "The entire system is based on the violation of human rights," a dissident now in the West said. "To agree to observe human rights would be like sawing off the branch you are sitting on for the Russian leadership." It is surprising, under these conditions, that anyone like Yuri Orlov or Shcharansky managed to have even a brief period of activism before being arrested.

The Soviet Union agreed to Provision VII, which binds it to "respect human rights and fundamental freedoms, including the freedom of thought, conscience, religion, or belief" not only as a desirable domestic condition, but as "an essential factor for the peace, justice, and well-being necessaryto ensure the development of friendly relations and cooperation . . . among all states." The second part, of course, is the answer to charges of interference in internal affairs, which is prohibited by another Helsinki Final Act provision. Yet another provision makes all the provisions of equal force, so that they cannot be selectively applied in interstate relations.

Russia agreed to these uncomfortable concessions because it wanted something else out of Helsinki and had, in fact, pushed for the conference in the first place in order to achieve it: Western agreement on the inviolability of the postwar boundaries of Europe.

That Helsinki turned into an advantage, or at least a standoff, for the West was also a result of the negotiating skills and commitment of the more or less anonymous diplomats who spent more than 2 years around the Geneva conference tables preparing the Final Act for signature at the Helsinki summit.

But would it not have been better to lose the human rights fight at Geneva and Helsinki, in the interests of better relations between the world's two great powers? The Russians, who have an estimated 10,000 political prisoners in camps and places of exile, believe so. Relations should not be based on interference in the internal affairs of the two partners, they say, in disregard of the not-very-fine print of Provision VII, but should be directed in a positive way, toward cooperating. The Russians then cite deficiencies in the American record on human rights, hastening to add that this does not constitute interference, since it is part of the legitimate Soviet concern for justice for oppressed peoples.

Moral and legal arguments could go on indefinitely. Is

pushing human rights issues in the Soviet Union good politics for the United States? Some Westerners do not believe that it is; they call instead for the measures, chiefly increased contacts among intellectuals, that will eventually make the Soviet Union a more open society and thus help its dissidents without outside prompting. The dissidents dissent from this view.

According to senior American officials, if there were ever any doubts about the political as well as the moral arguments for advocating human rights observance in the Soviet Union, they were resolved by the testimonials of the dissidents themselves. These men and women inside Russia get word back, through Western correspondents and other channels, that they do not want any letup in the pressure, even though it results in prison sentences, because without Western attention neither they nor their cause would be able to survive at all. Only through the continued focus of Western opinion on the human rights situation, they say, is it possible for the movement to renew itself, to find brave new people to take the place of those who go into the strict regime prisons or, if they are lucky, into the prisoner-spy exchanges.

What is more important to them is that they feel they are having some slight successes—the rise, perhaps temporary, in exit permits for Jewish dissidents is cited—and that the movement is bound to grow, despite the repeated inroads made by arrest, intimidation, and forced expatriation.

"There have always been those striving for human rights in Russia," a dissident writer said. "When the striving gets too great, the system is forcibly changed, since it cannot accommodate them. This was true when the emerging bourgeoisie ran up against czarist absolutism, whether in the performance of plays or the introduction of modern manufacturing and trade. The system was too inflexible to meet their demands. It had to perish. Sooner or later the present system will face this challenge and fail to respond to it.

"In any dictatorship there is a circle holding all the subject people. Most of them are in the middle of it, and some are on the edges, pressing out. In the middle, they never come up against the restrictions of the authorities. On the edges, they do. The number in the middle is huge; that on the edges, small. In Hitler's Germany, tens of millions lived through one of the worst dictatorships in history without ever being affected by its criminality. You were in no trouble unless you were a Jew or tried to publish a book or make a speech.

"The Soviet system today is not in any way as criminal as the Nazi system was, but it does affect more people, because it has its hands on everything. Not only on the scientist who cannot get permission to go to a specialists' conference at MIT, or the art historian who must see the originals of Degas or Michelangelo, but even the factory manager who wants more efficiency—all find themselves on the outer edge of the circle.

"And as the Soviet Union changes more and more from backward agricultural nation to industrial society, the group on the edges will grow and will include not only poets and Jews who want to emigrate, but larger and larger numbers of the Russian equivalent of the man in the gray flannel suit."

It is comparatively easy to lock up political activists, but not men in gray flannel suits, if their number increases as predicted, and if the economy is to be kept running. Even the rounding up of the most outspoken activists is difficult, however. The Soviet Union is a police state, but it does not like the world to see it acting like one. It is proud of socialist democracy and national unity, and arrests show the cracks in these façades. When dissidents are arrested, the authorities are usually careful to avoid any charges that could be interpreted as attacks on freedom of expression. Overt acts such as espionage are easier to punish, whether or not the charges are fabricated.

The Soviet dissident movement has been virtually wiped out several times by such waves of arrests, and yet new members keep coming forward. The United States could not control this phenomenon even if it wanted to. It fought for the human rights provisions of the Helsinki Final Act, and now Helsinki has taken on a life of its own, spawning monitoring groups and then groups to write and protest about the monitors' arrests. It is a process that started before the Carter administration began, and one that will continue long after it is history.

The adversaries in the most important relationship in the remaining years of the century have both tried, in their own ways, to get beyond the images dictated by propaganda or wishful thinking in appraising each other.

There is propaganda on both sides, but surely more of an effort in the Soviet Union, if only because the Russians, at official and unofficial levels, seem to spend more time worrying about the United States than the United States does about Russia. On the Moscow subway, as high school students head home in the afternoon, an English language paperback is a familiar sight. It is *Habits and Ways in Great Britain and the United States,* a mixture of misinformation, generalization, and an occasional insight. As young Soviet citizens learn English, they also learn that "the wealth most people seem to be enjoying in the United States is not theirs in reality," and that hippies are not really whole-hearted revolutionaries, but advocates of "passive inaction, or opting out." This may do for those who will never get a chance to see the West for themselves, but fortunately there is another, more sophisticated level of information for those who have to deal with the United States as a political adversary.

Since World War II, an entire generation of Soviet men and women familiar with all aspects of American life has entered public life. Their knowledge is direct. It comes from periods as exchange students, prolonged residence as diplomats, trade officials, or journalists. One need only count the size of the Soviet missions at the United Nations and in

Washington to understand the possibilities over the years of producing Americanists, in the families of diplomats as well as directly in government service. The nearly flawless American accents of some of the announcers on Radio Moscow's North American service is another indication. Some of the experts are young, products of the Nixon-initiated exchanges, but some of the senior ones got their first look at the United States during an earlier burst of exchanges in the Khrushchev-Eisenhower era.

Much of this expertise is concentrated in the old stucco villa and annexes of the U.S.A. and Canada Institute of the Soviet Academy of Sciences, under the direction of the oft-quoted Arbatov. But Soviet officials with a good sense of what goes on in the United States can be found at many levels in the ministries, the state industrial and trade organizations, the universities, the media, and embassies abroad. It is from all these sources that the following account is drawn.

At the end of the Second World War, the United States was extremely powerful. It had emerged from the war unscathed and even strengthened; the contrast with the Soviet Union's losses, in people, cities, and industrial capacity, is sharp. Instead of being nearly wiped out, United States industry was modernized with government help and war contracts. There were some war losses, but not enough to affect the manpower needs of the factories for the new peacetime push on the export markets. A fleet of ships that had been expanding all through the war stood ready at United States ports to deliver the exports and bring back cheap raw materials. If the regimes were progressive, like Czechoslovakia's after 1948, they refused to engage in this kind of trade or to accept Marshall Plan aid. American colonialism meant that there were assured markets and sources of raw material all over the world. The United States dictated the price without fear of contradiction.

To enforce its position, the United States had its atomic monopoly, and all these reasons added up to a correlation of forces very much in favor of the United States, which is why it insisted on waging the Cold War against the Soviet Union, dividing Germany, and leading a weak Western Europe into hostile positions against the East. In Asia the United States, failing to prevent the victory of Mao Zedong in China, attacked North Korea as a means of extending its foothold on the mainland and supported the French attempt to stifle Vietnamese independence.

At about the time of Stalin's death in 1953, however, the correlation of forces, that combination of political, social, economic, and military strength Russian analysts believe they can measure, began to tip against the United States, although not even the Soviet Union was aware that this was happening. Not only was the Soviet Union given a new, flexible leadership, but it also had time to begin to recover its strength from the bloodletting of the war. Its scientists ended the atomic monopoly and leaped into the lead in the race for space. These phenomena in the Soviet Union are easy to understand, because there was national mobilization to accomplish these tasks.

What is not so easily apparent is what happened to the United States' power. In 1953, the Americans did nothing to take advantage of the uprising in East Berlin. Three years later, the same hesitation was seen in the Hungarian uprising and the Anglo-French invasion of Suez. That double crisis in November 1956 in fact marked the real turn in world events in favor of the Soviet Union. It showed that Russia had the power to put down counterrevolution in Hungary, in what was, and would remain, its sphere of influence. At the same time it projected the threat of that power to a distant part of the world to demonstrate to everyone that it has rights as well as interests in the world at large.

More tests came in the sixties, and aside from the Cuban missile embarrassment caused by Khrushchev's recklessness, all showed how power had shifted. The Americans could not defeat the Vietnamese, but the Soviet Union showed how easily it could handle counterrevolution in Czechoslovakia.

Of course, the Soviet Union was not without problems during this period. There was the necessity to change leadership from Khrushchev to Brezhnev, and there were Khrushchev's revelations about the excesses of Stalin, although the latter is now being evaluated and appreciated more for his services to the Soviet state over a long career—particularly in the wartime defense of the Motherland—than for any shortcomings of character. One of the rare points of agreement between the Russians and the Chinese is the common appreciation of Stalin's skills at organizing a developing Socialist society.

The hostility of the Chinese, the fault of the Chinese leadership, ended a period of cooperation and friendship, but viewed in its entirety, Soviet policies toward the rest of the world have resulted in many net gains. One need only look at the growing liberation movement in Africa and Asia, or the sight of Soviet fleet units in the Mediterranean or the Baltic, or the strength of the Communist parties in the West.

Why the United States threw away this advantage is hard to tell. It is easy to explain the Soviet side of the equation of relative power; with the tools of Marxism-Leninism, one can predict the rise of progressive forces everywhere. The American shortcomings seem also to be systemic. Democracy means that the politicians must constantly worry about getting reelected, and thus their instinct is to adopt the soft policies that play to the consumer instinct among Americans and never to make the tough, necessary decisions. The United States' automobile industry is in trouble, and yet the Americans let the Japanese flood their market with imported cars and even permit the Germans to build factories in the United States. It is possible that the United States really controls these foreign firms, but it is more likely that consumer demands lead to such practices.

American business and industry are rich, incredibly rich by the standards of the Soviet state economy, but weak. United States heavy industry, for example, needs to be completely reequipped to compete with competitors like South Korea, whom the Americans themselves put in business. Yet the Americans, from Madison Avenue to Capitol Hill, spend their resources instead on the gratification of frivolous wishes. Soviet society may be excessively stratified, so that the consumer has too little say. But the Soviet Union doesn't want so much freedom that its citizens can't walk in the parks at night. The Soviet Union doesn't want the rock records, the blue jeans, the idleness, and the antisocial attitudes that spell Western ideology. Its leaders are quite frank about wanting to keep all that out. A nation in which everyone performs military service (unless there are valid and not so valid reasons for exemption) wonders why Americans afford the luxury of a volunteer army, and why they pay people for not working when their parks and streets are in such need of workers.

In this condition of relative weakness, in any case, the United States was forced to negotiate with Russia on the basis of parity, equality. President Nixon began these negotiations. He was a realist and a true statesman, able to put behind his earlier strident anti-Communism in the search for peace.

But Watergate removed him from the scene. It is possible that Watergate was the creation of the opponents of détente, but more likely it was—as reported in the American press—a series of very corrupt actions that would have gone undetected except for political rivalries.

Détente caught the Cold War element in the United States by surprise. Apparently this group did not believe that Nixon— who, after all, was at one time one of its most active and vigorous members—was serious in trying to improve relations with the Soviet Union. As a result, the cold warriors needed a few years to regroup their forces. Those were the years when détente really was effective.

This Cold War element, also frequently referred to as "certain circles," can be isolated and identified. It includes the military-industrial complex, of course, but more: old leftists, former military men and diplomats, so-called Soviet experts, all people with a vested interest in maintaining tensions. There is an old Russian saying that covers the subject: "For most people, war and turmoil are truly hell, but for some, they are like the Holy Mother."

The Russians see the Cold War forces in ascendancy again. The Senate is a basically reactionary body that will not ratify UN human rights conventions because its members fear that would cost them reelection. Of course, Soviet officials know there are many currents in the Senate, but they say they wonder why the administration must negotiate everything subject to its approval and changes. When the Kremlin leaders agree to something, there is no problem with the Supreme Soviet.

The United States' Cold War forces were able to revive when Jimmy Carter became president. The Carter presidency was difficult to figure out, because his first cabinet included many people committed to détente and better relationships. It included Cyrus Vance, Harold Brown, and Michael Blumenthal, along with those, like Zbigniew Brzezinski, who were out-and-out advocates of cold war. The National Security Adviser is an obstacle to détente and is influenced by his Polish background as well as by his previous career in anti-Soviet activities at Columbia and in the government. His policies may or may not be based on the well-known anti-Russian attitudes of the Poles, but the point is that whatever their basis, they are usually not friendly, and for such a person to have a close daily relationship with the president is not a good thing for United States-Soviet relations. It is even possible that he had a role of some kind in the election of the Polish Pope; certainly it is known that the American cardinals who went to the conclave had their political instructions, as usual, before they left.

It is difficult to judge from a distance whether Carter is truly religious or uses religion as an excuse for pushing the human rights issue. But it must be noted that his religious feelings did not affect the peasants on his plantation. In any case, human rights was used as an anti-Soviet provocation at the start of the Carter administration, and in this, the United States was completely at odds with the rest of the world, even with its own

NATO partners. Human rights in this sense is a deepening of the ideological struggle, and, more seriously, it is a unilateral escalation—it is not a reaction to any stepping up of the struggle from the Soviet side.

Above all, raising human rights questions constitutes interference in the internal affairs of the Soviet Union. It is, further, an attempt by the Americans to change the Soviet system to be what America considers its own image—although its own human rights record is greatly deficient. The Soviet Union cannot condone anyone's telling it how to conduct its affairs.

There is a difference between ordinary interference and the interference practiced by the Carter team and by elements in the Congress before his administration began. This new kind of interference is making a certain kind of Soviet conduct—the provision of exit permits and the like—the prerequisite for normal trade relations, something that every other nation has with the USSR as a matter of course. The Soviet Union does not try to use pressure to modify American behavior and will not respond to pressure against it. If exit permits for Jews were fewer in number in 1977 than in previous years and greater after that, it had nothing to do with human rights campaigns, only the travel plans of the Jews, which vary with conditions at home and abroad. Except for criminals and certain sensitive cases, Jews and others are free to leave the Soviet Union, but employment problems in the United States and troubles in Israel often keep them at home.

The president's religion and Brzezinski's strategic planning combined to produce the human rights issue, but that doesn't explain the domestic need for the policy. The United States needed human rights to attract the liberals, the anti-Vietnam faction, to the anti-Soviet platform, which until then had been the exclusive property of the generals and the hard-liners in Congress. But it also needed to distract attention from the shambles of American power abroad and policy at home. By telling the world about alleged violations of human rights, the

Americans thought they could make it forget about the leadership crisis that resulted from Watergate, the loss of face that the defeat in Vietnam brought, and the loss of moral position that was caused by the revelations about the CIA and FBI.

The human rights campaign failed because the Soviet Union did not change its policies, and the United States lost trade opportunities worth several billion dollars. Russia proved it is not dependent on the Americans, either for business or for advanced technology. It can get all it wants from the other Western partners and Japan. In some areas, such as oil-drilling equipment, there are advantages in dealing with the United States, but it is also possible to wait 2 to 4 years to be able to buy the same things from United States subsidiaries or license holders elsewhere in the world.

The period of détente ended, for all intents and purposes, when Nixon left the White House. Despite his arms limitation achievements at Vladivostok, Ford was too weak to accomplish much. That relationships worsened with the advent of Carter and actions such as receiving the criminal Bukovsky—who is not even a human being—is beyond question.

The touchstone of relations in the eighties is the way the United States plays its China card. It is normal for nations to have diplomatic relations, and the Soviet Union cannot and does not object to that. But arming an aggressive China or entering into any kind of defensive alliance with it would endanger Soviet security and not be compatible with the continuation of détente.

The United States does not realize the threat the Chinese pose, not only to the rest of the world (the Soviet Union included) but to the Americans themselves. The Chinese have turned on their Soviet allies and providers of aid and technology, and they will also do so with the Americans. Before that, they are likely to turn their attention to India and Pakistan—which lie in the traditional direction of Chinese expansionism.

To sum up, from a safe and promising relationship with the

Soviet Union, the United States has moved in less than a de-cade to a volatile and dangerous one with China. This has not been the fault of the Soviet Union, whose aid to Third World nations and other activities have been consistent with its inter-national duties and have brought it not economic gain but con-siderable expense, not the least in scarce energy resources. It has been the fault of the United States.

It is not surprising that the Americans who deal with the Soviet Union on a day-to-day basis in Moscow and other capitals follow a different line of reasoning about the decline of reasonably good relations and the prospects for their re-vival in the future. If their Soviet counterparts are well pre-pared to interpret the United States through their knowledge of the language, culture, and political system, and often through prolonged periods of residence, the same can be said for the career Americans.

These veteran American observers believe it is unlikely that the United States will ever have friendly relations with a nation governed as the Soviet Union is. True friendship and identity of aims must await a change, not only in leaders, but in the system of leadership. The United States does not advo-cate such a change, considering it to be the internal affair of the USSR, but it is not interference to suggest that as long as the systems are so vastly different, the best that can be hoped for is the absence of conflict, and that is the aim of United States policy.

United States officials do not have a particular theory to explain the origins of the Cold War or the background of détente. The Soviet system has enough critics without addi-tional voices being added. But any nation with a leader like Stalin—not in the dim past of the revolution or civil war, but the contemporary of President Eisenhower—certainly be-longs to a different stage of political development, particularly in view of its reluctance to come to terms with the contemporary manifestations of Stalinism in public life: the cult of the personality of the leader, the impossibility of criticism, the secrecy and conspiratorial atmosphere that pervade much of the decision making.

The decisions made in recent years have been harmful to United States-Soviet relations, no matter what one's interpretation of linkage is. The United States believes that progress in arms limitation is too important to be threatened by United States displeasure over Soviet and Cuban military moves in Third World countries. But it also recognizes that one, two, or a dozen Senate votes on ratification of SALT or other treaties could hinge on individual senators' dislike of what the Soviet Union is doing abroad. If the Soviet leadership isn't aware of this, it cannot be because it has no access to information. Its advisers are quite sophisticated about differentiating among the different strata in Washington. They didn't used to be, but now they can distinguish elements of conflict, for example, between the State and Commerce departments on using trade as a political lever, and they realize that the White House may be called in to resolve such cases. Ascribing everything to the generals or top-hatted Wall Streeters may be fine for *Pravda*'s cartoonists, but the leaders are better served.

Whether they make use of this advice is another matter. Soviet advisers complained privately to their American counterparts that at one important United States-Soviet meeting, it was embarrassingly clear that the Politburo members who took part had not even bothered to read the briefing books that had been carefully prepared for them. At other times, Soviet advisers seem overly impressed by the amount of influence they think they have.

A comparatively recent development in United States-Soviet relationships provides a direct channel between Washington and Moscow. More and more members of Congress have been traveling to Moscow, because of a genuine interest in Soviet affairs, a particular interest like emigration, or a need for help in getting reelected. These senators and congressmen and women sit down with top Kremlin officials, and they exchange views directly and forthrightly, without the filters of advisers or diplomacy. The channel is recognized as important by both sides, particularly in view of Congress' stronger role in foreign policy of recent years.

Working groups established in the first years of détente are also able to cut through the propaganda arguments and get down to the issues dividing the two sides, although some group members wonder how much attention is paid to their findings in the two capitals.

"We do manage a general airing of views and misperceptions," an American group member said. "We know each other well enough to skip the polemics. We are broadly based, and the Soviet side appreciates this—they know that decisions in the United States are made on a number of bases, not just by the military-industrial complex. The buildup in central Europe and activities in Africa and the Middle East are discussed, as is human rights. China gets brought in as a justification for the Soviet buildup, the need to be prepared to fight a two-front war."

In these and the hundreds of other meetings at all diplomatic and political levels, the United States has sketched out some constants in Soviet behavior in recent years, characteristics that are by no means a sure guide to prediction of similar behavior in the future, but that have served well in anticipating some moves. The main ones are the aforementioned caution and conservatism in relations in general, the concern with China, and an overriding desire to be recognized as an equal partner by the United States.

Despite flirtations, past and continuing, with West Germany and France, the Soviet Union knows that it cannot substitute any other single country for the United States as its main partner in international relations, however difficult the Americans may seem to be in the human rights or Afghanistan controversies.

A United Europe might have this economic strength, but not the political strength as yet, and certainly not the strategic. Neither Germany nor France nor Europe as a whole has the power to destroy the Soviet Union in a nuclear war. Nor does any of them provide the deterrent against the destruction of the Soviet Union that targeting Soviet missiles on the United States provides.

And only the United States can provide the Soviet Union with the repeated recognition as a great power that it seems to need. This Big Two club is closed even to nuclear powers like France and Britain, because they do not have the other membership requirements. Neither, some Americans argue, does the Soviet Union—it assumes too much in putting itself on a level with the United States. A great power it certainly is—a great power with a superpower military establishment— but in other areas, the USSR is just a big underdeveloped nation that is unwilling to admit it.

Nevertheless, the important thing is that the Soviet Union insists it belongs to the club, and that it has an impressive, if incomplete, list of membership credentials. When the United States forgets this or tries to ignore it, the Soviet Union has a way of reminding Americans of it, even if it is by means of flying another unit of Cuban infantrymen to a distant corner of Africa, or of Soviet infantrymen to Cuba.

This striving for equality and recognition as an equal can be seen in Soviet explanations of why détente was possible. It was not weakness, but parity, that brought about détente, the United States is told repeatedly. And détente, rather than being a radical departure, is the product of the best conservative minds of the Kremlin.

Détente means preserving the achievements of the Soviet state, through Helsinki's guarantees of the borders won by

Red Army advances in 1944 and 1945, and through SALT. Arms limitation and control might seem at first glance to be a liberal policy; in the United States, at least, the conservatives are not among the pro-SALT lobbyists. But, it is argued, the Soviet leadership entered into SALT because it needed the resources freed by the limitation on strategic stockpiles in order to do a number of things to preserve the status quo: to continue the present economic program of trying to provide consumer goods, and to build up its conventional and tactical nuclear forces to use against the West and China. As long as the strategic arms race continued at its unchecked pace, there was no chance of maintaining both military and civilian production at satisfactory levels.

Conservatism does not rule out expansion in Africa or Asia, but it does dictate that the Soviet and Cuban adventures be confined to countries where the conflict with direct Western interests does not present too clear a challenge. Conservatism was seen in the Southeast Asian wars of 1978–1979, when Soviet troops were shuffled around the Chinese border, but the real fighting was done, and the real risks taken, by the Vietnamese, the Chinese, and a few Cambodians. In Afghanistan, as will be discussed later, Russian soldiers took the real risks, but the Russian government risked very little.

And finally, the Soviet Union admires conservatism in others, not so much as a political identification, but as a characteristic by which a negotiating partner or adversary can be better predicted. Soviet officials like to recall Henry Kissinger as such a partner, forgetting some unconservative actions like his secret flight to Peking, and they contrast his methods to the volatility of the administration that followed.

The United States sees a certain disadvantage, however, to relations with a nation that moves, even cautiously, into areas that seem threatening to Western interests, and that insists that such maneuvers are the business of no one but small nations like Cuba, Angola, Ethiopia, and Afghanistan.

In its dealings with the Russians, the United States rejects this line, pointing out that the Soviets do, indeed, have control over expeditionary forces as well as the receiving nations, and that their actions do have a substantial dampening effect on the Moscow-Washington relationship.

The essence of the Soviet-American relationship, in this American view, depends on understanding what détente really means. It does not imply mutual understanding, or friendship, or good relations. Its definition is clear, both in French and in Russian: relaxation of tensions. The United States, and the world, will have to realize that there will be periods of good and bad relations with the Soviet Union. Where there are common interests, the Americans will try to reach agreements such as the ones in arms control, science, and trade. Where common interests cannot be found, there will be friction and competition.

The fact that the basic floor of détente survives means that, if both nations respect it and its limitations, none of these points of friction and rivalry will lead to direct conflict between Russia and the United States, a conflict that would engulf the world.

Part II

THE SOVIET UNION AND EUROPE

5

Western Europe

THE FIRST TIME or the twentieth, the passage from Eastern to Western Europe is an occasion for relief and wonder. The heavy iron barrier lifts slowly from the concrete roadblocks, officials in little booths return passports and masses of scribbled forms, soldiers touch their carbines in salute, and the East recedes behind the barbed wire. At first, the West seems to mean only the absence of things Eastern. There are no collective farms, no guardhouses and tank traps, no banners hailing the other achievements of Communism. But then the West begins to make its own impact with things normally considered an annoyance: advertising billboards, brightly lit show windows, election posters of more than one candidate, graffiti against nuclear power or other government actions.

The billboards invite people to fly to New York or Brazil, showing East Europeans that once the East-West border has been cleared, there are no others that really present problems in the rest of the world. Other advertisements offer cars at prices within the reach of ordinary workers, and, indeed, the thickening traffic includes many such drivers. The main task of the police seems to be to keep this traffic from jamming, not to pull drivers over for arbitrary checks of their papers, and soldiers are a far rarer sight in the militaristic West than in the peace-loving East.

It is impossible for a Westerner to get inside the skin of an Easterner at such a moment, but many have described their feelings to Western fellow passengers on trains or planes. They suffer a mixture of political and cultural shock. Travel always brings discovery, but most travelers have at least a vague idea of what to expect. Soviet and Eastern European citizens, however, are taught to expect the opposite of what they will see.

Thousands of articles, books, speeches, and broadcasts have drummed into them the idea that Western Europe is a disaster area, economically and politically. It suffers from inflation and unemployment, they are told. It is ruled by reactionary governments. It groans under the burden of a military-industrial clique and is frightened by its adventurist plans.

What they discover instead is a variety of social systems with a variety of problems, but none so bad as they have been led to expect, or as bad as those they have left behind. They are most impressed by the completely new (to them) concept that there are different ways of approaching these problems, and that it is best to discuss and argue about these ways in public. That is the main East-West difference, not the contrast between full shop windows and drab, half-empty state stores.

The comparative handful of Easterners who get to visit the West learn this, but their governments do not seem to. Soviet and Eastern European official attitudes remain focused on the Western Europe of the forties—still torn, politically and economically, by World War II and looking leftward for salvation. They do not see the new, integrated, and increasingly confident Europe that began to emerge in the sixties.

Soviet policy has been directed, from the start, at exploiting the divisions among European countries, and the differences that those countries have with the United States. But other Soviet actions keep getting in the way. When the Soviet embassy in Lisbon plays a key role behind the scenes in an attempted coup by the local Communist Party, or when Soviet navy landing craft hold maneuvers near the peaceful Baltic islands of Denmark, Western Europeans tend to cling more tightly to their international arrangements for economic, political, and military security and reject Soviet ideas for separate alliances or armament-free zones.

And then the Russians draw back with an air of injury, accuse Europe of wanting a return to the Cold War, and issue threats—these days reduced trade, a few years ago nuclear weapons—that only serve to confirm the fears of the Western Europeans.

Soviet inability to influence Western Europe did not come about because of lack of opportunity. The Russians were admired and appreciated in the early postwar years for their part in liberating Europe from Nazi Germany, and Communists entered the governments of Italy and France. Communist ministers were no better or worse than their bourgeois colleagues in coping with Europe's multiplicity of problems. What turned them out of office in the forties was the politics practiced in the East.

The death of democracy, which occurred after the war in one Eastern European government after another and which culminated in the 1948 Prague coup, was what consigned the Communists to permanent minority status in the West and, indeed, made it difficult for years for even moderate Socialists to attract votes.

Soviet political practices became such a liability, in fact, that Europe devised a new kind of Communism that denied their applicability and campaigned for election with promises that NATO would shield the Communist regimes that would be established in the West from Soviet attempts to undermine their independence.

Soviet relations with Western Europe will be examined, first from the standpoint of the Eurocommunist movement, and then from the aspects of nationalism, as practiced in France, the American alliance, as practiced in Great Britain, and the combination of both these political stances that characterizes West Germany.

The Eurocommunists are the first to say that there is no Eurocommunism. Their search for a way out of the blind alley of dependence on Moscow, they say, cannot lead them to the establishment of another center of authority, in East or West.

But there are Eurocommunist parties, and there is consultation, if not always agreement, among their leaders. Whether or not this constitutes a movement—many Eurocommunists deny that it does—there are common principles that link them. Whatever it is called, Eurocommunism flourishes in the political life of Italy, France, and Spain, where the three most important Communist parties of Western Europe operate. Being European and Communist, it must be stressed, is not enough to qualify as being Eurocommunist. Portugal's party is both, but staunchly loyal to Moscow and authoritarian in its internal structure. Germany has two Communist parties, neither of which is Eurocommunist. The first follows the Soviet and East German lines faithfully, and the second is a Chinese satellite.

What distinguishes Eurocommunism is its rejection of both the Soviet and the Western Social Democratic solutions for the problems of capitalist society, coupled with the promise of solving those problems democratically, through the electoral process and not revolution. These policies have attracted large numbers of intellectuals and young people, in addition to the working class, to Party ranks. They have also attracted the enmity of Moscow and the suspicion of Washington.

Manuel Azcarte, foreign affairs spokesman for the Spanish Communist Party, argues that anything mistrusted by both the Soviet Union and the United States must be all right. The Western contention that Eurocommunism is formally independent of Moscow but actually its servile tool, and the Soviet contention that it is an invention of the imperialists aimed at wrecking Communist unity are both wrong, he says: "Since it cannot be a maneuver in both these senses, it is not a maneuver at all." One could argue with Azcarte that it might be a maneuver in *one* of these senses. But it is better to examine Eurocommunism's background, professed policies, and likelihood of future political success.

The Eurocommunists say they are needed because capitalism has failed Europe and because the other kinds of socialists, Soviet-style or democratic like the Scandinavians, cannot do the job of fixing the economies. But it could be argued that the Social Democrats have had considerable electoral success in northern Europe. That, the Eurocommunists respond, is just the trouble. They have attained power but have made no real use of it. They have not transformed society; they have preserved capitalism. In fact, the Eurocommunists argue with a trace of envy, perhaps that is why they continue to get elected—the voters know that they are not going to change things very much. But, the argument continues, the voters are wrong: The economic misery and alienation in the Western world cannot be cured by any of the solutions tried or proposed to date by the ordinary bourgeois or slightly-left-of-center parties. Radical change is needed. But it cannot be imposed from above, which is why Communism doesn't work very well in Eastern Europe. It must come through the ballot box. And as important as the ability to vote Communism into power, the Eurocommunists insist, is the ability to vote it out of power again if it does not live up to its promises.

Historians and analysts of Eurocommunism, in and outside the Party, trace its birth to events outside Western Europe. One account calls it the illegitimate child of détente and the Sino-Soviet conflict. Without the first, Western pressure would have kept the most important party, the Italian, out of the "historic compromise" of the late seventies, in which it shared responsibility with the Christian Democrats for governing the country, without actually being in the cabinet. Without the second, the arguments and then the split with Moscow could not have succeeded. China's independence both encouraged the European parties and made the Soviet Union more reluctant to divide the movement even more by cracking down on them.

Others say Khruschev's 1956 denunciation of Stalin made it possible for the European parties to avoid practicing Stalinism, as they had had to do up until that time, in the highly inappropriate surroundings of Western electoral politics. Nevertheless, many of them waited some time before taking advantage of this freedom.

The Prague Spring is yet another influence. Czech and Slovak reformers produced the first model of Communism in Eastern Europe that was not based on Lenin's half-century-old rules intended for czarist Russia. This encouraged the Western parties to try the same.

In any case, there is general agreement that a long-term return to East-West tensions would make the atmosphere very difficult for Eurocommunism. That is why its leaders are also generally agreed not to follow any course of political action that might upset the East-West balance. For the Italians, this meant great reticence in entering the cabinet. Internal documents of the Italian Communist Party contend that

Washington would consider a major shift to the Communists in any European country as a product of Moscow interference in an area where Moscow has no business. The United States would be wrong, these documents say, but that is immaterial. The destabilizing effect would be the same. That is why the Italian party, both in these documents and in public pronouncements, argues that a flourishing, prosperous Western Europe, free of Soviet pressure, is the best climate in which to operate, to gain votes, and to bring about the changes they want to see.

This Western Europe also includes the shield of NATO, and Enrico Berlinguer, secretary of the Italian Communist Party, is on record as having said that he does not want to see the Italian experiment snuffed out as the Czechoslovak one was, with the clear implication that NATO tanks protect Eurocommunism from Soviet tanks.

Frequent and biting criticism of the Soviet system is an important characteristic of Eurocommunism, as these views * from leading members of the Spanish, French, and Italian parties make clear:

"The first socialist revolution in the history of the world turned into an authoritarian regime, a despotism in which power resides undemocratically in the hands of a small nucleus."

"Even today, the dead hand of Russian history inhibits the development of Soviet Socialism. That is why there is in the Soviet Union no democratic opposition, no free press, no freedom of association, no freedom of assembly, no freedom of opinion."

"For us today, the whole system of power-from-the-top, the entire idea of dictatorship, has become false, utterly false,

---

* Taken, with much of the other material for this section, from G. M. Urban's excellent *Eurocommunism* (London: Maurice Temple Smith, 1979).

even if in those early and terrible decades of Soviet isolation in a capitalistic environment and under Fascist attack, Leninism was the simplest way of maintaining unity at home and security abroad."

Since these sentiments are widespread, although not unanimous, among the leaderships of the three most powerful Communist parties in Western Europe, it can be seen that the Soviet Union faces a problem of some dimensions. Not only are these Communists trying to increase their vote by impressing voters with their democratic intentions, they are also using as one of their main arguments the glaring lack of voting rights in the countries of the East and putting themselves squarely against such practices, as they must if their professed commitment to democracy is to be believed. Such a policy would be called anti-Soviet and the work of dissidents if it were proclaimed in the East, but the dissidents of Eurocommunism cannot be silenced or locked up.

And when men like Berlinguer and his elegant young theoreticians and planners cross over to Hungary for meetings with Janos Kadar, the party leader, or to Romania to see President Nicolae Ceaucescu, the dangers to Moscow are clear. It could be argued that none of the Eastern European leaders needs Western advice on how to make Communism more popular, only the removal of Soviet troops or influence. But listening to mavericks with Eurocommunist Party cards might just make the Eastern European leaders a shade more independent and ready to take risks. If this is true for Western Communists out of power, it can be imagined that their arguments would carry even more weight if they attain power. A Eurocommunist government or coalition in Western Europe, if it would keep to its promises of wedding socialism and democracy, would be an example of enormous attraction to Eastern Europe. And this is why, from this aspect, at least, the Soviet Union has no wish to see the Eurocommunists in power.

This does not mean the Russians would oppose a Communist government in the West; too much would be at stake for that in terms of loss of prestige for the democracies and gains for the Communist world. But Russia would certainly hope, and almost certainly work, for less democracy in that government.

Many in the West suspect it would not be very difficult to rid the Eurocommunists of their democratic tendencies, since they contend that this commitment to democracy is very shallow in any case. No Communist regime has ever surrendered power voluntarily at the polls. Why, after the long years of exile, persecution, and powerlessness, before having a chance to get its new programs going, would a Communist party government want to do so now? The Eurocommunists argue that there are first times for everything.

Soviet officials do not have a very consistent line of argument on Eurocommunism, as perhaps befits a situation they are not equipped to understand. On the one hand, they quote with approval Moscow's official condemnation of the Spanish Party for abandoning Leninism in favor of more democracy: "It is impossible to renounce Lenin while at the same time declaring loyalty to Marxism." On the other hand, they contend that there is real democracy in the Eastern versions of Communism, as proved by the 99-plus percentages of votes cast for the Parties with absolute predictability in every election from Khabarovsk to Bratislava. And finally, they concede that even an un-Leninist Communist party would be a step forward for Western European voters, and that having voted it into power, they would be extremely unlikely to vote the Communist party out, since socialism is a higher level of the organization of society than the democratic pluralist forms it would have replaced, and it just doesn't make sense that people would want to reverse the course of history and revert to a less progressive level.

So, in effect, the Soviet Union comes down squarely in

favor of the undemocratic features of Eurocommunism and against the democratic, although, of course, officials do not put the argument in those terms. They do point out with some justification, however, that Communist rule in the East is a long-established fact and that Communist rule in the West has yet to be tried, and that perhaps the experienced Communists ought to be listened to more than the theorists in the cafés of Paris and Rome. Moscow calls this "established socialism," says it has "proved its undoubted advantage over the political system of capitalism and ensured constant progress on the road to social and economic development," and contends it is a logical if not obligatory model for the Western parties to follow. Those Western parties rejected the obligation to follow it at the last attempt at Communist unification, the Berlin summit of 1976, when the Eurocommunists and others refused to accept a general line valid for all parties.

This kind of democracy in inter-party relations disturbs Moscow as much as do the domestic plans of the Eurocommunists. And more and more, Soviet practices disturb the Western parties and hurt them at the polls. The French, for example, issued a statement assessing the general direction of development in the Soviet Union as positive and applauding "every success gained in the development of Soviet socialist society.

"But, at the same time," the statement added, "in the name of the Communist ideal, they consider it not only their right, but their duty to comment publicly on everything that could harm socialism. That is why they cannot remain silent about the serious differences they have with the Communist Party of the Soviet Union . . . mainly about the democratic component of socialism."

And thus democracy in the Western parties rubs the Soviet Party in three ways: by allowing criticism of the Soviet lack of democratic practices; by using so much democracy in their own elections in the West that they risk being turned out of power by the voters; and by advocating both these practices for Eastern Europe.

This leaves the Soviet Union with two equally undesirable alternatives: to abandon its support for the Western Communist parties and thus give up a long-sought opportunity to influence political life in the Western European democracies, or to put up with far-ranging criticism of Soviet society, both in the commentaries on current Soviet practice and in the plans for Western Communist models that specifically exclude Soviet practice. The Soviet response has been to do neither but to try to get the Eurocommunists to change.

But to the democrats in the West, there are disturbing signs that the Eurocommunists practice democracy too little, not too much.

Communist parties have always differed from the democratic parties in Western parliaments because of their adherence to a bundle of old rules and regulations, the legacy of the early twentieth-century interpretation of Marxism devised by Lenin to cope with the specific conditions of the Russian society he had to work in.

Illegal and harried by the czarist secret police, with only a tiny minority of the nation educated or eligible to vote, Lenin's party had to be organized on conspiratorial lines and had to seize power by violent revolution. It was able to retain power only through the continuation of this violence, in the Cheka terror, the Civil War, and the labor camps that Stalin introduced as an improvement on Leninism. Democracy in the internal life of the party was considered impossible under those conditions; policy was made at the top and carried out obediently by the rank and file. The system worked, or at least survived, in the highly specific conditions of the Soviet

Union, but it could never attract more than a minority in the conditions of the West—large minorities, as in prewar Germany and in the contemporary French and Italian Parties, with 600,000 and 1.8 million members respectively (almost all, in fact, of the 3 million Communists in the West), or powerless small groups such as Britain's 25,000-member Party. Sometimes, as in the Popular Front days of the thirties, the Moscow line made it possible to gain a larger following by playing down the Leninism and playing up the democracy and willingness to cooperate with other parties. But it was really not until the de-Stalinization signal was given in Moscow in 1956 that the Western Communists were able to escape these burdens from the past, and it must be noted that in the case of the French, it took a further 20 years finally to respond clearly to the signal.

After condemning the gulags and the terror, the Western Parties set out to peel away the layers of authoritarianism that the great figures of the movement—Marx, Lenin, and Stalin—had wrapped around the basic egalitarianism. Tacitly or formally, the Eurocommunists first shed the dictatorship of the proletariat, Marx's vague term that had been abused and transformed into the dictatorship of one man, and then Lenin's dictum to seek and cling to power through violence.

Terror is not a popular policy, and the critics of Eurocommunism are satisfied that the parties have indeed put Stalin behind them. They are less sure whether other antidemocratic tendencies do not remain. The Italians, for example, in forswearing the dictatorship of the proletariat replaced it with something that sounded quite similar—the hegemony of the proletariat—except that it was the product of Italy's own Communist thinker, Antonio Gramsci.

Does hegemony mean that, having gained power, the working class will not want to yield it? Not at all, the Italian Communists insist: "Once we accept the rules of the game and come to power through the ballot box, we are committed to respecting those rules, whether they benefit us or not," Italian Central Committee member Lucio Lombardo Radice told G. M. Urban, the Eurocommunism scholar, in an interview. He added, however, that "once the working class has acquired hegemony and led Italian society out of its almost permanent crisis, it would be difficult to envision anyone wanting a regression from a better state of society to a worse state."

The Communist president of the Italian Chamber of Deputies, Pietro Ingrao, has put forward a peculiar idea of a kind of parliamentary democracy in which there would be no opposition. It is purely a bourgeois concept that there must be opposition parties in a legislature, he maintains. Parliaments can also be unitary organizations, where the various groups of society—workers' organizations and schools, for example—are represented in a "higher level" of democracy that sounds a great deal like the Supreme Soviet.

The way a party runs its own affairs is a better guide to the way it might run the country than the theories and promises of its leaders. And in this respect, many democrats would have trouble with democratic centralism, an important tenet of Marxism-Leninism that the Eurocommunists have not seen fit to unload. In its pure form, it permits free discussion (although not the formation of factions) until the majority has decided on an issue or policy. At that point party members, high and low, of whatever view, must adopt the majority decision and defend it as if it were their own or risk exclusion on grounds of factionalism.

Democratic centralism enabled the French Communist Party to perform the amazing feat of voting to retain the dictatorship of the proletariat in 1975 by a vote of 1,700 to zero, and to abolish it in 1976 by exactly the same vote. In 1979, when the Italian Communist party sought to analyze its electoral losses, it permitted free discussion among the governing bodies and a great deal of airing of dissatisfaction, but only up to a certain point. A 6-day limit was imposed, under democratic centralist principles, and then the law of unanimity descended.

"It is necessary and possible to improve the Party's internal organization," the intellectual gadfly of the French Communists, Jean Elleinstein,* has said. "But . . . I am not saying that democratization will, or should, result in the organization of majorities and minorities. . . . We must conserve certain rules of centralism. It would be dangerous to introduce and formally legalize splinter groups and minorities, because they would divide the Party and impede decisive action.

"After all," Elleinstein concludes, "we are not talking about rules for the organization of society; we are talking about the reorganization of the internal life of the Party." But if a Party is concerned with eliminating minorities and splinter groups in its internal business when out of power, could it be expected to be any more tolerant of them if it gets its historic chance to direct French society?

Western critics also worry about the effect of Eurocommunist electoral victories on the West's defense capabilities. French forces are not under peacetime NATO control, and Spain, where the Party has only a 9 percent following in the electorate, is not a NATO member as yet, and so attention focuses on Italy. Could the other NATO partners count on a Eurocommunist-governed Italy? Urban put this question to the Party spokesman, and the response was not reassuring.

"The Italian Communist Party would not want to commit itself to either side," was the first reaction of Lombardo Radice. "It would be for peace." But if a choice did have to be

---

* That there are limits to the gadfly role was shown by Elleinstein's decision to leave the Party in 1980 to protest the Soviet invasion of Afghanistan and French Communist backing for it.

made, the Italian Party would "certainly oppose anti-Soviet-ism. It would be against any move to roll back the present frontiers of socialism and *a fortiori* to destroy it." In other words, a Communist-governed Italy would, or might, support NATO in a purely defensive war. But the Communists would reserve their right to withdraw support if, in their opinion, the war was not purely defensive, or if it changed its character while in progress.

The prospect of Communists in the government of Portugal, another NATO member, caused the organization to withhold secret military information from Lisbon in 1975 and 1976. But Portugal's Communists are different: unequivocal in their loyalty to Moscow and remote from power, since the failure of their *putsch* attempt and the support for democratic parties from, among others, the Social Democrats of Northern Europe. With 30 of the 247 seats in the Lisbon parliament, the Portuguese Communists can influence NATO planning no more than the Spanish can.

Equivocal about Western defense and about democracy inside and outside the Party, the Eurocommunists, for all their criticism of Soviet practice, have a long way to go before convincing skeptical Western observers about their moderation and commitment to playing by the political rules.

But there are skeptics, too, on the other side—rank and file Party members who increasingly find their leaders too moderate and too committed to the rules.

On the walls of Italian buildings, the graffiti formula PCI = DC (Italian Communist Party equals Christian Democrats) is a familiar sight, even outside local party headquarters offices. It signifies the dissatisfaction of the radicals in Italy—whether PCI members or Party opponents in the splinter groups further left—with the policies of cooperating with the Center and, in general, with the whole game of parliamentarianism and moderation.

The Italian Communists' first postwar loss in a national election, when they dropped from about 34 to 30 percent of the vote in 1979, was widely seen as proof of this disillusionment. Election analyses, including some by the Party, showed that people who wanted a more radical, vociferously anticapitalist line either voted for the splinter groups further left or stayed home. The resultant vote loss for the Communists was 3 million. This feeling was apparent from the shouted questions and heckling in some of the PCI's factory and big city electoral rallies. It came out, too, in the postmortems conducted by Berlinguer.

The French Communist Party was unable to overcome the tradition of suspicion and distrust of everything to the right, even (or perhaps particularly) if it is the Socialists, and the 1978 electoral coalition fell apart as a result. A strong streak of antibossism runs through European workers. They vote Communist because they want to shake things up, not necessarily because they approve of Moscow's human rights policies. The Communist vote is a protest vote against the establishment in the country voting. And when the Communist Party seems to be joining the establishment, or moderating its tough, quasi-military structure, the protest vote might just go to someone else or might not be cast at all.

The dilemma for the parties is clear: if you drop the Soviet-style trappings and agree to work within the system, you win voters at one end of the political scale but risk losing them at the other. If you go back the other way, you make the Party a great deal easier to run and smooth relations with Moscow but lose the moderate backers as you pick up the protest voters.

The parties must move in one direction or the other, if they are not to remain in the minority forever. And here the dilemma emerges again, as Urban notes. Eurocommunism, he says, "must either end in Social Democracy or revert back to some form of Leninism. In the first case it will cease to be Communist; in the second it will no longer be Euro."

Despite past Soviet support, financial and political, for Western Communist parties, Moscow has chosen to work mostly at the government level for influence in Western Europe, sometimes at the expense of the Communists, as in the case of its preference for Gaullism in the sixties in France. Playing one political party against another in a nation is consistent with Soviet policy for the entire western part of the continent, where—with alternate promises and threats—it encourages German to distrust Frenchman, Frenchman to distrust Briton, all nationals to distrust the integration of Europe, and integrated Europe—as well as its individual components—to distrust the United States.

In this respect, Soviet policy toward Western Europe is no different from its policy toward Eastern Europe. Every attempt of the Eastern Europeans to form their own political or economic units, separate from or equal to the Soviet Union—such as Tito's Balkan Federation with Bulgaria, the several attempts at Danube Federation, and the Little Entente revival scheme of Czechoslovakia, Romania, and Yugoslavia in 1968—brought trouble from Moscow.

Western Europe cannot be brought into line in this way, but it can be pressured and wooed with trade, and this has been the pattern of Soviet relations with Europe for 30 years.

A Soviet official more familiar with the Western European political landscape than most concedes that there may be some misreading of the trends there by the people in Moscow. Western Europe, in his view, is unique in containing strivings for both greater unity and greater diversity. Despite the repeated suggestions of those Soviet diplomats who deal regularly with Western Europe, no systematic attempt has been made in the Soviet Union to try to understand the phe-

nomenon better. There is no Western European Institute on
a level with Arbatov's America think-tank, these Europe-
anists say, but there ought to be if the Kremlin is to receive a
better grade of policy advice.

Until then, it seems likely that the old policies of divide,
with the ultimate hope of rule, will continue, with nationalist
France at once the most attractive and the most elusive of
the targets.

The Russians have looked on France as an instrument useful in several ways. Russia's first concern was to keep alive
France's old and justified suspicion of Germany; the second,
to achieve French independence from the United States; the
third, to spark French resentment of the special relationship
Britain enjoyed with America; and the fourth, to encourage
French espousal of national rather than federal Europe, including national armies rather than the European Defense
Community or even NATO.

In and out of power, the key to France was Charles de
Gaulle, and long before de Gaulle's return to the government in 1958, Soviet embassy limousines would make the
long trip to his home in Colombey-les-deux-Eglises in eastern France, to wait while ambassadors and ministers from
Moscow conferred with the General. De Gaulle had some
drawbacks, as became apparent after 1958. At home, he was
a relentless opponent of the Communists. Abroad, he would
tolerate no tampering with his solution for Algeria and
above all, no foreign recognition of the Algerian rebels.

The Soviet Union complied with this wish, but with enormous difficulty. Nonrecognition went against all the Third
World policies the Russians were beginning to pursue at that
time, and it ran directly against Peking's open support of the
Algerians. Here was an early example of the differences in
Peking-Moscow relations. To avoid being counted for or
against the Algerians, Moscow was forced to the extreme of

voting for procedural loopholes at the United Nations Security Council.

It was worth it to the Russians, because they saw de Gaulle, the leader of the Free French struggle against Nazi Germany, as their guarantee of the permanence of French-German enmity. But not for the first time, or for the last, de Gaulle upset his partner's calculations. He began a series of meetings with Konrad Adenauer, the West German Chancellor, in the first year of his return to French politics. And, despite warnings from Khrushchev that this was comparable to the Hitler-Mussolini talks, he began to lay the groundwork for Franco-German reconciliation.

The Russians were far more pleased with the emerging Gaullist policies toward the United States, and they encouraged every new show of independence with praise for the general as a realist of broad vision, and for France as a great power. Soviet recognition of the Algerian provisional government in 1960 did nothing to slow the Gaullist drive for less dependence on the United States, a drive that culminated in the removal of NATO headquarters from France and the withdrawal of French troops from NATO's operational control. That was because Gaullist policy had a vast momentum and rationale of its own and was far from being a tool of Russia, as was frequently contended at the time.

The individuality of French policy became all the more clear when de Gaulle, to the surprise of the world and the Soviet Union in particular, launched his concept of a Europe of nations from the Atlantic to the Urals, and his formula for East-West relations: détente, leading to entente, leading to cooperation.

It was an abrupt departure from all the Cold War policies and practices up to that time, since they were based on a divided Europe and a Western refusal to make the first move toward the East as long as the regimes there remained hostile and challenging. De Gaulle took the step with his 1966 visit to Moscow.

The Russians welcomed de Gaulle (the first French head of state since Napoleon to sleep in the Kremlin), but for reasons more of triangle politics than of Napoleonic power. France stood for a great many policies the Russians agreed with and opposed a great many they opposed. Both were against the nuclear arming of Germany; both favored recognition of Communist China. Both opposed the United States' intervention in Southeast Asia, and both sought to remove Europe from American influence.

The Soviets talked of a special relationship with France, and Soviet communiqués of the period referred to "the two Continental great powers." Trade grew, and there were plans for cooperation even in space. A *Pravda* editorial at the time of de Gaulle's Moscow visit laid bare, probably unintentionally, Soviet hopes for the ultimate goals of the relationship. The Soviet Communist Party paper told the French they ought to be masters in their own house, that Americans stationed on their territory undermined their sovereignty because the Americans acted as if France were their protectorate, not a proud, independent nation. NATO itself, *Pravda* continued, was a danger to peace, and France was particularly in danger, not only from NATO but also from European integration under the Americans. Fortunately, however, creation of a "rump Europe" had been prevented by French action, and the "day of the American protectorate over this or any other state in Europe belongs to the past."

In the Moscow talks, the Russian line ran thus: "No one in Western Europe thinks there is a danger from the East anymore, and yet the Americans are acting as if there were, trying to dominate Europe as they do Vietnam. We, the Russians, and you, the French, oppose that kind of domination in Southeast Asia, so why not extend this opposition to the

American domination of Europe, recognizing that you are finally big and strong enough to defend yourselves without the United States?" De Gaulle answered, in effect, with a completely different proposition. He explained what he meant by a Europe from the Atlantic to the Urals, and the Russians did not like it. It would be a Europe, he stressed, with freedom of movement for all the individual nations inside this vast area, whether Communist or democratically ruled, and that meant an end to blocs, whether in the West or in the East. The Soviet side was not prepared to respond to this, and the final communiqué, although it bore the lofty title of the Declaration of Moscow, said very little about either side's proposal.

In the meantime, de Gaulle was being overtaken on the right. A few months after the French-Soviet summit, Lyndon Johnson, in an October 1966 speech written by a State Department adviser named Zbigniew Brzezinski (not very well known then outside academic circles) called for a policy of building bridges between Western and Eastern Europe, with the impetus to come from the West.

The Soviet leadership was wary, but it began to take notice. "If the United States is ready to extend cooperation," the argument went, "why not explore it? France is, after all, a useful irritant in Europe, but a second-rate power that cannot measure up to the United States in nuclear potential, trade, or the space race." Vietnam made it impossible to go too far in this direction, but in the meantime the General was showing the Russians some of the dangers of his new Europe that stretched to their Ural mountains.

In state visits to Poland and Romania in 1967 and 1968, de Gaulle made speech after speech condemning the restraints imposed by the membership of those two nations in the bloc system. He offered a special relationship to help the breaking up of blocs. Watching the reaction of Wladyslaw Gomulka, then Polish Communist chief, as he replied in the Sejm (the Polish parliament) to de Gaulle's offer was a lesson in the depth of Eastern Europe's dependence on Russia. Only in the West can one defy the dominating power and survive. Gomulka's savage, frightened response to de Gaulle showed how little vague talk about the future weighed against the realities of enforced loyalty to Moscow.

Had de Gaulle remained in office, the probes into the Soviet backyard would have continued, as they did, but with less drama, under his successors Georges Pompidou and Valéry Giscard d'Estaing. The probes were not well received; this is not the kind of bloc-free movement the Soviet Union has in mind. It wants all the movement to take place on the Western side of the bloc lineup. But in any case, by 1972, Russia had all but abandoned France as an important lever in the attempt to divide Europe and diminish American influence. From that time on, it was possible to deal with the real rival power, the United States, and, incidentally, to concede it a permanent role in Europe in the process.

Decades of Soviet diplomacy in France had brought very little lasting result, despite the drama of the de Gaulle era. France had left NATO, and NATO France, but this was hardly an achievement for Soviet diplomacy. France's feeling of nationhood, its conviction that no one else could be counted on to defend it, played the main part. Despite all sorts of hedges that ensure a French commitment to the West in case of war, it is clear that the French action hurt NATO and helped the Soviet military. But it also made the alliance more responsive to the wishes of the smaller European members, and it did not cause its collapse. On the other side of the bloc borders, France might have played a role in Romania's independent actions within the Warsaw Pact.

Other Soviet hopes were disappointed completely, above all, the attempt to keep France and West Germany apart.

The two nations are now such close partners that the rest of
Europe worries about their dominance.

The Common Market is alive and vigorous. Only the
French Communists oppose its admitting Spain, Greece, and
other Southern European nations, since their proletarian internationalism does not extend to the workers of those countries who would be able to threaten French jobs if they were
European Economic Community (EEC) members.

De Gaulle did shake things up, and he probably played a
role in the decisions of other leaders to end the Cold War.
He might have been the inspiration for the Nixon visit to
Moscow. Nixon claims full credit for taking the initiative
with the Russians, but, after all, another unorthodox conservative had been there before him. The French prepared the
way, in Peking as well as in Moscow, but then they had to
stand aside for the Americans. It is not that the French have
disappeared from the scene in the Soviet Union and Eastern
Europe or China; they are as active as ever. It is a tribute to
French diplomatic skill that Paris manages to have, at the
same time, a treaty of friendship with the Soviet Union and
an agreement to sell arms to its enemy China.

The landscape of British-Soviet relations looks simple indeed compared to the complicated features of French-Soviet
relations. Britain had no de Gaulle; it did not want to be
number one in Europe; it had no rivalry with the United
States; it was and is a loyal NATO member and eventually
even joined the EEC.

This set of British positions meant that a different set of
Soviet initiatives had to be used, although the tactics, in general, followed the old carrot-and-stick rule.

Some of the latter were particularly crude, such as Premier
Nikolai Bulganin's letter to the British people warning that
the use of nuclear weapons against "such a comparatively

small and densely populated territory as the British Isles" would be grave indeed, but hastening to assure his readers that "nothing could be further from the truth than possible attempts to interpret my words as threats and intimidation." Bulganin's aim was to persuade the British people not to let the United States station nuclear submarines in Scotland; it failed.

The carrots were appropriately generous. From time to time, Britain enjoyed the position of being the Soviet Union's leading Western trading partner, relinquishing the position later to the French and the Germans, for other sets of political reasons.

Britain has always been troublesome for the Soviet Union because of its close relationship with the United States. But at the same time, that relationship makes the British important for the Soviets to try to influence.

A British official summed up the Moscow interests as follows: "Rightfully or wrongfully, they consider us a pipeline to the United States, able to influence American actions or, at the very least, to interpret them to the Russians. They also use us as a proxy target when they want to hurt the United States but not hit it directly."

The Russians had high hopes, for example, as did the British themselves, that former Labour Prime Minister Harold Wilson would be able to use his influence on the United States to end the Vietnam war. But in the end Britain proved too closely tied to the United States, and de Gaulle, who was opposed to the war and outspoken about it, proved more valuable than the loyal Wilson.

Britain proved to be a handy surrogate target in 1968, in the repercussions over the Soviet invasion of Czechoslovakia. Britain protested with official statements and spontaneous demonstrations, as did much of the rest of the world. But unlike the rest of the world, Britain was selected to bear the main burden of Soviet wrath. The Russians said the British reaction was inconsistent with recent attempts to improve relations and constituted "anti-Soviet hysteria." The Soviet role in disturbing those relations wasn't mentioned.

When the British public refused to quit objecting to the Soviet occupation, the Russians went a step further and charged that London was using Czechoslovakia as a pretext to undermine the carefully improved climate of the previous 2 years. Why was Britain singled out? The French, too, had protested with demonstrations and statements, but the French government moved quickly to patch up relations, considering the needs of practical politics and détente more important than the moral satisfaction of condemning what was in any case a *fait accompli*. France did not take part, as Britain did, in the NATO buildup that followed the invasion. The main reason the British bore the brunt, in the view of diplomats involved with the Russians during that period, was the Soviet need to strike out hard at the West for its moral defeat in Czechoslovakia without posing any direct challenge to the United States, where a new president-elect held out hope of improved relations.

Four years after the occupation furor, British-Soviet relations plunged even lower when Britain expelled or refused to let return 105 Soviet diplomats, trade officials, and journalists on charges of espionage. It took 18 months to restore even cool relations after that. But the patterns of ups and downs have continued, with fewer dramatic dips, whether Labour or Conservative prime ministers live in No. 10 Downing Street.

The patterns contain something of a contradiction. On the one hand, as Soviet officials concede, Russia's aim is to get Britain to act more independently of the United States, to feel less bound to NATO and particularly to the West Germans who, the British are constantly reminded by the Russians, would like to dominate them. On the other hand, if the Russians really succeed in dividing Britain from the United

States and other members of the alliance, a great deal of Britain's value would be lost to them, because then the United States would not have to pay attention to British interpretations of Soviet intentions or listen to British counsel against rash acts that might damage détente.

The dilemma is not a very great one. In the British view, the advantages of detachment from the special relationship with the United States are so slight, and the disadvantages of any closer relationship with the Soviet Union so great, that no real movement is likely. And although this viewpoint is not shared by the Soviet Union, there is evidence that the Russians accept it.

Britain's, France's, and, as will be discussed later, Germany's relations with Russia have direct bearing on the kind of relations they feel able to have with China. Those with less to lose in Moscow are in a position to try to gain in Peking; those with much at stake in the Soviet relationship must be proportionally more cautious with the Chinese.

But China does not make these choices easy. It has no reason to wish for smooth relations between any of its new Western contacts and the Soviet Union. That is one of the dangers to the Europeans of playing triangle politics: to find themselves being used against each other by one of the Communist powers.

But for Britain, France, and Germany, the other danger is paramount. The Soviet Union is a great continental power, and on their continent. It is easily able to rain rockets, even medium-range ones, on their cities, and China is not. As a result, the China card must be carefully considered.

Britain, France, and Germany do give their relations with China careful consideration, although they are also careful not to be intimidated by Soviet thundering. The picture that has emerged is of a Britain tilting toward China, a Germany tilting toward Russia, and a France managing rather well in balancing relations between both Communist powers.

Britain goes about its China policy in the realization that, over the years, Moscow has lost much of its leverage with London. Trade no longer has the importance it once had, particularly if trade with China can replace or exceed it. The coldness of Soviet-British relations may show the great power of retribution Russia has against a nation too closely tied to the United States, but it also exhausts Soviet possibilities of influence. It is a diplomatic axiom that if one lets relations sink close to zero, one also loses leverage for influencing the other nation's actions.

The Chinese, for their part, make it difficult for the British by insisting on the sale of arms as a sign of good faith. You cannot be trusted partners, they say, unless you trust us with some weapons. The Germans are able to resist such blandishments; they would have too much to lose from the Russians. The British have very little.

But in any case, British officials say, Britain does have an interest in a strong China, able to defend itself, as a stabilizing factor in world affairs. This is why the arms deal most under attack by the Russians, involving Harrier vertical take-off jets, has such a decidedly defensive character. (On the Chinese-Soviet border, the Soviets contend, nothing is defensive, and everything, including the Harriers, which have only a 30-mile range, can be used to attack Soviet positions.) This is also why British officials are convinced that some kind of Western role is necessary to overcome China's military weakness—not at all in the sense of an alliance that would goad the Russians. The China Britain is working for would be able to buy arms but would also gain the confidence to begin to attend international disarmament talks and consider nuclear test bans.

For the French, commercial, nationalist, and defense considerations enter into the relationship with China. France is able to deal with Peking and Moscow on roughly equal terms, although French officials contend that their reputation for enjoying good relations with both is clearly exaggerated.

"There isn't any such thing for France as good relations with Moscow or Peking," a French diplomat said, "or for Germany or any other country in the West. From time to time to time our relations are less cool, and from time to time there is an injection of trade, but nothing that really constitutes good relations in the sense that we have them with Western countries. They view the capitalist world as one. They have no real favorites or real enemies, and the proof of this is the rise and fall, and further rise and fall, of one Western nation after another in their esteem.

"They do, however, choose to play us off against each other, with America always in the background, and the Franco-German relationship often in the foreground."

This playing off contains the secret of France's success. Unlike Britain, France has left some room for maneuver. The Soviet Union thinks there may be some leverage left in the French-American relationship, but not in the British-American.

France's reaction to Afghanistan was a good example of this diplomatic finesse. Giscard joined his German allies in condemning the invasion, but balked at taking part in a Western European foreign ministers' meeting with Vance to present a united front. That would have undercut French freedom of action. France felt it did not have to join in a chorus of anti-Russian voices; its condemnation was individually thought out and individually presented. If, at the same time, its actions ameliorated Soviet displeasure a bit and reminded the United States of French independence, that, too, was part of the calculation.

France has not acted this way in international affairs for the sake of its ties with China or Russia, but for the sake of its independence in foreign affairs. Britain, for what it considers equally valid reasons, has remained a close ally of the United States and has suffered for it in its dealings with the

Soviet Union. But this is a positive factor in developing ties with China. France, by maintaining distance from the United States for its own reasons, benefits from both the Soviet Union and China. It can offer defensive rockets to the Chinese and open up further markets for the hard-pressed French armaments industry, which cannot survive economically with only the home market. At the same time it can hold off Moscow's displeasure, through frequent consultations and effective diplomacy in the first place, but in the main through being able to offer Russia a glimmer of hope of another move that might discomfit the Americans.

France is able to do this, too, without harming its close alliance with Germany, even though Germany takes a far different view toward arms sales and other attention-attracting dealings with China. Germany does this because it is much more concerned than France or Britain with the state of its relations with the Soviet Union. In trade, in its handling of the dissident problem, in its reticence in condemning Soviet adventures in the Third World, and particularly in its relations with China, Germany pursues a far different line from Britain's or France's.

6

Germany

"WE SHOULD BE FORTUNATE to find a power, given our present situation and history, with which there is so little conflict of political interest as there is with Russia," Bismarck wrote in 1891. For that reason, the old Chancellor had earlier concluded, behind the backs of his Austrian allies, a secret reinsurance treaty with the Russians that provided for Russian neutrality in the event of a falling out in the German-Austrian alliance.

Now there is a new reinsurance agreement between Germany and Russia, the two most powerful nations in Europe. But this new agreement is in the form of mutual understanding rather than binding secret clauses. Like the old agreement, it is based on Germany's uneasiness with its main partner: at that time, Austria, now, the United States.

Reinsurance is not to be confused with reunification, although that perennial of German politics has returned to active discussion in East and West. Reunification could turn out to be the ultimate step in Soviet-German relations in the very long run. But it would be under terms and conditions far removed from those under current discussion.

Historical parallels are uncertain guides, but there is a continuity of policy and political thought in Europe often missing in American politics. It has produced some natural and some surprising partnerships in the past, arrangements that manage to transcend ideology.

"There have always been continental alliances and rivalries," a Soviet diplomat in a Western capital said. "Russia has always had a part in them, sometimes against, sometimes with Germany, France, Austria, or England."

In Bismarck's time, reinsurance was based on German worries about Austria's volatile and unpredictable policies, and on the fact that its interests in other parts of the continent sometimes conflicted with German interests. The Austrians, too, seemed too willing to follow fluctuations in public opinion. Germany no longer trusted the Russians but, despite their massive arms buildup and ambitions of European hegemony, thought them unlikely to attack. Above all, they seemed in need of assurances from the West.

Comparing the time of Kaiser and Czar to the present would have little point if it were not being done by the officials and advisers of today's Germany and Russia. Before the parallels are explored further, however, there must be consideration of the differences. Germany's present ally, the United States, can scarcely be compared to the Austro-Hungarian empire. The United States is far stronger and is not the rival of Germany in the sense Austria was. Germany itself, strong as it is, no longer has the relative position with Russia it had under Bismarck. Russia is a different place, too, not because of Communism but because of its worldwide interests.

The three modern powers are equal in some fields but not in others. Germany is Russia's largest Western trading partner, as it was a 100 years ago, and Germany is Western Europe's most formidable military power. But under the new conditions in the world, this isn't enough. One must have nuclear weapons to have real strength and bargaining power, and Germany does not have them. Finally, the Germany of old, as Bismarck stressed, had no real quarrels with Russia. Modern Germany has put its quarrels behind it in treaties with Russia, Poland, and East Germany, but they have not been settled forever. Russians live in Königsberg and call it Kaliningrad; Poles are in Szeczin, the former Baltic port of Stettin; and Russian-dominated Germans are in part of Berlin.

Nevertheless, within the limits of this relationship that is equal in some ways and not in others, there are good reasons for both sides to seek reinsurance. For the Germans, these reasons are based in part on strength and in part on weakness, on pragmatism and European tradition, and on the wishes of political parties to win elections.

The division of Germany and the isolated position of West Berlin is a weakness the Russians can exploit at will. A further weakness is Germany's dependence on the United States for the nuclear shield against Russia as well as for the main responsibility in maintaining West Berlin's status. This German-American alliance has worked remarkably well for three decades, but no relationship can be so tight as to exclude differences and resentments. The Germans benefit, however, from not being counted among the strategic nuclear powers with worldwide interests, particularly in their dealings with the Russians. The United States gets blamed for dictatorships in South America and the Middle East; the United States must leap in with protests when new kinds of MIG fighter planes are sighted in Cuba or Ethiopia; the United States takes the blame as well as the credit for Israeli-Egyptian settlements and oil price squeezes. It is not always a frustrating and troublesome thing to be a middle power, and not always a good and easy thing to be a superpower.

Middle powers like Germany fit more easily into the traditional relationships of European states. Since the founding of modern European nations, there have been combinations, structures, alliances, rivalries, leagues, and benevolent neutralities, with the perceived benefit to the treaty-making governments outweighing every other consideration, to the point where despot would side with democrat, uncle against nephew, Slav with German against Slav. No nation was powerful enough by itself to stand against the most powerful coalition of the others, and, as a result, diplomacy was a constant process of planning and plotting, switching partners and enemies, and making treaties and secret agreements that often contradicted them.

But this is more than remote history. The combination making did not end with the Second World War and has not ended with the forging of the two apparently permanent postwar alignments, NATO and the Warsaw Pact. The alignments that seem to divide Europe so neatly are by no means free of gaps, with nations that do not belong (Yugoslavia, Sweden), or belong half-heartedly (France, Romania), or have strong internal forces questioning membership (Eastern Europe, Italy).

Even if the division of Europe into two more or less inflexible alignments is accepted, there is plenty of room to play the old European game of alliance building. General de Gaulle was the most prominent practitioner, but France was no longer able to offer all the attractions of a major power in trade, political leverage, and technology. Germany could. It is no accident that the Germans were next in the Western line for an opening to the East, picking up where de Gaulle failed. Trade with Germany meant major projects; French industry, for all its individual achievements, simply did not have the depth required by the vast Soviet market and pent-up needs. For this reason, Germany became the focus of attention, first in the capitals of Eastern Europe, and then in the Soviet Union itself.

The drawback was the unsettled questions of World War

II, the Königsbergs and Stettins. Only when these were out of the way could the path to Russia be opened fully for the Germans. The first small steps were taken in 1966, just as the French were having their greatest success but laying the foundation for failure with the ambitious design of bloc-free nations in East and West. The Germans had no such design, not even for Königsberg. Part of their approach was to give up the territories farthest to the East—the former East Prussia, Pomerania, and Silesia—which had been incorporated into the Soviet Union and Poland.

But the problem of "Middle Germany," known to most of the world as East Germany or the German Democratic Republic, was not solved through these concessions. It became a part of one of the two models brought forward for the future relations of Germany and the Soviet Union.

The first model is German reunification, granted by the Soviet Union in exchange for permanent neutrality. The second model is a special West German–Soviet relationship, to be achieved without neutrality. The first is loosely associated with the left wing of the Social Democratic Party of Germany (SPD), above all, with Egon Bahr, former Chancellor Willy Brandt's adviser and go-between in the crucial days of the Eastern Policy at the end of the sixties. The second model has emerged as the more or less unarticulated line of Chancellor Helmut Schmidt's centrists in the SPD.

The Bahr Plan has become the favorite weapon of those opposed to the Social Democrats' Ostpolitik as well as the favorite panacea of those political forces worried about the Soviet threat or excessive military influence in West Germany. The principle opponents, the conservative Christian Democrats of Franz Josef Strauss, contend that neutrality on the pattern of Finland's is the ultimate aim of the socialists in coming to an accommodation with the East. In the view of Soviet diplomats in Bonn, however, much of the hue and cry over the supposed Plan is the work of the conservatives themselves, in an attempt to undermine the modest gains of détente with threats of where it could lead to. In this view, the German Left becomes the unwitting ally of Strauss's forces.

The Bahr Plan foresees the neutralization of Central Europe, with a reunited East and West Germany at its heart, and Czechoslovakia, Poland, and Hungary forming an eventual widened neutral zone to the east, in exchange for a neutral Belgium, Holland, and Italy in the west. The eastern neutrals would leave the Warsaw Pact and the western ones NATO; reunited Germany would, of course, be disarmed and restricted in its links with the West, but details are vague. Britain and France would not be included in any future neutral zone to the West because of their nuclear arsenals.

Despite newspaper scare stories based on leaks of secret memoranda, and speculation about Bahr's meetings with the Russians in Moscow and Berlin, Bahr himself says the plan is only a theoretical sketch of one development that could or ought to take place in Europe in the future, but probably not in this century. Every time there is a new leak about Bahr's or others' thoughts on German neutrality, the outcry from the conservatives is loud and the tone ominous. But objections to German reunification and neutrality do not come from the right alone, nor do they come from West Germany alone.

The head of any rejectionist front would be East Germany, which would simply disappear under such an arrangement, with token posts in the new government to its leaders and token—or perhaps greater—acknowledgment and retention of some of the fixtures of socialism in a United Germany. This loss of the 17 million people on whom so much attention and resources have been spent by the Russians is, of course, one of the main obstacles to reunification plans. For this reason, Soviet officials like to recount the sacrifices their nation has made for the unwilling East Germans and to stress, as one did, that "now, the two parts of Germany are like fire and water—one firmly socialist, the other just as firmly capitalist. Under such conditions, how can they be mixed?"

There is no need, practical or historical, for reunification, a Soviet political commentator stressed. Germany was a unitary state for only a few decades of its history, he pointed out; no one was talking about the need for Austria or the German-speaking parts of Switzerland to be put under a single political system. That argument ignores the point that these regions never were part of a nation, as the two German states were.

It is also a line, as a Polish Party member said, that can be switched off and on if the Soviet Union ever changes its mind about Germany, and the Poles are clearly worried that someday this might happen. For Poland, the specter of a German nation of some 80 million on its borders is a disturbing one indeed. If commentators in other countries recall Rapallo,* the German-Soviet deal of the twenties, in talking about the prospects of a change in the German-Soviet relations of the eighties, those in Poland refer privately to the Hitler-Stalin pact, which permitted the Russians to march into Poland from the east as the Germans were marching in from the west.

Many Poles fear that a neutral Germany, even if it did not directly or immediately threaten Poland, would have an indirect effect on Poland's internal politics. That is because Soviet troop strength in Poland could be expected to increase

---

* In the Rapallo Treaty of 1922, Germany and the new Soviet state agreed to establish trade and diplomatic relations and to mutually renounce reparations claims. The agreement was made behind the backs of the Allies and did much to strengthen both the war-shattered Weimar Republic and the Soviet Union—to the later regret of France, Britain, and the United States.

enormously to make up for the loss of the East German buffer state, with a consequent dampening effect on Poland's relatively successful attempts to operate independently of Soviet control. As the Bahr plan proceeds, these troops might not be permitted under the provision of the East-West zone of neutrality. But Poles know that the Russians have ways. The Red Army units stationed in their country since the war are not supposed to be there for occupation duties, after all; they are only protecting the communications lines between the Soviet Union and East Germany. Why this protection is needed in a fraternal socialist partner country is not clear. In any case, it is feared that some similar formula would be found to handle the neutral areas.

Each new wave of neutralization talk brings differing but essentially negative responses from Germany's neighbors and allies in the West. Neutralization would rule out any influence in German affairs for France and Britain, which now share responsibility for Berlin and have troops there and in West Germany, as well as for the United States. The French and British attitudes toward a powerful united Germany are even more critical than those of the United States, which would not feel threatened by 80 million hard-working but neutral Germans the way the 53 million neighboring French would. No Western nation, including the United States, would be pleased with the loss of Germany as a partner and its gain by Russia. Smaller NATO countries with memories of the German occupation would have the added worry of being dominated by instead of allied with Germany.

All would be justified in fearing the collapse of NATO and probably of the European Community, since the withdrawal of Germany from both alliances would doubtless be part of the Soviet price.

When these Western fears and objections are added up, the benefits to the Soviet Union of dumping its East German state and alienating some of its other East European partners begin to appear clearer. But no reunification or neutrality scheme is going to get off the ground unless the main figure, West Germany, permits it to. To the lineup of those who are against reunification on neutralist terms, or who say they are (East Germany, Poland, France, Britain, the United States, and the Soviet Union) must be added a large majority of the West Germans themselves, including the leaders of the main governing and opposition parties.

Their position can best be summed up by a conversation diplomats say was held at a high level with the Soviet ambassador to Bonn, Vladimir Semenov, who came to the Rhine at the end of 1978 with the reputation of an advocate of neutrality. Semenov, in a previous posting as political adviser to the Soviet commandant in East Germany, was believed to have had a major role in drafting the last concrete Soviet offer of reunification in exchange for neutrality, made in 1952 in a final fruitless effort to halt West German rearmament and entry into NATO.

As he took up his new assignment, Semenov was brought up to date by the Germans on what had happened since 1952: West Germany chose the guarantees of NATO and its other Western links at that time, Semenov was told, and as a result of its European and Atlantic orientation, the Germany he was returning to was a far different place from the one he had known in the fifties. It is a Germany, Semenov was told, with contacts all over the world, regardless of political systems. Even at previous peaks of German power, the British or the Americans were always able to keep German trade and influence out of their spheres of interest. But now the Germans were back, not as occupiers but as businessmen, diplomats, scientists, engineers, and development helpers, in Eastern and Western Europe as well as in the Third World. Often they are preferred to the Russians or the Americans because they attach no political strings. This is a Germany that has not existed since the turn of the century, an altogether different place from the weak, defeated state Semenov had known, a state that might have been much more ready to listen to reunification offers—above all with its army then in existence only on paper—but that now was the strongest in Europe. Now it was a question of whether this new Germany would want to give the Soviet Union veto rights on its European and world role.

There are problems, Semenov was told, as well as achievements, and one of the problems is the Eastern province the Russians call the German Democratic Republic, and where 17 million Germans live. Not for the first time in German history has there been such a detached province. But the Ostpolitik of recent years has made it more possible to maintain contacts with it, to emphasize the common belonging to the German nation that binds the people of the two German states together.

The question that was put to the Soviet ambassador in conclusion was this: If we subscribe to one or the other of the neutrality-for-unification plans, we would have to give up much of this network of connections, this new world reputation, or at least we would have to submit our plans and actions to the Soviet Union, which would remain our rival and adversary, for approval. Would this approval be very likely if it could be seen to affect Soviet interests? And should we give up all that we have worked for so hard for the sake of the recovery of a *province?*

With so much against a neutral Germany, why is the question being discussed at all? From the Soviet standpoint, causing unease and reviving old fears in Western capitals, and quite possibly in East Berlin and Warsaw as well, is not wasted diplomatic effort, even if the impact is lessened by Soviet assurances at all levels that there is really nothing to the neutralization plans but talk.

Diplomats in the West and in Poland have paid enough

attention to the talk, however, to have constructed some tentative models of the advantages and disadvantages to the Russians. The alliance, passive or active, that might develop between a united Germany and the Soviet Union would end the Soviet Union's isolation at the same time that it would remove an adversary from the opposing coalition. The costly occupation of East Germany—where, after more than 30 years, Soviet and East German officials are on terms that border on open hostility, where soldiers are largely confined to barracks and have to be rotated every 12 to 18 months to keep them from forming contacts with the more prosperous East German people, and where confidence in the East German regime is still so slight that even after token troop withdrawals the Soviet occupation force of 350,000 troops outnumbers the East German army by more than two to one—could be terminated. All these are reasons enough to sacrifice a province.

In West Germany, many in the left of the Social Democratic party say that the current division of Europe into armed camps cannot and should not last forever, since in the short run it wastes money, resources, and manpower and in the long run carries a heightened risk of war.

There are other factors, less rational, in Germany that may enter into the future course of German-Soviet relations. In an era when holy men turn out powerful Shahs and nationalist, separatist, and splinter organizations kill and kidnap to win small bits of territory in dozens of other countries, the impact of patriotism, national consciousness, and other elements less easy to describe or defend than membership in the Common Market may be felt. Germany still is a nation without a national holiday, unless one counts the anniversary, celebrated in East Germany, of the date Russian troops marched in.

When traveling to Germany from Scandinavia, one is always struck by the fact that the bright Danish and Swedish colors flutter from most farmsteads and villages, but when the German border is crossed, flags are few and far between. Thoughtful Germans reply that their nation had enough of enforced flag flying during the 12 years of the Nazi Reich, and that everyone ought to realize that giving up old and worn-out ideas of nationalism in favor of the new hope of a united Europe and the Atlantic alliance is the only course of reason for Germany.

Opinion polls over the years have supported this view with increasingly wide margins. The percentage of those even interested in reunification, let alone the advocates of it, gets smaller and smaller each year. As Germany's population becomes more and more dominated by those born after the war, fewer people have memories of the old homes in the East. The successful efforts of the Communists to cut off most emigration mean that no sizable new groups of refugees from the other part of Germany are entering the public opinion statistics to call for reunification.

A final argument against Germany's embarking on some irrational crusade for neutrality and national unity is perhaps more rational. Unlike the Palestinians, the Germans have long had their homeland, even if it is a smaller one than it was before Hitler began his conquests and met his defeat. Germans, even East Germans, do not live in refugee camps or in temporary residences in other nations. It would have been easy for Germany to keep the national question alive the way it has been kept alive in the Middle East, using the 6 million refugees from the East for leverage. The West German politicians of that day, although accused, then and now, of being the worst apostles of the Cold War, chose instead to integrate the refugees from the East as quickly as possible, sacrificing some political advantages, perhaps, for domestic unity. The refugee-based political parties of the right that were healthy in the fifties died out as this integration progressed.

In those days, however, it was axiomatic, in Bonn and Moscow, that the East-West aspect of German foreign policy had to be a question of either-or. If you tied yourself to the West, to NATO and the beginnings of European coopera- tion, Germans believed, then you cut yourself off from the East. After all, the Western alliances were aimed at contain- ing the Soviet Union, which meant conceding to it the ter- ritories it had won in the war, at least temporarily, pending a final peace treaty, but drawing a line that said no more. The Soviet Union, in the note from Stalin that drew on the advice of Semenov and other German experts, made its final offer in 1952, before the Bundeswehr, the new German army, be- came a fact. The tone and the terms were clearly either-or. No army and reunification, or army and no reunification. The Germans replied, army.

It was only at the end of the sixties that Brandt began to try to overcome the inflexibility of the equation. First as for- eign minister and then as chancellor, he had to argue, ma- neuver, and debate on three fronts at once in launching his Ostpolitik. On the domestic front, he had to convince the Germans that they had indeed lost the Second World War and ought to give up hope for the return of their lost eastern territories, as long as there was a powerful victor nation watching over them. In foreign policy, Brandt's main task was winning over the Soviet Union to the idea that Germany was not a revanchist, military nation waiting its chance to resume the war, as Soviet propaganda so frequently con- tended. That was the second front. The third was the Amer- ican. The United States and Germany's other Western allies had to be assured and reassured that Ostpolitik was not being conducted behind their backs or at their expense, and that Germany intended to improve relations with the East without worsening them with the West.

Brandt succeeded where others had failed. Was this be- cause he was a better negotiator than Adenauer or Ludwig Erhard? Part of the answer does lie in Brandt's background as an anti-Nazi exile and the fact that he brought the socialists back into the government for the first time since the war. This counts for something in Soviet eyes, as officials stress in evaluating German politics. They are less ready to concede that Moscow has conducted and will conduct deals with people anywhere in the political spectrum, the only real need being a brief period of time to permit the propaganda machinery to shift gears. And thus the biggest factor for change in Soviet-German relations was Soviet needs in the sixties, when, because of the break with China, the USSR was left without a major ally for the first time since the end of the Second World War and had to turn westward in its search for new partners, if not allies. The opening to the East that Brandt pushed was fortuitous indeed for the Russians. Russian support, at first cautious, was essential to the success of the move. And if it had not existed at all from the Bonn side, it is likely the Russians would have tried to invent it.

After preliminary tests of Ostpolitik in Eastern Europe, the Germans turned to Moscow in 1970, and in August of that year, West Germany and the USSR signed an agreement renouncing the use of force in settling political disputes. West German exports for the year shot up by 44.8 percent, and further spectacular rises were to be registered in the years ahead. The following year, the four powers came to agreement over Berlin, easing freedom of movement for West Germans to and from the city and reducing a considerable source of irritation.

The East-West trade bank was founded in Frankfurt and the first meeting of the Soviet-German commission for economic and technical cooperation held, in 1972, to prepare for the conclusion of a long-term treaty of trade and economic cooperation. By the time Brezhnev paid the first visit of a Soviet leader to Bonn in May 1973, more economic, cultural, and scientific agreements were ready for signature, and the trade curve kept rising, with great leaps registered by giant deals such as the three to sell natural gas transmission pipes to the Soviet Union in exchange for the gas produced in Siberia and piped to the West.

Brezhnev's second visit, in May 1978, set targets of trade and industrial cooperation into the next century, with a somewhat vague 25-year agreement, but also underlined the business results of the previous 8 years: trade had quadrupled, reaching an annual volume of about $6 billion. It was not an alliance in any sense, despite the warmth of some of the toasts, but as a consolation for the Soviet loss of China it wasn't bad, because this new partner in the West built factories and bought raw materials in huge quantities, helping Russia in the process in three ways at once: by ending its isolation, increasing its trade turnover (and in hard currency), and improving its technology.

And so, by the end of the seventies, the West Germans found that they were wanted not only in the West, but also in the East, and that they did not have to neglect either direction to benefit from the other. Germany's voice in NATO and the European Community has grown, and the German representatives at the United Nations and other world councils have become more active, in part because one of the side issues in the East-West agreements was to grant both East and West Germany full UN membership.

The fact that West Germany could continue to have good relations with both East and West is the least noticed but most important aspect of Ostpolitik. It means that German-Soviet relations were based on a far different set of conditions than those of the deal the Russians offered Kurt Schumacher, the one-legged concentration camp survivor who led the socialists immediately after the war on a platform of neutrality and antimilitarism. Schumacher's successors, and those of Adenauer, who accepted the military and rejected neutrality, managed to achieve more than either man had because, in that later period, their aims and those of the Soviet Union coincided.

By the end of the seventies, however, the policy of being able to have your cake and eat it, too, developed its own problems. The Soviet Union found itself more and more pushed into the corner by China's reaching out and by the American human rights campaign. The Germans felt the pressure from both sides. Bonn saw its own human rights efforts being undermined by the more publicity-conscious but, in the German view, less effective campaign of the United States. The Germans wanted Soviet and Polish citizens of German background to continue to be able to leave those countries in large numbers on the basis of private arrangements made during official negotiations on trade and politics. The Carter spotlight, Bonn felt, endangered this emigration.

There were also disagreements on Western defense, some of them arising out of the natural reluctance of the Germans to have their nation used as the battlefield of Europe in the next nuclear war, and some of them natural resentment against not having full control of their own foreign policy.

The Soviet Union exploited these differences, contrasting the volatility of the United States with its own reasonableness in permitting the Volga Germans to continue to emigrate, in keeping its hands off Berlin's transit routes to the West, and in continuing to buy and sell record amounts in the German trade.

These problems were the genesis of the new Ostpolitik tailored by Helmut Schmidt for the eighties. It is the policy of Brandt, his predecessor as chancellor, taken a step or two further in relations with both the United States and the Soviet Union.

None of the parallels to earlier pacts—Rapallo, Locarno,*

---

* The Locarno conference of 1925 and resultant treaties guaranteed Germany's western borders and provided arbitration with Germany's eastern neighbors. The sense of security Europe felt as a result was called the Spirit of Locarno.

Molotov-Ribbentrop—fits the policy at all. There is no hint of Soviet-German alliance; the Germans, in fact, took pains to resist Russian pressure in 1978 to make their agreement one of friendship as well as trade and cooperation. The much less friendly French had agreed to this provision, but the Germans thought that friendship would have said more than they wanted to, not only to the Russians, but to the United States.

If there is no alliance, there is at least a tilt toward the Soviet Union, taken, it is stressed by German officials, not in any measure as appeasement, but to protect German self-interest at a time when the United States does not seem overly willing or able to do so.

The Germans insist that this tilt means no lessening of the German commitment to the network of Western ties in the European and Atlantic alliances, and Germany's vigorous role in all of them bears out this contention. But at the same time, there is a definite wish to put a bit of distance between German policy and American policy toward the Soviet Union. Indeed, the Germans wish to establish some distance from the policies of Britain and France, too; Germany has gone out of its way to keep armaments out of its trade with China, in contrast to the British and the French, with the reaction of the Russians in mind.

The rationale for this German policy is Bonn's assessment of American policies and capabilities, in both the near and the distant future. In the long term, the Germans have realized for some time that the United States does not command the power to police the world. In the short term, they contend, it is doing rather a bad job with the strength it has left. German assessments of the first years of the Carter administration were slightly less critical of the president than of his advisers, particularly Brzezinski, who is thought in Bonn to have played the China card disastrously by choosing the wrong time to revive talks on United States normalization of relations with Peking. By coming to the side of Peking at a time of turmoil in Southeast Asia, the Germans believe, the United States encouraged the Chinese, probably unwittingly, to attack Vietnam. That there was no counterpressure from the Soviet Union against states like Germany, which were not implicated in any way but were nevertheless easy targets, is considered at once good luck and an illustration of the risks the United States' allies have to put up with.

The national security adviser also was blamed for making a crusade of human rights, endangering the quiet diplomacy the Germans had been using to achieve the emigration of as many as 10,000 a year of the 2 million Volga Germans and more than 100,000 ethnic Germans from Poland. German criticism is tempered by the belief, justified or not, that after the first turbulent period of human rights confrontation, the United States switched to the quiet German method.

At the beginning of the Carter administration, the Germans were so worried that they seriously considered going it alone in their relations with the Soviet Union, whatever the cost that would have meant to their ties with the United States. They were certain that the United States would antagonize the Russians on issues that did not necessarily concern Germany but would have a harmful affect on the general atmosphere of détente and thus, after all, on Bonn's successes or failures in the East.

German policy became one of building a separate line to the Soviet Union, avoiding public issues such as human rights. It did not mean necessarily taking the Soviet side, or the American, but only putting forward an independent set of policies based on advantages to Bonn.

The Germans' main fear was that the human rights furor would harm not only the Volga Germans but also the chances of SALT II and the further arms control steps that depended on it. The German position in the middle of Europe, as well as military position in the Western alliance, puts arms control in the forefront of German political considerations, and Bonn was afraid that previous SALT gains were going to be sacrificed for an ill-conceived but popular human rights drive that would alienate the Soviet Union.

After the first Carter years, the Germans began to trust the Americans more. Their leaders got to know each other—although, apparently, not to like each other very much—at summit meetings. The absolute necessity for going it alone that was perceived in the first days was gone. Nevertheless, the idea of some kind of reinsurance, although not in the strict Bismarckian sense of a secret treaty behind the back of an ally, is deemed essential.

If the relative loss of power by the United States and the unpredictability of policy from Washington are the reasons the Germans thought they ought to seek some form of reinsurance, the existence of Berlin and East Germany are the reasons they must.

For years, the conviction in Bonn has been strong that France and Britain, two of the three Western guarantor powers for Berlin, would not lift a finger in its defense in a real crunch. Of late, despite repeated American assurances, the feeling has been growing that even the Americans would be unwilling or unable to come to the aid of Berlin if the Russians decided to "peacefully reunite" the 2-million-population Western sectors of the city with 1-million-population East Berlin. The American paralysis when the Berlin wall was built, in violation of every four-power agreement on the books, is still remembered. Even fresher are the television images of the Americans scrambling for helicopters in Saigon and the Vietnamese they were leaving behind. If the Allies won't, then the Germans must look out for Berlin for themselves, not through the use or threat of force of arms, but through political skill and the extension of economic possibilities to the Russians.

Berlin's history has been one of crises and calms, but for the near future, at least, Bonn thinks that its Soviet tilt has paid off in more secure links between the city and the West, 110 miles distant. One clear indication of this is the new Berlin-Hamburg Autobahn. Together with the reopening of canals previously blocked by the city's division, which save barge crews 3 days of travel and controls, the $1 billion road is valuable as a new connection between Berlin and the main German port of Hamburg. It replaces 4 hours of tortuous back-road travel with 2½ hours of expressway driving. Although the new highway and canal arrangement falls short of the corridors envisaged by some Western planners as the ultimate solution to Berlin's access problem (and the refugee problem of the East Germans), it is a long way from the sonic booms of Soviet fighters and the crisis blockades of the highways that have been so much a part of Berlin's postwar history. When the Soviet Union wanted to make a particular political point, it always had the power to put the squeeze on Berlin.

It still has the power. But the aim of German policy is to make it more advantageous for the Russians to desist than to persist in the harassment of Berlin.

This kind of aim involves the tangled relationship between the two German states, about which a separate book could be written. Suffice it to say that in the past, it served the interests of the East Germans to threaten the position of West Berlin, as it often served the Russians. No nation with a pretense of sovereignty wants a city with diametrically opposite political and economic outlooks, guarded by the troops of three nations, in its midst, particularly when the city is a show window for Western prosperity and such a magnet for refugees that only a wall can keep them out. But now that East Germany has gained recognition throughout the world as a real country, it might be better served by accepting West Berlin's presence with more grace and trying to benefit from it. Accept it East Germany must in any case, if that is Russian policy, but the East Germans in the past have been given some room to maneuver and have usually gone in the direction of harassment and instability. Now, with a new free road handed them—East German as well as Western use is foreseen for the Hamburg highway—they have given evidence of their interest in stability by allowing for the impact of the highway on their next 5-year plan.

Certainly the West Germans wish to maintain ties as close as possible with the East Germans. By close ties they mean not only trade (which has reached the point at which East Europeans call it the secret pipeline between Comecon—the Soviet-dominated council for Mutual Economic Assistance—and the Common Market) but also cultural and family relations, and political ones as well, if possible. The heads of the two German governments meet infrequently at international summits, but the idea of any more official visits was dropped by the East Germans after they saw the wild reception accorded Brandt on the first such venture in the East German city of Erfurt. All these ties, Bonn believes, keep alive the complex and emotion-laden idea of a single German nationhood, despite the existence of two German states with opposing social and political systems. If the idea of a common nation is maintained, then one day, when European politics make it possible, Germans in East and West can be reunited without having grown too far apart. Until then, the key to whether they live next door to each other in Europe in isolation, or whether there are family and other contacts, is the attitude of the Soviet Union.

How reinsurance works was dramatically demonstrated early in the Carter administration when Schmidt refused to receive the dissident Bukovsky shortly after Carter had invited him to the White House. That was as much a gesture to the Moscow conservatives, who distrust their own centrists' good relations with Germany, as it was to the United States to slow down and play down the publicity, Bonn officials said. And that has been the pattern of subsequent policy actions: On the one hand, to try to convince the Soviet Union that the German tilt is still in position, and on the other, to try to persuade the United States to follow policies that would make a more extreme tilt—and perhaps even going it alone—unnecessary.

Schmidt makes use of the frequent Western summits to talk to the other leaders about a favorite idea he has about dealing with the Russians. That is to put oneself in the Russians' place, trying to imagine how they think and react when a particular move is made by the West or China. Schmidt's attitude is doubtless why the Soviet leadership is so high on this Social Democrat and former Wehrmacht lieutenant. Their approval comes out in every conversation on Germany with Soviet diplomats and officials. This centrist understands the centrists in Moscow, and they him. He stands solidly in the middle on Ostpolitik, as little influenced by the mystical talk of reunification on the left as by the thundering against Russia on the right. The centrists in Moscow have their problems, too, and that is well understood in Bonn. Some opposition was sensed, for example, on the Berlin-Hamburg Autobahn, from conservatives who thought it a concession to the West rather than a help to the East. All the more reason, in the Bonn view, to consult regularly and reassure the Russians there is nothing to worry about in the general pattern of the relationship.

Afghanistan tested the relationhip severely. Schmidt, like Carter, was facing an election campaign in which charges that détente was a failure was a leading issue. His reaction had to be firm, but at the same time, he had to resist pressures from Washington to join in what the Germans considered the United States' overreaction.

He managed to placate the Americans and not anger the Russians too greatly by adroit use of Germany's strengths and weaknesses. He used the first to remind the United States how important German and European cooperation was in drawing the line against further Soviet expansion. The second, Germany's division, was used to justify Bonn's reluctance to lead the anti-Soviet campaign.

In a briefing for American specialists on Germany early in 1980, Schmidt indicated that the Germans were solving their dilemma by considering Afghanistan a *fait accompli* and by moving on to prevent future expansionist moves by the Russians: "How do we *contain* the Soviet Union after Afghanistan? Europe must have unity to be successful. It's not sufficient if we, the Germans, join the Americans, if the other Europeans don't. Only by Western unity and the military balance in Europe will there be no illusions for the Soviet Union about being strong enough to overwhelm the West. Where you have equilibrium, there is no invitation to the Soviet Union to extend its power and influence."

What would happen to the Bonn-Moscow pattern if changes of leadership took place in one or both capitals is hard to predict. Both nations do have a reputation for down-the-middle kinds of leaders. Of more concern in Bonn is the next generation of politicians and the directions some trends are taking within the Social Democratic party. The most important of these for the East-West relationship is the heavy skepticism on the part of the radical Young Socialists that NATO is necessary at all, or, as the ancient SPD parliamentary leader Herbert Wehner put it, the contention that the Soviet army, and therefore the Soviet buildup in Central Europe, is purely defensive, or the feeling that the draft and the Bundeswehr are wasteful (although there is no shortage of young army volunteers), or that NATO, anyway, is run by the Americans and the generals.

Associated with this German revisionism are the forces, mostly youthful, who occupy nuclear power plant sites, worry about the power of the multinationals, and consider the army and NATO a part of this same vast establishment, and such disparate elements as farmers whose fields are torn up by maneuvering tanks and who find support for their complaints in the views of Bonn defense officials who want to scale down the size of NATO maneuvers. It is not a political movement, not a coalition, not a cause. It is not strong enough for the politicians to give it any real attention. But no one can rule out the prospect that in a decade or so there might come into existence such a movement, coalition, or cause, one that would turn Bonn away from the center and back to talk of reunification, reunification that could be had in exchange for giving up something the Germans were preparing to give up in any case—a strong army and close ties to the West.

Against this possibility, the Bonn government can do no more than try to keep defense spending in line with other national needs, to urge a stronger political role for NATO— here it agrees with the dissenters—and to make Europe as much a factor in its own defense as the United States.

None of this brings Bonn into conflict with the Soviet Union, and even if it did, the Germans would probably push ahead. They know they cannot possibly avoid offending the Russians some of the time. They are limited, too, in what they can get the Russians to agree to. There is no alliance with Moscow that the Germans can threaten to pull out of. Reinsurance and separate policies are fine phrases, but how do they work? Is it a question of nuances and atmosphere, or are concrete actions involved?

Even before Afghanistan, tests were frequent. One came with human rights, and the Schmidt government is satisfied it passed it. The Schmidt government managed to extract emigration concessions from Russia and Poland without a public fuss that would have upset other parts of the relationship. It managed to accomplish this, too, without undercutting any allied position, despite its disapproval of American tactics.

Another test came from China. When Chinese diplomats, cabinet ministers, and trade officials began descending on Europe with pragmatist enthusiasm, one of their main targets was West Germany. Even in Mao's last years, the enemy-of-my-enemy idea had worked to the extent of bringing invitations to Peking to Bundeswehr generals and politicians. The generals were forced to decline, although their retired counterparts could go, and the politicians visiting China included both the chancellor and his rival, the conservative Franz Josef Strauss.

The new initiative of Hua Kua-feng and Deng Xiaoping met with similar caution. The Chinese delegations were firmly but politely told that their colorful shopping lists of high-technology armaments could not be satisfied in Germany but that straight industrial deals were fine. The Chinese got a different reception in France and Britain, since these countries have no Berlin or divided nation to worry about. If the Chinese did not understand this, there was always a final argument to fall back on, that Germany has a policy of not supplying armaments to troubled areas of the world.

In their talks with the Soviet Union, the Germans take great pains to show how little they are playing the China card. As far as diplomatic relations and industrial help, including plans for a $15 billion steel mill, Schmidt has said that this poses no problem for the Soviet side.

"The Soviet Union understands that we are dependent on exports and the international division of labor in order to provide employment," he said.* "We do not intend to use diplomatic relations with the People's Republic of China as a flanking tactic in the development of German-Soviet relations. The Soviet Union, geographically, is our immediate neighbor. At the same time, it is an immediately neighboring factor, politically and militarily, in world politics. There is nothing for West Germany in an intensification of the current differences of opinion between Moscow and Peking."

Is there anything for West Germany in replacing the United States as the main object of Soviet attention in the West? Many Moscow moves and much talk point in this direction from time to time. German and American officials tend to dismiss them as attempts to drive wedges between the Western partners, or to produce desired behavior from one by praising such behavior in the other. In the past, the German militarists were the bad example most of the time and one of the other Western allies the good example of how to behave toward Russia. Since 1970, Germany has more often than not won most of the praise. The relatively short distance between Germany's industrial regions and Russia's raw materials is another argument in favor of Germany's playing such a role; the two nations are natural trading partners. Add to this the mutual interest in maintaining the status quo in Central Europe. Berlin is there. The Germans must consider it in their dealings with the Russians. And the Russians, although they are hesitant about admitting it, must also consider it in their dealings with the Germans. The Germans develop trade and technology in Russia, in part, because of Berlin. If the Soviet Union changes Berlin's status, this development can be slowed down. Both sides know this. They are like powerful wrestlers on a cliff, trying to gain advantage without forcing themselves over the edge.

---

* In an October 17, 1978, interview with the *Süddeutsche Zeitung*.

More fuel for the argument is provided by Russian ambitions for a Europe less under United States influence. A Germany closely tied to Russia would play a key role in such a Europe.

A Soviet diplomat in Germany put the argument this way: "There is a realization by the bourgeoisie in Germany that the Soviet Union is here to stay, cannot be defeated. It took two world wars for them to realize this. Now, since they can't do anything about it, they ought to accommodate themselves to it, and, except for certain circles, they are.

"We think the United States fears an independent Europe, an independent Germany, because those governments are going to get closer to their natural partner, the Soviet Union, also a 'European country.' By forcing or urging a heavier burden of armaments on Europe, the United States hopes to keep its economies from expanding too rapidly and thus keep it from becoming more independent. Parallel to this effort, the tightening of the NATO structure makes Europe knuckle under to the Americans."

In light of all these arguments, political, geographical, and economic, does it make sense for Moscow to cut its losses in the troublesome relationship with America and build up a substitute one with Germany, the more reliable partner? Surprisingly, the view from Moscow is different.

In Russia, a good deal of stress is put on how satisfactory the Germans are as partners, as in this summation by a Soviet official: "The Germans were our enemies; you [the Americans] were our allies. Our relations with them, however, are better. That is because they understand détente better than you do. They didn't make a big fuss about human rights and got both trade and the release of their people. They are now our leading partner, and our trade with you is in a shambles."

This approval, however, is more than balanced by considerations of superpowerhood. Superpowers can really deal only with other superpowers, especially when one of them has fought hard to reach the status and is never quite sure of its recognition as such. Americans may have forgotten the linkup of United States and Soviet astronauts in space. To the Russians, it was one of the main events of détente, if not of recent history, because it demonstrated cooperation on the basis of *equality*. It is cooperation, but not equality, when American farmers make up for the inefficiencies of the collective farm system with shipments of grain, or when Italians are called in with the blueprints and the machine tools to make Russia's national car. It is cooperation, not equality, when Russia pairs with Germany instead of the United States.

The prime consideration, of course, is strategic, not psychological. The United States and only the United States has the power to blow up Russia. The Germans will remain an eminently useful partner for the Soviet Union, and the Soviet Union will have to tolerate the ups and downs of its relations with the United States. The Germans can help the Soviet consumer by shipping in machinery to make more goods for the shelves and take hard-to-transport raw materials in payment. They can counsel a softer course on East-West controversies, because they want the Berlin lever to stay in neutral.

Germany's best use to the Soviet Union is as a hedge against isolation, as a part-time ally, perhaps, in a dangerous world in which everyone has strong friends except the Soviet Union, and in which it is better to have good relations with someone who has great misgivings about the whole affair than to have no relations at all.

The development to date, from Cold War to partial trust, shows that the relationship will be no more static in the future than it has been in the past. Which way it will turn in Germany depends in large measure on factors outside the realm of foreign relations—domestic issues like the rate of unemployment and inflation—that could bring pressure to bear on defense costs (and that are pushed, not too effectively, by the Soviet-line German Communist Party) and eventually make neutrality seem attractive.

Much depends, too, on the leaders on the Rhine, men holding hatfuls of cards labeled "United States," "Soviet Union," "China," "Europe." They have played them well to date, so well that they have managed a few modifications in the behavior of the United States and the Soviet Union, no small achievement for a middle-sized power.

In the case of the United States, the Germans say, the change was the return to quiet diplomacy in human rights questions, with the larger issues of arms limitation and the prevention of nuclear war in mind. In the case of the Soviet Union, Germany's achievement has been to get the lesson across that moderation in crisis spots like Berlin will be amply repaid, not only in a handsome level of trade and technical help for modernization, but also in an offer of a partnership, or half a partnership. To Russia, a nation alone in a big-power world, even half an offer is a great deal.

7

Eastern Europe

EVERY 10 YEARS, with a regularity that must be disquieting to the Communist rulers, something happens in Eastern Europe to upset the enforced tranquility and change the course of the following decade.

Such an event was the election of Karol Cardinal Wojtyla, Archbishop of Cracow in southern Poland, as Pope John Paul II in October 1978. There was no uprising and no tanks, but the effect, in the long term, is likely to be as powerful as that of Tito's split with Moscow in 1948, the Hungarian revolution of 1956, or the Prague Spring of 1968.

This is not to suggest that John Paul, a man who has devoted his life to peace, will precipitate the kind of violent change that the region has known so often. But his capacity to bring about peaceful change is a much greater hope to the people of Poland, the other nations of Eastern Europe, and the Soviet Union itself. The reason is that Eastern Europe is not a place containing a few dissidents, but an entire region of dissidence in which everyone from the peasants and factory workers to the intellectuals and national leaders is dissatisfied in some way: with the size of their pay packets; with governments that can double the price of gasoline and heating oil overnight; with what they can and cannot read, write, and paint; or with what Soviet strategic considerations do to local 5-year plans.

To all these members of the more-or-less loyal opposition in Eastern Europe, Pope John Paul was the right man at the right time. As the first Pole and first citizen of a Communist country to become head of the Roman Catholic Church, he knows and understands the problems of life in an authoritarian system. As an outstanding humanist and thinker, he is concerned as well with the alienation and despair that industrial societies, Communist or capitalist, seem to produce.

But most important of all is his commitment to human rights, expressed in his first encyclical, in his historic 9 days in Poland, and in his record as a courageous partisan of individual freedoms through 36 years in the service of the Church in a Communist nation, as divinity student, parish priest, teacher, bishop, and cardinal.

No pope and no revolutionary is going to shake the Communist grip on Eastern Europe, at least as long as the Soviet Union is able to maintain its strength in the area and to keep its own dissidents and nationalists quiet at home. Those seeking liberalization understand and accept this. But the leaders of the six countries have also tacitly accepted the idea that there can be a struggle, within carefully prescribed limits, over the details of how their power is administered.

Human rights is the platform, the weapon, the opening wedge. It is not just an effective way of expressing opposition to the abuse of power by the regimes; it is the only way. This is because human rights are guaranteed by the constitutions of all the Communist states, but other means of protest taken for granted in the West—forming political parties, picketing against government policies—are just as clearly forbidden.

Zdenek Hejzlar, one of the leading Prague reformers of 1968, described the problem in this way: "The trickiest part of the whole process of democratization is the opening move, since the prevailing social system includes not one single mechanism making such a move possible."

But that analysis was written before the unexpected accession of Karol Wojtyla to the throne of Peter and the new situation that created for Eastern Europe. Triumphal journeys and crowds of many millions do not, of course, change politics overnight; the Pope's sermons and speeches on human rights and a Europe of free nations, both Eastern and Western, were promises of a hard fight rather than an idyllic future.

This may not sound like much if one lives in the United States or Western Europe and can exercise the divine right of the enfranchised to get rid of leaders who are not responsive to the nation's needs or wants. It may sound even less interesting to the advocates of power from the barrel of a gun, the liberation movements that Moscow is always helping if they are far enough from its borders. But if one lives in the Russian backyard, as do the 100 million people of Bulgaria, Czechoslovakia, East Germany, Hungary, Poland, and Romania, it is a heady prospect indeed. And if the doctrine that the rights of the individual are at least as important as the directives of the government can spread from Eastern Europe to Russia itself, it is possible that a reverberating effect might be set in motion, with one careful concession in Poland causing one in the Soviet Ukraine, and that one affecting Slovakia or Hungary.

Paper guarantees of rights have been on the books for decades in the Soviet bloc, going hand in hand with the cynical and systematic repression of those rights. But in addition to the emergence of the pope as conscience and guarantor, there is another new factor the regimes must reckon with in the Eastern Europe of the eighties. That is the failure of what had been a fairly successful attempt by Soviet and local Communist leaders to compensate for the lack of political freedoms with consumer goods and a more relaxed attitude toward the duties of the citizen to the state. Until economic difficulties overtook it in the late seventies, this policy kept the peace in Eastern Europe, and, if it didn't manage to create happiness, at least it ameliorated the depths of despair in the region that followed the sudden ending of the hopes of Czechoslovakia.

Eastern European intellectuals call the Communist policy the specific social contract. Its terms are these: You, the intellectuals, are not to engage in politics or even literature; leave that to the regulars. We, the regime, will give you a reasonable standard of living, will build more apartments and fill the highways with Western-model cars made in our factories, will provide places in the universities and jobs for your children, and will even import (as in the case of East Germany) $10 million worth of Levi's for them, if they can afford $75 a pair, or (as in the case of Hungary) will set up a factory and make them ourselves.

Carrot and stick have always been the basic policy tools of these regimes in their relations with their constituents, but there are important differences between the old ways and the contemporary, according to those who have lived under both. The most important one is the restraint shown in the use of police terror to achieve obedience. Another is the disregard of many of the bothersome trappings of Communism—the phony egalitarianism, the forced attendance at the frequent and dreary political rallies, the job and college quotas for workers and peasants, and the resultant fabrication of such backgrounds. People found out, at last, that they were beginning to be treated as adults.

They also discovered that it cost the state no more to paint cars red and yellow than to paint them gray or black, and that if some of the ambitious plan targets for heavy industry were scaled down so that more consumer goods would be on the shelves, people might work harder. Poland trebled its automobile production, with machines from Italy's Fiat, in the last decade. And in the same period, the number of private cars in Hungary increased from a few hundred thousand to more than a million.

There is no such bright spectrum in the cultural field, although some Eastern Europeans benefit from Western imports that, in contrast to the Fiat technology, are not government-authorized. The amount of benefit depends on geography. Border areas of Hungary can receive Austrian television clearly; Czechoslovakia gets both Austrian and West German television. Coastal Poland receives a clear signal from Sweden and Denmark, but East Germany is the best served of all: Not only is the language the same, but in 80 percent of the country the two West German national channels and the various regional channels can be seen.

East Germans thus can choose between the Communist channels and a vastly more objective account of what is going on in the world—the Communist as well as the West—in news, analysis, drama, and music. So many watch Western television, despite regime disapproval, that protest letters from the East helped prevent a change of the West German late-night movie to an even later hour (Communist societies go to work earlier than Western).

It is likely that the Western commercials make as much of an impression on the Eastern viewers as the uncensored news and theater. Not only do the products they are pushing seem to be better than those sold in the East (and the East German consumers, in their innocence, believe the claims of the ad men) but the way of life they depict goes far beyond the dreams permitted under the social contract. The slim and beautiful Westerners in the commercials are filmed on the Riviera, in the Alps, even in Tahiti and Hawaii. Thus it is not only their shampoo and lawn mowers that are envied; it is their freedom to cross borders.

A small trickle of tourist traffic does manage to get to the

West from the East. Currency restrictions play a part in limiting such travel; most Eastern Europeans are permitted to take so little foreign currency out of the country that a modest lunch in Zurich would wipe them out. The big barrier, however, is political. As one Eastern European put it, you must be careful to advance your career to the point at which you can afford to apply for a tourist visa to the West, but not so far as to make the government suspect you might be valuable if you decide to stay.

Hungary and Poland lead the bloc in their willingness to permit travel to the West, and they also lead in the cultural freedom they grant at home. Polish and Hungarian newspaper readers have a better idea of world events than do readers in other Eastern countries, and the flow of ideas from the rest of the world in the form of books, plays, and films is less restricted by these two nations.

There are few writers in prison in contemporary Eastern Europe. Part of the reason, as one of their leading representatives said, is that administrative punishments have replaced pure terror as a more efficient means of control. "Instead of locking us up," he explained, "they expel us from our writers' union, fine us for any income our books have earned in the West—not censorship, you understand, just enforcement of the foreign currency laws—take away our teaching or translating jobs, and, finally, evict us from our apartments. Even though some of us do get taken in for questioning or for long months of prison under the excuse of pretrial investigation, the days of the spectacular show trials and confessions, the executions and long forced-labor sentences, seem to be over."

The key to this new Eastern European social arrangement is whether or not it is accepted as permanent. If it is, then people will put away their reform plans and try to make the best of things. If it is not, they will try to enjoy their car trips and blue jeans and still work for a better way of ordering the political life of their nations.

For a decade after the tanks of August 1968 stopped reform dead in Prague, acceptance was all but universal. A few optimists waited for changes in Moscow; the pessimists agreed that such changes were a prerequisite for change in Eastern Europe but were unlikely to come in their lifetimes. This attitude seemed to be the ultimate victory of the Brezhnev Doctrine, that proclamation in the ruins of the Czechoslovak experiment that the Soviet model is the sole acceptable one for Eastern Europe, and that any attempts to tamper with it will be greeted by armed force, with Moscow, of course, the one defining what constitutes tampering.

The ruins of the Hungarian Revolution 12 years earlier had produced a Moscow doctrine diametrically opposite. Its author, Nikita Khrushchev, displayed a flexibility surprising to those in the West who considered him a blusterer and a tyrant. Khrushchev, in November 1956, promised the leaders, if not the people, of Eastern Europe that they could follow their own roads to socialism, because of their differing conditions, if only they did not stray too far. :

Under this Khrushchev Doctrine, the battered Hungarian nation took the first steps in economic reform, laying the groundwork for the mixed-plan market system that is now the envy of Eastern Europe. Romania embarked on its independent foreign policy, an Eastern mirror-image of Gaullism. Poland and East Germany launched consumerist movements, from the top. Bulgaria remained cautious, tradition-bound, and tough—a little Russia in the Balkans. Czechoslovakia tried to squeeze into its 8 months of unchecked freedom all the rights and liberties won by any of the others: a radically reformed economy, political independence, good relations with countries Moscow did not like, and,finally, a free press to write about it all, in case the Soviets had missed something.

When all these freedoms were eliminated in Czechoslovakia, a freeze descended on the rest of Eastern Europe, as chilly as the visages of the Kremlin leaders posing for pictures on top of Lenin's tomb. Reform was frozen but not revoked: Hungary was allowed to go ahead with its economic pragmatism, and Romania, more grudgingly, with its foreign policy acrobatics. No one, however, was permitted to embark on any new experiments.

East German and Polish consumerism was extended to the rest of the bloc, as a palliative, and became one of the few elements in Soviet-East European relations genuinely desired by both parties: for Moscow to keep the lid on, for the Eastern Europeans to be able to enjoy life more. Not, however, without a certain amount of resentment on the part of Soviet citizens well traveled or well informed enough to realize that their Polish and Bulgarian neighbors have higher living standards than they do: "It's one of the most charitable acts in history, isn't it, that we've subsidized their standards of living at our own expense," a Soviet industrial manager said. "It's too bad they're so close to the West, but we do have to make concessions."

As a result of the new social contract (and of a different set of circumstances in Yugoslavia), Eastern Europe produced some dazzling, by local standards, displays of affluence in the late seventies.

The Warsaw Ghetto monument, the understated commemoration of so much human tragedy and suffering, became, with its park and traffic-free streets, a convenient place for driving instructions for the thousands of new car owners of Warsaw.

The Hungarian *puszta's* traditional landscape of plains broken by the silhouettes of thatched-roofed cottages and wooden wellsweeps was brought up to date with the addition of television antennae.

East Germans went to the foreign-currency shops in their cities and along their highways to buy not only the necessities their stores did not provide, but also luxuries and frivolities like racing stripes and rally driving lights for their cars—in a country where the driving is as regulated and humdrum as everything else.

A Czech in political trouble since 1948 found that the remote little summer house he had managed to build during periods when he could get no work became part of a summer colony with a population density approaching Hong Kong's. Many of his new neighbors are 1968 dissidents, and one of their reasons for building in the country was to hear Western broadcasts, free of the jamming directed at the cities.

Yugoslavia, operating with many of the constraints of Communism—but none of those of Soviet Communism—on its economy, went the furthest of all, producing the phenomenon of Marxist millionaires with yachts on the Adriatic, as well as the more frequent one of migrant workers who return from Germany and Scandinavia with useful skills and respectable hard-currency bank accounts.

"There have been two Yugoslav miracles," a Party member in Belgrade said. "The first was defeating one big power, the Germans, and defying a second, the Russians.

"Miracle number two is that someone like my mother, a Partisan fighter who lost all five of her brothers in the war and lived in a single room for years after that, now has her own villa on the Adriatic, can cross freely into Italy to buy furniture and equipment, and finds that the Italians are happy to change her Yugoslav *dinars* at a good rate."

Except in Yugoslavia, the policy of affluent Communism began to run into trouble in the mid-seventies. Poland tinkered with wages and prices so inexpertly that twice the streets exploded, in 1970 and 1976, resulting in rare examples of worker protest bringing about a change of government or policy in the bloc. Elsewhere, the limitations of central planning and the general waste inherent in the Eastern models of socialism began to interfere more and more with the goal of keeping the people happy and quiet.

International factors played an important role in the ups

as well as the downs. Within 2 years of the Soviet invasion of Czechoslovakia, United States-Soviet détente, West German Ostpolitik, and French, German, and Italian business enterprise combined to produce a spectacular rise in East-West trade. Western companies built hotels, sold whiskey and buses, and provided formulae for producing Coke and Pepsi and deodorants. Less obvious but far more important, Western machine tools and manufacturing processes began to take hold in Eastern consumer goods industries, often through the delivery of entire plants and personnel to train locals, causing an across-the-board improvement in the quantity and quality of goods on the shelves of department stores and supermarkets. In one such store in Hungary, a Swedish cash register checked out purchases wheeled up in a shopping cart designed by Austrians. The purchases included detergent made locally by a West German process, a British cooking gadget, and a frozen Hungarian chicken, processed and wrapped in peasant-design plastic by an American machine bought by one of the large collective farms.

No sooner had these trade, licensing, and exchange patterns started, however, than the West began to export the ills as well as the benefits of capitalism. The first was the mid-seventies recession. As a Polish official explained, his trade organization bought American shoe machinery with a promise to pay for it with shoes sold to the American market. The recession all but eliminated the market, leaving the Poles with the ability to make shoes too high-priced for domestic customers, a great deal of expensive equipment, and a debt that had to be paid back in dollars. Poland's hard-currency debt, in fact, reached $16 billion before reduced purchases began to whittle it down. The $4 billion annual interest bill alone was bigger than the entire national budget of Communist pauper nations like Albania.

Then came bad news from the East, in the form of oil price increases from the Soviet Union. Soviet propagandists were put to work rewriting their material about Eastern Europe's having a stable and assured supply of crude oil from Siberia at prices far below that of the world market. As the Russians caught up with OPEC rates, the Eastern Europeans became increasingly resentful. They had, after all, paid as much or more to the Russians in the days of cheap oil than they could have paid in the Middle East. In addition, they had invested heavily in the pipelines and other development costs of the Soviet oil and gas fields, putting their money in, as a Hungarian economist complained, at interest rates as low as 2 percent, which, allowing for inflation, meant receiving no interest at all.

Inflation was, in fact, the third part of the economic problems that descended on Eastern Europe to interfere with the social contract. Bulgarians, whose average monthly income of about $150 puts them near the bottom of Europe's scale, suddenly found themselves at the top of another index when the price of gasoline rose to $4.25 a gallon. All across the bloc, the rise in energy costs fed inflation and slowed growth. There were Western exports of inflation, too, in the form of higher prices for machinery and equipment, licenses, and technological help.

Domestic policies hurt rather than helped. Wage increases without commensurate gains in productivity were a fixture of the social contract. Government-fixed prices were supposed to mean that this newly printed money represented real gains in earnings. But the scarcity of food and other goods in the state stores forced customers to the officially tolerated "free" market, where prices were four times as high. The Polish government went into the automobile black market itself, to siphon off some of the extra money and to undercut the private entrepreneurs operating illegally.

A Warsaw schoolteacher described how the system works: "You put down your 69,000 *zlotys* (about $2,200) for a Polski Fiat 126 (a tiny four-seater). You count on waiting two years.

Or you can buy a car from someone who has already waited, for twice the price. That, of course, is illegal. Now the government will sell you a new one, too, for twice the price, and a wait of only a month. If you're really lucky—a textile worker who makes some production record, a miner—then you can have both: the regular price and immediate delivery."

With all its problems, however, the East European economic situation is a bright, happy landscape in contrast to the Eastern European political situation. The enterprise managers who spend millions of dollars, hire and fire hundreds of employees, and argue their cases for resource allocation at the highest Party levels have no more political influence than the poorest-paid janitor, or indeed the most detested dissidents. They vote with the 99-plus percent. They read what the Party writes: they sign Party petitions about Vietnam and Chile.

Reading the Party press and listening to the radio for any length of time produces an eerie sense that nothing at all is happening in that particular country that is really news, but that in the world outside, things are in constant turmoil. Much is written and spoken about, of course, but it all concerns the arrival or departure of delegations, the pledges of workers to fulfill plans, and the opening or closing of exhibitions. In the West, critics are attacking the governments, demonstrators are marching, journalists are making revelations, legislative commissions are conducting investigations. All is movement, conflict, questioning, and this is always presented as a sign of democratic weakness. In the East, all is serene. There is no opposition. There are no negative votes in parliament.

Not even the officials believe this, of course, and there exists an unofficial network of communications in all the bloc countries that is amazingly efficient at informing interested citizens about what is going on. Unfortunately, the real news is mixed with a lot of gossip and rumor, none of it reflecting very favorably on the march of Communism or the reputations of the rulers. (Unfortunately, because the truth is bad enough.)

From these informal communications networks sprang the dissident movement—men and women in the Soviet Union and every country of Eastern Europe, including Yugoslavia, more or less loosely organized around the goal of using the truth as a means of making the regimes more responsive to the needs of the people. By issuing *samizdat* (self-published and therefore illegal) material about the true state of things, as they see it, by holding press conferences or contacting Western journalists, they make sure that the message gets out to the world, and sometimes comes back, through the broadcasts of Radio Free Europe, the British Broadcasting Corporation, the Voice of America, and Radio Liberty.

Making the regime responsive means different things to different dissidents, in Eastern Europe as in the Soviet Union. Some simply want to leave the country, particularly Jews and members of other minorities. If the minority is too big to move, like the 1.6 million Hungarians in the Transylvania region of Romania, then they want the right to literature, education, official dealings, and cultural life in their own language.

Those without ethnic grievances call for more freedom, in specific areas or in general, whether it is the importation of a few more books, or a little less censorship of what is written locally, or the whole new deal of a pluralistic society in which the Communist Party would have to compete for political power instead of having its leading role written into the constitution.

Where religion is strong and well organized, such as East Germany's Lutheran church and Poland's Roman Catholic

Church, the dissidents get support from some of the pulpits and publications. The relationship between the secular dissidents and the churches is a complex one; some goals are shared and some diverge. All are interested in freedom of speech and conscience, but the intellectuals and political activists are not interested very much in new church construction, and the churches are always wary about going too far in a confrontation with officialdom that might help the dissidents' cause but harm the long-term interests of the church members.

This does not mean that tests of the system should be avoided, but that the ground and the issue should be chosen carefully. The East German Church took the regime by surprise when it used its newly won rights to Sunday radio broadcasts to criticize the introduction of compulsory military training in the grade schools. That stand coincided with that of the dissident intellectuals, but it could be justified on moral grounds and thus be defended against charges of political interference.

The Polish cardinal who was to become Pope John Paul II defined the issue: "The mission of the Church does not call for carrying on politics, for that would be encroaching upon the competency of the State. However, the Church has the right and the duty to participate in political matters from a moral aspect, to speak out even if it should cause her suffering and difficulty. Christians cannot be mere onlookers."

I interviewed and corresponded with Cardinal Wojtyla in the early seventies and in the process became familiar not only with his thinking, but with the way the Church works, from parish to national level, in the defense of individual rights threatened by the state's power and lack of concern.

The cardinal, in those days, could command only a fraction of the diplomatic, political, and moral power he was granted later, but he pushed the power he had to the limit.

To illustrate the problem, and the opportunity, facing the Church under Communism, he used the Biblical phrase: "Render therefore unto Caesar the things which are Caesar's; and unto God the things which are God's" (Matthew 22:21). From the time he began divinity studies under the German occupation in 1942 until the time he left Cracow for the 1978 consistory, he devoted his considerable courage and intellect to enlarging the second sphere and diminishing the first.

That the state is strong and enduring, irrespective of ideology, was demonstrated by the fact that Wojtyla began his Church career in an underground university established by the Church to keep the national cultural heritage alive under the Nazis, and he ended his career in Poland as a principal supporter of the "flying universities," those dissident seminars conducted underground to teach and discuss subjects forbidden by the Communists.

The God-and-Caesar formulation does not mean that Wojtyla sought to win people to the Church or away from the regime. Proselytizing is hardly necessary in Poland, where nine of ten are already Catholics. And despite its unpopularity, the government is backed by such power, Polish and Soviet, that no one would seriously consider its overthrow.

A better arrangement of the existing power relationships is the aim, and defining what is God's and what is Caesar's—every day, anew—is the method. Wojtyla's historic contribution to the process was to claim for his side the issue of human rights. The freedom of the individual, he stressed in his sermons and his writings, is the natural state of mankind, not something that can be parceled out in little pieces by the authorities and then snatched back again. If this is so, then it is the legitimate task of the Church to strive for individual freedom. When police clubbed students in the narrow cobblestoned streets of Cracow in 1968, and when troops fired on workers rioting in the Baltic ports in 1970, killing forty-five, the Polish bishops could do no more than repeat this stand. Their statements, largely written by Wojtyla, could be distilled into a phrase that was at once a cry of anguish and an expression of hope: "Freedom is God's basic gift to man."

As cardinal, Wojtyla worked to secure this gift in two main ways. The first was to support the human rights movement. Cracow, with its ancient university and liberal Catholic weekly, *Tygodnik Powszechny,* became the intellectual center for human rights in Poland, and indeed in Eastern Europe. Every one of the outspoken Cracow leaders depended on the cardinal for support and protection.

The movement grew out of the discussion circles of intellectuals organized by Cracow churches in the sixties. They were not clubs or political groups—that kind of activity is against the law. But it is impossible to talk about morals and theology without bringing up the problems of daily life under Communism and trying to find some answers. There is the secret of the power of the Church in Poland. When an office manager in the state economy or a teacher spends an evening at a Catholic discussion circle, no one in their Party unit can know whether it was to talk about religion or the shortcomings of the Plan.

The Cardinal's other level of work for human rights was more basic and, like the clubs, is of course still being carried on by his Cracow successors. Cracow families come to the archbishop's palace, a Renaissance building not far from the city hall, for help on personal, school, and housing problems. The Church thus steps in to help where the State cannot or will not help the individual and, by doing this, aligns itself with the individual in his or her relationship with the State.

Every afternoon in every Polish city and village, children and teenagers walk in chatting groups from the schools of the State to the schools of the Church. It is estimated that a third of Poland's 34 million people have gone through these classes in church buildings, basements, and private homes. The story of religious teaching since World War II is one of gains and losses, government harassment followed by concession, depending on the mood of the populace or the state of the economy.

The regime presents its side of the story in terms of separation of Church and State, an argument that might be convincing in other societies, where university lectures are not censored. The Church argues that part of its rightful mission is to teach about religion as well as to preach.

But the effect of the religion classes has gone far beyond knowledge of the Bible. A good part of Poland's population has benefited from a dual education, from the Party and from the Church, and has learned that there is more than one set of answers to the problems of contemporary life. It has learned to question dogma (religious, in many cases, as well as ideological) and to value the individual. Every effort in the state schools is aimed in the opposite direction, and in the Soviet Union and most of Eastern Europe, there are only state schools. It is no wonder that the dissident movement in Poland is by far the strongest of the region.

When Wojtyla became pope in October 1978, his field of battle for human rights suddenly enlarged from the old towns and farming country of the Cracow archdiocese to the whole world, but particularly, because of his background, to the eastern part of it. His adversaries changed from the low-key Polish Party officials in Cracow to an impressive array of dictators, with the old men in the Kremlin again being given special attention.

Few men could have been better prepared for the challenge either by intellect or experience. Born in a poor family in Wadowice, a village near Cracow, in 1920, Wojtyla went to the village school and a nearby high school. Shortly after he enrolled at the university in Cracow, the Germans invaded Poland, closed the schools, and sent the professors to concentration camps, where few survived the war. Within a few weeks, however, the underground university was in being, and Wojtyla was one of its students, constantly under threat of discovery and arrest. In 1942 he decided to begin study for the priesthood, and, during the same period, the underground seminarian helped to found an underground theater, the Rhapsody, to present plays about Polish patriots in the vaulted cellars of Cracow while the German soldiers patrolled above.

Wojtyla could not escape being rounded up by the Germans for forced labor. He was sent to the Solvay soda plant near Cracow but managed to keep studying, writing plays, and acting in the theater. The factory work was hard but the experience valuable, he said: "I consider those four years especially important in my life. I believe that divine providence prepared me in that way for future tasks."

Ordained in 1946, he went abroad for 2 years, to study in Rome and to work among emigré Polish miners in France and Belgium. He returned to a country parish near Cracow and then to a city one, at the height of the Communists' war on the Church. Priests were arrested by the hundreds as spies and saboteurs, and the Polish Primate, Stefan Cardinal Wyszinski, was placed under house arrest. But the young priest of St. Florian's, Cracow, managed to continue his preaching and education. Wojtyla became a doctor of theology in 1951, a professor at the Catholic University of Lublin in 1954, and acting archbishop of Cracow in 1962. And as priest, scholar, teacher, and Church dignitary, he remained close to his parishioners, particularly the young. Former members of these student circles recall fondly the mountain hikes and canoeing with Father Wojtyla. But above all they remember the discussions in which he would draw on all the resources of his intellect, learning, and deep faith to help guide their lives in a society trying to subordinate all these qualities to obedience and acceptance.

In 1967, at the age of 47, Wojtyla was made a cardinal by Pope Paul VI and began to gather the international experience and reputation that led to his election as pope 11 years later. In 1956, one of Poland's frequent worker upheavals had ended the Communists' war on the Church, as well as many other unpleasant features of Polish life, and it was thus possible for both Wojtyla and Wyszinski to travel freely to and from the Vatican. Nevertheless, the regime still was able to keep Pope Paul from visiting Poland in 1966, on the thousandth anniversary of Christianity in the nation.

That kind of resistance crumbled after the election of a Polish pope, and the issue of a papal visit became only a matter of when, not if. But the Polish Communists showed that, despite the power and authority of the pope's office, there are still times when the Church must bow to the State. Pope John Paul had planned to visit Poland in May 1979, on the nine-hundredth anniversary of the death of St. Stanislaw, the Cracow bishop executed for opposing the Polish king. His Christmas letter to the Cracow archdiocese called St. Stanislaw "an advocate of the most essential human rights," someone who "did not hesitate to confront the ruler when defense of the moral order was called for."

The contemporary parallels were too clear for the Communists to accept. The Christmas letter was heavily censored—although later allowed to appear in full—and diplomatic pressure was put on the pope to visit at a time less charged with emotion. The pope gave ground but gained in other respects in keeping with the rules of Church-State warfare in Poland. He got 9 days instead of 3, a meeting with Party chief Edward Gierek, and, as it turned out, ample opportunity to commemorate St. Stanislaw a month later.

If there was any doubt about the importance of human

rights for the new papacy, Pope John Paul's first encyclical removed it: "The rights of power can only be understood on the basis of respect for the objective and inviolable rights of man. . . . The lack of this leads to the dissolution of society, opposition by citizens to authority, or a situation of oppression, intimidation, violence, and terrorism, of which many examples have been provided by the totalitarianism of this century."

And, as expected, when he landed in Warsaw for what the Church (but not the regime) described as a pilgrimage "during the year dedicated to celebrating the martyrdom of St. Stanislaw," human rights appeared in his statements and sermons. The most moving was his sermon at the site of the Auschwitz death camp, where the Nazis exterminated 4 million men, women, and children, and where he spoke of "those inalienable rights of man which can be trampled on so easily and annihilated by man."

But no one was prepared for his moving the rights issue to a higher stage, to demand nothing less than the rights of nations, not only the people in those nations, to be free.

Poland, he told Gierek and the nation, had suffered long enough from the lack of respect for its independence and sovereignty; it and other nations must be guaranteed the "right of existence, to freedom . . . and also to the formation of its own culture and civilization."

At Gniezno, Poland's ancient capital, he made it clear that he considered it his duty as a Slavic pope to extend the hand of Christianity—from the West—to the peoples of all the Slavic countries: "Europe, which during its history has several times been divided; Europe, which toward the first half of the present century was tragically divided by the horrible world war; Europe, with its present and continuing division of regimes, ideologies, and economic and political systems, cannot cease to seek its fundamental unity: It must turn to Christianity."

Since all the Slavic nations are presently ruled by Communists, the challenge was clear. But Poland and its neighboring Communist states reacted by trying to ignore what the pope had said. Polish television, radio, and newspapers could hardly keep from covering such a major news event, although television producers were instructed to focus cameras on the pontiff and not on the crowds, which sometimes ran into the millions. Czechoslovakia sent a special correspondent to file stories on industrial achievements in Poland on every day of the pope's visit; he managed not to mention the visit at all. Throughout the bloc, television coverage was limited to seconds, and the one-paragraph newspaper stories were relegated to inside pages. And hastily instituted border restrictions kept most people from neighboring countries from seeing the visit for themselves.

The Soviet Union has tried since the election of the pope to pay him as little attention as possible. It dismissed as wishful thinking by the West the idea that the Slav in the Vatican might continue to be a powerful advocate of the individual and a powerful adversary of Communism.

But the papal visit to Russia's borders has certainly caused concern. The pope achieved a number of things in Poland, none of them desirable for the Soviet Union: He made it plain that his human rights campaign would continue; he called for the freedom of nations under a kind of pan-Christian umbrella linking West and East in a decidedly non-Communist fashion; he served notice on the Polish regime to grant more religious concessions; he brushed aside Communist claims to legitimacy based on the past 35 years and made his own claim on the basis of more than a thousand years of the history of church and nation; and finally he showed, by holding court like a Polish king, by attracting the largest crowds in the nation's history and the greatest outpouring of emotion, how shallow the roots of Communism are in Poland and how deep the roots of the nation.

Soviet officials, in public and private statements, contend that none of this is very worrisome to the one Slavic nation with nuclear rockets and a huge army, especially when this strength is compared to the celebrated lack of any military divisions supporting the pope.

There is, all the same, the vague and uneasy feeling that the Poles, the old enemies, have done something behind the Russians' backs. And the Soviet Union must be wondering whatever happened to all the money spent for 30 years on the collaborating PAX "peace priests" movement, if someone like Wojtyla nevertheless manages to emerge.

Roman Catholicism, active or latent, is a strong force in the western provinces of the USSR, above all in the Baltic. The much larger Russian Orthodox Church was all but destroyed under Stalin; its priests pose no present human rights challenge to the regime.

But religion is only one facet of John Paul II's challenge to the regimes of Eastern Europe and appeal to the people—to Catholics most of all, but to the aggrieved members of other religions and those of no religion as well.

At a time of declining faith in the power of the governments to provide a better life, economically, politically, or spiritually, the pope has come along to say not only that improvement is possible, but also that it is the fulfillment of God's design for mankind. That message may prove to be as powerful as the one preached in Eastern Europe three-quarters of a century ago by another Slavic intellectual with no divisions of troops, Vladimir Ilyich Lenin.

What the pope seeks for the individuals of Eastern Europe he also seeks for the states—"the dignity and rights of nations"—and this doctrine of national sovereignty and independence poses as great a challenge to the Soviet Union and as great an opportunity to the Eastern Europeans in the future as human rights does in the present. Right now, it is far easier to win concessions within the existing structure of Russia's European empire than it is to change the structure.

The pope's own Poland would be the leading candidate for national independence, were it not landlocked between the Soviet Union and the Communist part of Germany, with Soviet troops supposedly guarding the supply lines between the two. Geography and history are no more favorable to Bulgaria, Hungary, and Czechoslovakia, but they do favor Romania somewhat and Yugoslavia a great deal. Both these Balkan nations are exceptions to many rules in Eastern Europe, but perhaps the most important is that neither has Soviet troops stationed on its soil.

To agree with a term much used by Communist commentators during national holidays and military parades, Soviet power in Eastern Europe is indeed awesome. It extends beyond the obvious signs of troops and tanks of the Red Army in every country except the aforementioned and Bulgaria. These soldiers back up local soldiers, and they, in turn, back up armies of police, both ordinary and security. At the top are leaders chosen for their loyalty to the Soviet Union and Communism, loyalty that has usually been tested by prison terms, often administered by the Communists themselves.

Encountering Soviet advisers in Czechoslovak ministries was a shock for journalists like me in the early days of the occupation, although in fairness it must be said that Soviet influence on the six governments is exercised more subtly in normal times. The best way is to let the local leaderships carry out the policies the Soviet Union wishes and, if possible, to anticipate those wishes. Sometimes, in the fifties and sixties, the leaders were far too willing to ignore local needs, and the people went on strike, rioted, or rose in revolt, disregarding all that military power. East Berlin and Pilsen, Czechoslovakia in 1953; Poznan, Poland, and Budapest in 1956; Warsaw and Cracow as well as Prague in 1968;

Gdansk in 1970 and Warsaw in 1976; and the miners' strike in Romania's Jiu valley in 1977 are the main examples.

This record of unrest in an area supposedly happily marching toward Communism shows that the Communist leaders of the six countries are men caught in the middle, trying to please the Soviet Union on one hand and their people on the other. There are solutions to the domestic problems of economic inefficiency and lack of freedoms, but the solutions call for less Communism of the Moscow variety, and this the Soviet Union is reluctant to permit. It seems clear that men like Czechoslovakia's Gustav Husak, Poland's Gierek, and Hungary's Janos Kadar must be much more than the mere puppets they are often accused of being in order to be able to survive so long.

Nationalism cuts both ways in the Soviet bloc; if any member of the six leaderships gets too ambitious in that direction, he is reminded that the Soviet Union holds the ultimate judgment over national survival. It might be thought that so much sovereignty has been conceded to the Soviet Union that no one could get very excited about the loss of what little remains. But national hopes and prides are very much alive and are therefore very sensitive to pressure.

Poland can be frightened with talk of German reunification, as can East Germany. The Polish nightmare is a reunited Germany with reason to be grateful to the Russians.

Romania and Hungary are kept apart through the Transylvanian question. Transylvania's 1.6 million Hungarians have belonged to Romania twice and Hungary once since World War I. Returning Transylvania to Hungary once again would considerably reduce Romania's power and importance and considerably increase Hungary's. Bulgaria and Yugoslavia have longstanding differences over Macedonia; Czechoslovakia could be divided into its two components, as it was under the German occupation and as some Slovak Communist extremists suggested that it be in 1968, with the difference that the Slovak part would become the sixteenth Soviet republic.

If all this sounds like the wildest emigré gossip that ever came out of the cafés of Paris or Munich, let it be remembered that it is the Soviet Union and the leaders of Eastern Europe who periodically renew plans and speculation about all these issues.

Most of the time, these questions of territorial integrity and national survival are brought up to counter nationalist thrusts by one of the six countries, or even by Yugoslavia. The most frequent target is Romania; part of its nationalist appeal, after all, includes designs on a piece of the Soviet Union that used to be Romanian—Bessarabia, now known as Soviet Moldavia. Yugoslavia, freed from the bloc in 1948, must be treated as a sovereign state. It is free to choose its friends and enemies and free to experiment with its economy and social structure. Its success has made it a model for its Eastern neighbors to aim for if they are ever permitted that much freedom to experiment. They consider it an example within reach: Poland and Hungary will never look like America, but they might someday look something like Yugoslavia.

After Stalin's colossal blunder in expelling Yugoslavia from the Cominform in 1948, the nation paid heavily for its independence in the grim blockade days of the late forties and early fifties. But it benefited in far greater measure by being able to throw off the dogmatic rules of Soviet-style planning and strict Party controls. Liberalization brought prosperity, political life loosened up, and the populace became a great deal easier to govern. Many problems remain, with the leadership question and the conflicts of the nationalities only the two most prominent, but these are problems the other states of Eastern Europe would gladly cope with if they could enjoy some of the other advantages the southern Slavs do.

Yugoslavia has two final advantages its neighbors would like to have: an independent, tough little army and mountainous terrain that together mean the determination and the ability to fight. Soviet troops could be in Romania's capital, Bucharest, the same day they crossed the Danube from Moldavia. There is only a broad plain and a small army in their way, and everyone on both sides of the border knows it. Soviet troops, even with a Bulgarian supply base, would have no such easy time in Yugoslavia, and this, too, has been generally appreciated by both sides since 1948.

This feeling of cocky independence, with its shadows of worry about Soviet intentions, comes out in conversations as well as in public statements in Yugoslavia. One striking illustration of both elements was a factory visit by Leonid Brezhnev in the late seventies. Brezhnev shook hands with the workers and then, in the course of a 45-minute speech, grew warmer and warmer in his praise of the friendship that linked Yugoslavia and Russia. Finally, departing from his prepared text, he blurted out a warm invitation to all the workers present to spend their vacations in the Soviet Union. He was astonished and flustered when this was greeted with laughter and shouts of "No, no." His speech then took on a hard and cold tone. Yugoslav officials present said the incident told more than a pile of treaties would how suspicious the two nations are of each other. Russia continues to treat Yugoslavia as an erring brother who someday will be welcomed back in the fold. Yugoslavs look on Russia with apprehension, wondering what it will try to get them back.

Both Yugoslavia and Romania try to take out as many insurance policies as they can against the Soviet Union. Yugoslavia started its independent course with the help of the United States but was alienated from China for years for ideological reasons; the Yugoslavs were far too liberal in the practice of Communism to suit the Maoists. The deepening Sino-Soviet split brought them back together. Romania was able to count on both United States and Chinese support from the outset.

Moscow considers China the more dangerous partner for both nations, although it condemns with equal vigor the threat of American or Chinese "bridgeheads in the Balkans." Washington, after all, is only following the same rules of détente it followed with Moscow if it tries to improve relations with Romania and Yugoslavia. The Soviets can find no such comfort, however, in looking at the increasingly frequent visits of high-level Chinese delegations to these two countries, and they were particularly alarmed at the 1978 trip of Chinese chairman Hua, which was called an attempt "to instigate the Balkan nations against each other, to sow dissent, to exploit the temporary misunderstandings between individual countries."

The increase in tensions in the region that followed the Hua visit left many diplomats in Romania and Yugoslavia wondering what the two regimes had gained. China's gain was clear: its new leadership had demonstrated to Moscow that its hold on the Balkans, the traditionally volatile part of Europe, was tenuous indeed, and it underlined this with a flurry of trade agreements and proclamations of friendship.

Yugoslavia won tacit recognition from the Chinese that its pragmatic Communism had been right all along, and the Chinese kind wrong, but that was not a great consolation when weighed against the displeasure of the Russians, the rumors of troop movements, and the other weapons from the arsenal of the war of nerves the Soviets are so adept at waging. Yugoslavs were reminded, in fact, of what Chou En-lai had told the independent Communist states of Europe in 1971: "We are a long way from Europe . . . one of our popular proverbs says, 'Distant waters cannot quench fire.' "

The other Yugoslav insurance policy, with the United States, has a guarantor nearly as distant, but perhaps more effective. Russian pressure on Yugoslavia can harm détente between Moscow and Washington. Moscow and Peking have no such reservoir of relations to empty. Yugoslav officials admit they have no clue as to what will happen when the next generation of Soviet leaders takes over, but they do have faith in the permanence of the United States as a Yugoslav partner. It is a low-key partnership, with the United States always counted on to come through when needed, whether it is to agree to resume some arms sales or to crack down on Croatian terrorists operating from the United States. The Yugoslavs say they can believe what the Americans tell them, and that if something slips in the relationship, the United States can be reminded and counted on to make things right. "Our relationship with the Soviet Union, in the past, has been good when relations with the United States have been bad," an official said. "But now we think we have reached the point of permanent good relations with the United States, and perhaps Moscow can rise and fall within that framework."

All this is possible, in the Moscow view, because of a technical error in the construction of the power blocs. Yugoslavia really belongs to the East, but because of Stalin's 1948 mistake, it managed to join the nonaligned and thus, in the Soviet scheme of things, is open to all sides, with the exception of China.

But Romania is a different story entirely. Despite its foot dragging and verbal defiance, it is firmly a member of all the alliances—military, econonic, and bilateral—that bind the states of Eastern Europe to the Soviet Union and constitute the formal lines of the Soviet sphere of influence. The United States has shown again and again that it will not step too far into this sphere.

China has been more reckless than the United States in intruding across these lines, because it is an avowed enemy of the Soviet Union, not an adversary more or less pursuing détente. And the Romanian leadership has been equally reckless in responding to the Chinese, even coming to their defense in Moscow.

The phenomenon of Nicolae Ceaucescu's pleasant but poor and backward country, 21 million Latins in a sea of Slavs, is the most interesting of all in Eastern Europe. Any examination of the phenomenon usually ends up with two questions: Why does he do it, and how does he get away with it? The answers are complex.

Any discussion of Romania ought to begin with what it is not. It is easy to confuse defiance of the Soviet Union with a general commitment to liberal policies. Romania has no such commitment. Its record in human rights is dismal; its domestic politics are conducted with authoritarian zeal. The press not only overlooks the failures but goes far beyond the rest of Eastern Europe in extolling the virtues of the leadership, above all of Ceaucescu. Despite impressive growth rates, the economy has failed to provide decent living standards.

What Romania might become is another matter, especially if it is ever able to follow the Yugoslav formula. Tito's independent state was as Stalinist at the start as the nation that had expelled it from the Cominform. But gradually, as its international contacts widened and its economy gained, domestic conditions also improved. No one, least of all its dissidents, would call Yugoslavia a model society, but it has many freedoms not yet found in the bloc, freedoms Romanians hope to gain for themselves someday.

For the present, Romania is constrained by the unwritten law of behavior in the socialist community, which says that one may be able to get away with unusual behavior in one sphere, but that it is dangerous to try departing from the pattern in more than one way. The anchor for Romania's adventurous foreign policy is domestic practices so orthodox that one exile calls them "Stalinism without the graves."

This kind of approved domestic behavior earned Romania

the tolerance, if not the complete acceptance, of the Soviet Union through most of the seventies. Romania's flirtations with China, the United States, and Israel among others, and its refusal to be more cooperative in Comecon, the Eastern Common Market, and in maneuvers of the Warsaw Pact produced invasion scares and coup rumors regularly at the close of the sixties. But then relations with Russia improved, in part because Ceaucescu had to wait out the turmoil in the two countries he counted on for protection. There was Vietnam and Watergate in the United States; in China there was the power struggle in Mao's last years and after his death.

The post-Mao leadership began sending delegations to liven things up again, with the culmination being Hua's visit. The Soviet Union charged that the visit constituted interference—in whose affairs it was not made clear, but the inference was in those of the socialist community, with Moscow at its head. Ceaucescu responded that Romania wanted to have good relations with all socialist countries. But the Soviet propaganda attacks continued. It was clear that Moscow considers the delegations that shuttle between Peking and the two Balkan capitals to be a sign of the limitations of Soviet power on the continent rather than the threat of war it claims to see. But limits of power are bad enough.

Ceaucescu was called to account half a year after the Hua visit at the regular Moscow meeting of the Warsaw Pact. Although the Pact is supposed to be a defense alliance for Europe only, China and other outside issues dominated the agenda.

The Soviet Union, alarmed over the rapprochement between China and Japan as well as China's Balkan incursions, fearful of being isolated in the Egyptian-Israeli negotiations, and concerned by NATO talk of military buildup, submitted draft decisions to take care of all these contingencies. The command structure of the pact was to be strengthened, at the cost of the individual nations' freedom of decision; the joint budget for armaments was to be raised; the possibility of using the pact for duty outside Europe was to be discussed (it was at a time of warfare, in progress and threatening, in Indochina); the Middle East settlement was to be condemned; and all the pact members' voices were to be added to Moscow's in condemning China. The usual communiqué issued at the end of the meeting gave no hint of disputation on any of these points. But it soon became clear from Romanian sources that Ceaucescu had defied the Soviet Union and all the other partners on every one of the points, refusing to sign in the end.

He did so because every issue went against some facet of Romanian policy. Romania avoids condemnation of China as well as Israel because it sees such group actions as infringements on its own sovereignty as well as impediments to its good relations with the nations involved. As any independent country might be expected to do, Romania resists putting other nations' generals at the head of its armies and ordering them to foreign fields. As an advocate of disarmament, it does not want to increase its own arms budget.

The Soviet Union and its allies turned up the volume of propaganda, but there were no more serious repercussions, and this brings back the question of how Romania manages to defy such an overwhelming array of power when no other nation in the bloc feels it can risk even a mild dissenting view.

The answer inevitably involves comparisons with the last, unsuccessful, defier—Czechoslovakia. Unlike the Prague reformers, Romania has forged ties with nations all over the world. Two visitors more different than Michael Blumenthal, then Secretary of the Treasury, and the pro-Soviet Ethiopian leader Mengistu Haile Mariam are hard to imagine, yet they visited Bucharest within days of the Moscow summit furor, Mengistu to get aid and Blumenthal to offer it. The Prague reformers had no such international network; they never had time to do much but try to explain their policies in their own backyard, getting sympathy only from Hungary, Romania, and Yugoslavia. When the crunch came, the first was forced to join in the invasion and the other two were powerless. China condemned the Russians but was too torn up by its internal struggles, and too far away, to do anything else.

But China today, as officials of both nations stress, is an important guarantor of Romania's independence, even though it could not be expected to send arms or troops. Its arms and troops are, however, occupying the Russians on the other side of the world, lessening the pressure on the Danube.

In the view of a Communist diplomat who sympathizes with the Romanian outlook, Romania is in better shape internally than Czechoslovakia was, even though its cohesion is based on authority rather than democracy. "There was dissension in the Czechoslovak ranks because not everyone agreed with the reform program; some competing politicians wanted the old way," he said. "The Romanian program of nationalism, pure and simple, is sure-fire. No one in Romania is pro-Russian. This unites the people in the factories, farms, and ministries, and it makes an invasion unlikely."

If these are at least partial answers to how the Romanians seem to be getting away with independence, the question of why they do it remains unanswered. A short answer would be that they must: that nationalism unites the nation not only as a deterrent against invasion, but as a means of taking people's minds off the failings of the regime, the lines for meat, the restrictions on travel, and the censorship. The circuses, in other words, make up for the lack of bread.

A longer answer would involve some of the general trends discernible in Eastern Europe as it goes into the fourth decade of its existence as part of the empire of the Soviet Union.

Nations, like people, want to assert their individuality,

their talents, and their peculiarities, and for more than a generation, all these differences have been submerged in the false homogeneity of a bloc of countries supposedly marching in step toward a Soviet-defined goal of socialism.

But on closer examination, each has tried, and continues to try, to express and assert itself: Bulgaria in being obstinately backward and traditional; Poland in being emotional, nationalist, and religious; Czechoslovakia and East Germany in attempting to compensate for lost dreams of political progress with consumerism; Hungary in trading its way to prosperity; and Romania, as the Eastern version of France, in claiming the right to leave blocs, act as broker between quarreling nations, and have an interest in politics in Wall Street, Africa, and the Chinese mainland.

The Soviet Union resists all these centrifugal tendencies, but its power, too, is limited, and it cannot impose complete obedience any longer. It must contend not only with its six wards, balancing threats and permissiveness, but also more and more with the growing influence of outside forces: the United States and China, far away as they may be, the oil-producing and exporting countries and the other arbiters of the shape of bloc economies, and, finally, the Polish priest from Wadowice who became Pope John Paul II.

Part III

THE SOVIET UNION AND DÉTENTE

8

Trade

WHEN PRESIDENT CARTER responded to the Soviet invasion of Afghanistan by blocking delivery of 17 million of the 25 million metric tons of grain ordered by Russia and by banning sales to the Soviets of an estimated $200 million worth of high technology goods, chiefly oil-field equipment, computers, machine tools, and other electronic equipment, he was acting in accord with a venerable tradition in Soviet-Western relations: Using trade as a political weapon.

Both sides have used the trade weapon many times in the past, and both have condemned it, during periods of smooth relations, only to return to make use of it during periods of stress. The monolithic nature of the Soviet economy and political system makes it easier for the Russians both to promote and to withhold trade. As the Americans discovered soon after the Carter embargo was imposed, the West is far too diverse a marketplace to permit an airtight embargo.

In good times and bad, trade with the West, or the lack of it, has so many advantages for the Soviet Union, in fact, that it is surprising that only in recent years has it amounted to very much.

The Russians say earlier opportunities were blocked by Western embargo policies, and the West says those policies were caused by the previous round of Soviet expansionism and the fear that Western sales would help the Eastern military posture. In any case, when the knot was cut in the sixties and Western salesmen in real numbers returned to the Moscow trading offices and the elegant dining rooms of the old National Hotel across from the Kremlin for the first time since the Second World War, the advantages immediately became clear.

Trade helps create happy political partnerships with Western countries. It fills Soviet highways with Italian-designed cars. It brings about the efficient extraction of oil and gas, coal and ores; it explores for more deposits with modern technology; and it pays for the necessary investment in pipelines and equipment with part of the raw materials delivered.

And trade is a useful auxiliary to politics. The Soviet Union can make the volume of trade dependent on the political actions of a France or a Germany. France and Germany are only partly able to use the trade weapon in retaliation, because their governments do not have a monopoly position in business and industry, as the Soviet Union does. Sometimes a Western trading partner does have something the Soviet Union cannot obtain elsewhere, but usually the only effect of a Western attempt to use trade as a weapon is an immediate and well-publicized decision by the Russians to go to one of the competitors.

Trade and politics are closely intertwined in the Soviet system, and the trade relations between Moscow and its partners rise and fall regularly with the needs of politics. Good political relations are generally accompanied by good trade relations, and vice versa. But sometimes the needs of the Soviet economy take priority over political considerations, and, in a situation where trade normally would be reduced as political punishment, it is allowed to continue and even expand. On the other side of the politics-trade equation, the Soviet Union considers a certain minimum level of trade essential as proof of good political relations.

If trade is such an obvious attraction to the Soviet Union, the conclusion of its policymakers might seem to be to have it form a very large part of the Soviet economy, to give it the highest priority and the lowest index of bureaucratic hindrance. This is not the case, except perhaps in priorities, and the reason it is not requires some explanation.

In the first place, the Soviet Union, like the United States, has a continental economy, not only vast but also engaged in manufacturing and selling mostly for itself. Even including the enormous increase of East-East trade between Moscow and Eastern Europe that the creation of the Soviet-dominated Council for Mutual Economic Assistance (Comecon) has brought about, foreign trade with all nations, East and West, still amounts to only about 5 percent of the Soviet gross national product, about the same figure as for the United States.

But unlike the United States, the Soviet Union has considerations of prestige and ideology to weigh when it considers and then rejects joint ventures with Western companies, when it lets the Germans build the new Moscow airport terminal and the Yugoslavs and Swedes the new hotels, and when it tries to get American computers to help Tass, the Soviet news agency, cover the Olympics, and ends up with French ones.

When the Communists took power in Russia, they were determined to sever the Western trade and business links the czarist governments had maintained. Western banks and businesses were expropriated; Western traders and engineers were sent home. But shortly afterward, Lenin invited the Western experts back, sweeping ideological considerations aside. The economy needed the innovation, licenses, and patents of the West—not to make it function, because it manages that without Western help, but to make it function better. Apart from a few show trials of Westerners blamed, as saboteurs, for the failures of the Soviet economy, Stalin also remained open to Western business. In 1936, for example, 3 years after Hitler came to power, Germany continued to be the Soviet Union's most important Western trading partner, despite the hostile propaganda on both sides. It was an early example of how trade needs can cancel political considerations. World War II supplies from the West were followed by a nearly complete break in business after the Cold War started.

Not until the final months of Nikita Khrushchev's period in office was it possible for a Soviet leader to admit that this business was not only desirable but necessary if the Soviet Union was to modernize. Khrushchev's earlier "We will bury you" rhetoric had taken the line that Soviet industry was vast, strong, and modern and didn't really need anything from the West, which, in any case, it was soon going to catch up with and pass. But the Soviet Union wanted friendship, and it wanted to help the struggling workers of the West, who were hit by recession, unused capacity, and unemployment and thus, as a favor, was willing to do business. Soviet commentators in those days were fond of recalling how their nation had come to the aid of Western Europe's industries during the real crisis of capitalism, the depression of the thirties. The offer was still good, they stressed. Taking this line seriously did involve some prestige factors for the West, just as Soviet prestige was to become involved later. The early trade openings by Britain and France were viewed with disfavor by the United States as succumbing to Soviet blandishment. These Western businessmen, the Americans contended, were agreeing to sell the Communists the rope with which they would be hanged, as Lenin is supposed to have said.

But, as sometimes happens, the Soviet line changed, abruptly and completely. In Khrushchev's final year in power, 1964, he said while on a trip to the prosperous and advanced countries of Scandinavia that cooperation with the West was very much needed, not for the old reasons, but to raise living standards and increase industrial progress in Russia. There was no hint from Khrushchev that worries about the growing rivalry with China had any role in this change, of course. But 1964 was a crucial year in the Soviet-Chinese relationship; the Suslov Commission's report that year was a sober assessment of the depth of the split as well as an account of how all previous attempts had failed to heal it. Nothing very sober at all was coming out of Peking; the war of words was escalating and there were reports of border incidents, long before the famous clash on the Ussuri.

Before turning completely to the Western economies, however, the new Soviet leadership made one last attempt to squeeze more technology and advanced industrial equipment out of its Eastern European allies. East Germany, because of its own higher technical level and its trade links with West Germany, was the particular target, and a tragic footnote to the East-West trade story was recorded in the suicide in 1965 of Erich Apel, the East German minister of foreign trade. Apel was unable to reconcile conflicting sets of orders from East Berlin and Moscow: to keep the East German economy expanding while at the same time shouldering much of the task of modernizing the huge Soviet one. The immediate dispute that led to his death was a Soviet demand for increased deliveries of complete chemical plants, something the East Germans needed for themselves. The Russians also stepped up orders for machine tools and electronics technology. But Apel's suicide showed the limits of squeezing the German Democratic Republic.

If the East Germans could not help enough, perhaps those

other Germans could. West German trade had followed the rule of politics until the fifties, at which point its trade was practically nonexistent. A year after diplomatic relations were instituted, trade between West Germany and Russia had reached the $125 million mark. Those present at the 1955 Moscow talks establishing relations recall how trade would be brought into the discussions as an incentive, with frequent reminders of the prewar days when Germany sold Russia 40 percent of all its machinery exports. But when the political progress faltered, talk of trade was dropped. The rise in trade that followed the successful conclusion of the Moscow meeting showed that politics was still linked with trade.

The United States' dealings with Russia in the seventies provide another aspect of the trade-politics linkage. When United States-Soviet trade rose from $200 million in 1971 to nearly $2 billion in 1975, after the Nixon visit to Moscow and the resultant political agreements, a Soviet commentator saw no other conclusion: "The dramatic increase is, of course, attributable to the improved political climate between our nations in the wake of the Soviet-American summitry." And when the Jackson-Vanik amendment coupling human rights and trade scuttled the trade treaty, it was noted that trade "hits rock bottom at times of political strain, and picks up in an atmosphere of friendly relations."

There are those in the West, diplomats as well as traders, who deny this premise, among them old hands in the business in Moscow. Through thick and thin, they insist, their orders have continued. There is no real way of checking this claim, but some of the statistics seem to contradict it. There is also a suspicion that such claims are intended to show the business acumen of the claimants.

Soviet officials do not deny the role of politics in trade, in general, but they do make an important distinction between day-to-day ups and downs and a broader framework of agreement. If relations in general are good and are regulated or institutionalized by some agreement or treaty, then the daily fluctuations have little effect. Within the Soviet-German agreements begun in 1970, there can be major or minor irritants, such as the harassment or expulsion of a German correspondent or the arrest of some Soviet spies, and diplomatic protests, but the level of trade continues.

The Soviet Union likes and seems to need treaties and signed agreements more than does the West. But the Russians sometimes have other, overriding needs that skew the whole trade and politics linkage. The most glaring exception to the formula is the way American grain sales flourished at a time of political chill, until the final blow of Afghanistan. But German and Japanese experience gives other examples.

The need to import grain, a Soviet official in a Western capital said in 1966, was a temporary one, caused from time to time by freak harvest conditions. After that period, however, imports became a regular fixture of East-West trade, with the United States shipping Russia 5 million tons of wheat and 10 million tons of coarse grains, most of which is for animal feeding to produce meat to eat with the wheat bread. In bad years, the figures doubled. Soviet officials cite their difficult climate as the reason for the shortages and say that although it is true that czarist Russia was an exporter of grain, the exporting was done at the expense of an adequate diet for the peasants. Diplomats in Moscow agree that the Russians, in common with most peoples, eat better than their grandmothers and grandfathers, but that much if not all the blame for the chronic grain shortages can be laid at the door of the inefficient system of state and collective farming. Bad weather is unavoidable but waste is not, and some studies show that as much as a third of the crop has disappeared by the time it gets harvested, goes in and out of storage, and ends up on the state market.

And so American farmers continued to produce for Russia, the dollars flowed out, and the grain flowed in, through spy trials and human rights controversies, missile rattling and political attacks. After the grain price scandals in 1972, sales were put on a regular contractual basis, with the Soviet Union committed to buying at least 6 million tons a year. Purchases can go to 8 million tons without further formalities, and higher if the Americans agree.

Until the 1979 invasion that shocked the world, it was the actual weather, the droughts and rains in the Soviet Union, not the political weather, that made the grain trade figures rise and fall, and it seems likely that agricultural climate will again count more than political climate in the future.

Trade overrode political considerations in 1962, when the Soviet Union needed to buy large-diameter pipes to exploit Siberian natural gas discoveries. The Germans made the pipes, but the Germans were militarists and revenge seekers who threatened the Soviet Union. The deal was nevertheless concluded; Soviet economic needs outweighed political distaste.

But then a curious sequence of events took place. The NATO committee that oversees the sale of materiel to the East that might enhance Soviet military capabilities ruled that the pipes constituted just that kind of goods. It blocked the sale. The Soviets then cut imports by 20 percent—but from the Germans, not the other Western countries that enforced the pipeline embargo. Political retaliation seems the only explanation for the sudden cut in what had been an expanding pattern of German sales to Moscow. The logical kind of retaliation would have been directed at the other NATO partners, whose motives, it was suspected at the time, were based on business competitiveness as well as strategic considerations.

Officials in Siberia who deal regularly with the Japanese and the Americans in the series of projects for exploiting oil and other minerals say that trade is both a reward for the Soviet Union's partners and a duty, part of maintaining détente. The Japanese have been fulfilling the duty and receiving the reward. In the Yakutia region, for example, Japanese equipment and engineers are involved in the digging and shipping of 100 million tons of coal. The Soviet Union can use part of the coking coal to smelt iron in the area. The Japanese provide the technology and get paid in the raw materials they need at home.

The flaw in the whole arrangement is the sorry state of political relations between the Soviet Union and Japan. The Russians refuse to discuss the return of the four tiny Japanese islands, harass Japanese fishermen in the area, and send so many warships into the waters off the Japanese coasts that diplomats call the maneuvers the Moscow Express. When Japan signed its peace treaty with China, reluctantly agreeing to Chinese insistence on a mild clause indicating that the Soviet Union might have designs on the area, Moscow responded with a propaganda attack reminiscent of the Cold War or the Russian reaction to Japan's anti-Comintern pact with Hitler.

It is clear that the economic needs of developing Siberia overrode the political needs of punishing Japan. There is also another factor in play that did not exist at the time of the German pipeline case. That is the competition of China for Japanese and Western business. It will be discussed at the conclusion of this examination of the relationship between trade and politics on the bilateral level.

France was rewarded amply in trade for Gaullist détente-entente-cooperation, but when these policies soured, so did the volume of business. De Gaulle's network of treaties with the Russians in the sixties was followed immediately and spectacularly with gains in the marketplace. Although Soviet exports to France remained at about the same level, since quality and consumer choice cannot be changed by political climate in free market countries, Soviet imports from France, which can be expanded or decreased at will by the Russians, nearly doubled between 1966 and 1968, the peak years of de Gaulle's opening to the East. The figures were 144 million rubles to 265 million. It was, to be sure, a time of a general increase in Soviet purchases from the West, but, among its competitors, France gained markedly, from eighth place in Western sales to the USSR in 1964 to first place in 1968. And then the de Gaulle boom in Russia collapsed, and France sank in the trade standings as Germany rose.

Britain's experience in Soviet trade shows the opposite effect: how unfavorable political conditions can throttle trade. Britain was in first place in trade in the fifties but in the sixties and seventies headed the Soviet enemies list instead for its protests against the invasion of Czechoslovakia and its spectacular expulsion of 105 alleged Soviet spies. Nevertheless, British businessmen thought the trade links were too firm to be shaken by such political occurrences. For one thing, Britain had, and has, a different trading position from those of the other Western partners. Its imports from the Soviet Union outweigh its exports because of the large trade in Soviet diamonds and furs that go to London for resale. It was thought that the Russians would not want to risk these markets by a punitive cutting of the amount of goods they purchased from Britain.

The businessmen were wrong. Soviet sales to Britain stayed at high levels; only in 1972, the year after the embassy spy scandal, did they fall, but they soon regained their earlier volume. British exports to the USSR, however, were another matter. At a time when other Western nations saw their sales curves going sharply upward, Britain's went sharply down. Between 1968 and 1973, sales to Russia fell from 245 million to 175 million rubles.

France and Britain, it may be unnecessary to add, were at the front of the line when the door to the China trade reopened.

The loss of Western and Japanese business to the Chinese is a constant concern to Soviet officials, although little is said about it in public. Much of the concern centers on the ambitious Soviet plans for development of Siberia.

The climate, the bureaucracy, and the huge investment needs of Siberia, the same factors that have hindered development since the czars, are the reasons Westerners and Japanese cite for the failure of the grand promises the Russians made in the early seventies. In the north of Siberia, an American-Japanese crew assembling giant trucks for coal strip mining reported that it took 4 months to put together three of the trucks. Six weeks would have been ample in normal weather, but there is no normal weather in Siberia if you are trying to make machines work or build things. Local boosters say that cars and equipment stop working at 50 below but that good Siberians never stop. That philosophy may work for cutting wood, but not for the technical and mechanical work Siberia needs now. Most of the year, the ground is frozen so hard that ordinary heavy-duty equipment cannot work it. In the spring, the surface layer of the permafrost melts, creating 3 feet of mush in which equipment and vehicles can—and do—sink. Americans, many of them veterans of Alaska conditions, have learned to cope. But they cannot cope with the Soviet bureaucracy. An American diplomat who wanted to check conditions at the truck assembly site was refused permission by Soviet authorities—not because the site was off limits, but because a small city where he would have to wait briefly to change planes was.

Soviet negotiating partners move cautiously, and sometimes erratically, their opposite numbers contend. Japan spent 8 years, at Soviet invitation, working out a $5 billion project to find and produce oil in the rich Tyumen fields of western Siberia and to build a pipeline across the continent to transport it to the Pacific. The deal collapsed when the Russians reduced the annual amount of oil they would sell Japan from 40 to 25 million tons and decided that, rather than a pipeline, they wanted Japanese help in building their new Siberian railway, the Baikal-Amur Magistral or BAM. The Japanese got their oil from China.

British Petroleum (BP), too, spent 8 years negotiating over Tyumen oil without result. In 6 weeks of talks, they had a contract with the Chinese.

"There were four Soviet ministries handling four basic functions: one for oil drilling, one for gas drilling, one for transport, and one for ancillary construction," a BP executive said. "When we first went there, we were taken to a field that was probably their best. Of the six drill rigs, five weren't in operation, and while we watched, the sixth broke down.

"But to the Russians, these eight years must have been well spent. They tried their best to soak up all the free information they could from us on the frequent visits of their delegations. We don't think this was their main aim. Their bureaucracy was the real cause of the breakdown."

International contracts for building something like a steel plant are complicated documents, an American steel man who trades in the Soviet Union said, and, in deals with most nations, normally run around 80 pages. One such contract concluded with the Soviet Union, he said, totaled 7,000 pages.

Americans and Japanese have spent close to the apparently obligatory 8 years on a gas project around Siberia's Lena river, the gold-mining area that gave Lenin his Party name. Everyone agrees that there is a great deal of natural gas in the area. At issue is the eventual price of extracting, piping, and liquefying it on the Pacific. More than $200 million has been spent just to find out how large the reserves are; a further $4 billion will be needed to develop them. Although the Americans and Japanese complain about the Soviet delays, the Russians argue, with justification, that it is hard to put a price on natural gas in the next century—the contract is to run for 25 years from 1985.

The final obstacle to Siberian investment, and the attraction of Chinese, is the amount of capital the Russians want from the West and Japan. Brezhnev once estimated that foreign investment alone would total $100 billion. BAM, which parallels the old Trans-Siberian railway 300 or more miles to the north, opening up a virgin area of mineral and energy resources twice the size of France, costs $7.5 million a mile to build and has nearly 2,000 miles to go before reaching completion sometime in the eighties. The Tyumen oil fields will be swallowing $3 billion a year for exploration and production for the next 15 years.

The potential returns are as great. In all of Siberia, the language of description is pure superlative. Siberia and the Soviet Far East are larger than the United States and Mexico. It is 4,200 miles east from the Urals to the Bering Sea and 2,100 from north to south. The territory has 80 percent of the Soviet Union's wealth in natural resources, including at least 4 billion tons of coal, 12 billion tons of oil, half the world's wood, and the largest deposits of natural gas to be found anywhere. Whether the Russians, with or without their Western and Japanese partners, succeed in recovering these riches, and at what price, will have a great deal of influence on the world energy situation in the years ahead.

But outsiders have to consider whether the benefits are worth the risks. Businessmen do not deny the importance of Siberia—to the Soviet Union. But their own interest is really in making a profit rather than in developing a subcontinent. No one suggests that China's resources can measure up to Russia's, but for most investors, they are enough and, in the present climate at least, are far easier to tap.

An American with long experience in Soviet-American trade and raw material ventures said that every one of the 25 United States companies with permanent offices in Moscow got into negotiations with China as well when conditions made that possible under the new leadership in Beijing. Businessmen and engineers frustrated with fighting the Soviet bureaucracy come back from China with cheering tales of friendliness and cooperation. It takes a year to conclude a deal of moderate size in Moscow, they say, but in China it can be wrapped up, with cash, in 3 months.

Despite Chinese retrenchment from some of the grand plans announced when the opening to the West and Japan began, China still offers many advantages the Soviet Union will not or cannot offer, because of ideology or long practice. Chief of these is joint ventures—possible in China, impossible in Russia. And to top it off, China is warmer. "Hell, we'll go south," one American said at the end of a tale of frustrations with visas, housing, and official run-arounds in Moscow.

Can the Russians develop their natural resource potential without the trade and technology of the industrial nations? It is really a question of degree. Despite the bogged-down projects, many others have been successful, and most are long-term compensation deals that will ensure cooperation into the next century. Austria, Finland, Italy, West Germany, and France are supplied natural gas from Soviet fields through Western pipelines paid for by the gas. Outside help will certainly speed up development, but development will come without it, too, although more slowly. Western estimates say Soviet oil production could be doubled within 10 years through massive introduction of American technology. This could mean a doubling of exports, too, which, at $6 billion a year, already account for half of Soviet hard-currency earnings. But some Soviet officials argue that they shouldn't be in such a hurry; the nation's resources are like gold in a vault, there to stay, and theirs to keep. They will become rarer and more valuable as time goes by, so why rush to exploit them?

It is possible that this attitude is intended to cover up concern about possible oil production declines. The Russians say there is no truth to CIA predictions that reserves are being used up so rapidly that the nation will have to import oil by the mid-eighties. But official figures do show a decline in the rate of increase in oil production in recent years.

In any case, the treasure chest reasoning goes against all the other trends in the Soviet economy and society, which point to increasing consumption of oil and raw materials, both in industry and in the private sector. These resources will have to come more and more from the fields and mines harder to reach, develop, and transport from, and that means investment and technology, Soviet or foreign.

The decade of the seventies brought an 80 percent increase in the number of vehicles in the Soviet Union. The Fiat-built plant at Togliatti turns out one Fiat-like Zhiguli every 20 seconds. Only one Soviet citizen in fifty owns a car now, but waiting lists stretch for 5 years. The current 5-year plan calls for an annual 8 to 10 percent increase in the production of cars and trucks, which is now around 2 million per year. The government encourages private car ownership as one of the benefits of "developed socialism." But it must pump more oil to fuel them. Current production quotas foresee an annual rise of 20 percent in oil output.

There are no shortages, both ordinary Russians and government spokesmen insist. They talk about lakes and seas of oil and gas under them, thousand-year supplies. But each year, it becomes more costly to tap them.

There is a real shortage, too, of technology, investment capital, and engineers and experts willing to go to distant places to work under difficult conditions. The United States, Western Europe, and Japan have a great many of those scarce assets right now, but they are going to use them where there is the least difficulty and the greatest chance of profit. Soviet managers, used to producing on orders from the state, find this hard to understand. But in a world where there are many claims on them, people are likely to choose the best climate, and, in both senses, Russia falls short.

China has its own problems. After the first flush of enthusiasm and multibillion-dollar orders, China imposed a sudden moratorium on projects agreed to with Japan. It was clear that China had overextended herself, and Western and Japanese assessments have been more cautious, too, since then. Then, according to Chinese sources, complaints began to multiply from the countryside about poverty and government price policies. Some of the leading complainers were the young urban men and women sent out during the cultural revolution to raise the consciousness of the peasants. The answer seemed to be to pay more attention to the nation's agriculture and less to grand steel plant projects, at least for the present. The peasants were given price raises for their produce, and other money was diverted from the modernization drive to provide a better consumer goods industry for the goods the peasants would now be able to buy.

Soviet diplomats have pointed to these developments as evidence of the unreliability of the Chinese as trading partners for the West and Japan. But the Chinese have gone far beyond the Russians in removing the ideological blocks to admitting capital from the West into their economy—not only as loans or investments to be paid back by shipments of raw materials, as is done in the Soviet Union. Russia permits joint ventures only in other countries. China allows foreign companies to invest jointly with the state, with no upper limit specified, profits to be shared by the Chinese and foreign partners, and the whole enterprise to be controlled by a joint board of directors.

And so, despite some loss of momentum from time to time, the fact remains that the United States, Japan, and

Western Europe are embarked on an ambitious program to build up China as an industrial power. This means that Russia will have to deal with a stronger China in the years ahead, but it also means that the loans, expertise, and ventures that go into the Chinese economy will not go into the Russian economy. It is not that there will be a cutoff of foreign trade or investment from the Soviet Union, but that at some point, if there has to be a choice, that choice is more likely to favor China.

The Soviet Union reacts to this prospect with two contradictory responses. The first is to deny that Russia needs Western trade, particularly American. We are doing very well, the Russian line goes. If we need to buy abroad, it is on the basis of mutual interest and no strings like Jackson-Vanik. And even within the ranks of the Western alliance, there are plenty of opportunities to buy from one partner if the other won't sell. Troubles with Soviet-American trade are, in fact, sometimes an advantage in furthering other Soviet aims. "When you look at it in a certain way," an American businessman said, "they really don't have too great an interest in a certain high level of trade with us. They can use their limited hard-currency resources to do business with our allies and drive wedges between us. They can accuse us of bad faith in not living up to the promises of that Nixon Moscow summit."

In the view of Western business and commercial circles in Moscow, piggy-backing human rights conditions onto the trade agreement, which resulted in denying the Soviet Union Most Favored Nation status, had more of a political effect than a business one.

And this ties in with the second Soviet response to the possibility of America's turning more to China. A good summation of the political aspect of trade was provided by a Soviet specialist on the subject, who maintained that there is a qualitative difference between the United States and the

Soviet Union's other trading partners. It may be all right for Belgium and Sweden to transfer some or most of their business to China, but not for the United States.

The two great powers share responsibility for peace and security on a world scale, because of their size and nuclear war-making capabilities. None of the other Soviet trading partners have this responsibility. But the world wants normal political relations between the two great powers, so that the risk of war is reduced. Peace, then, is dependent on the maintenance of these relations, and they, in turn, are dependent on a number of components, among them a normal level of trade. It is abnormal for the United States not to have a trade treaty, and not to have more of a share of Soviet trade.

The specialist was unable to put a quantitative floor or ceiling on the normal level of trade the Russians desire. When the United States ranks ahead of Finland, which it sometimes does, in the order of Western trading partners, is that sufficient, he was asked, since Finland has excellent (if not entirely normal) relations? The definition of what was normal seemed to be up to the Soviet Union.

And what has hindered the normal growth of trade was almost exclusively the fault of the United States. It is true, the Soviet specialist conceded, that there were a few justified complaints about the length of time the United States had to wait for answers from the Soviet ministries and about delays in deliveries, visas, and other minor matters, but they were details that could be fixed, not structural deficiencies. On the part of the United States, however, the dropping of the conditions that have encumbered trade would mean more than dollars and cents. It would show there was a will for peace rather than hopes of reviving the Cold War.

The prospects of China's receiving Most Favored Nation status and Russia's continuing to be denied it has made these arguments somewhat shriller. There is also puzzlement. Soviet specialists admit they cannot understand what is really behind the struggle for profits and markets among the capitalists. They know that big business controls the American government. But if this is so, why don't the profit seekers fix up the political situation so that more trade is possible? There is an answer, but it doesn't seem to be entirely satisfactory, and that is that "certain circles" are more interested in opposing détente than in making money. It must be a difficult choice for them.

But is the Soviet Union capable of sustaining a high or even a normal level of trade with its Western partners? Even with optimum political conditions, there are many economic and commercial conditions that make this difficult. In order to buy, the Soviet Union must sell, and it has trouble selling very much to the rest of the world—except for its arms exports, which are much wanted, and its raw materials, which are much needed—because of the generally low quality of its goods. It is not that Soviet designers and workers are stupid. They can produce high-quality merchandise that would sell anywhere. The trouble is that the central planning system does not allow enough flexibility to permit innovations and does not have the same concern for quality that it has for quantity. Production processes that are suited to the central controls of the plan work well in the Soviet Union; the generation of electric power is one. No new models need be brought out to attract Western buyers; the huge electrical grids are best run by a central authority, and their performance is best measured by quantity of output. But unfortunately, the Soviet Union can't sell electricity in Macy's or the Galeries Lafayette.

One advantage of central controls in offerings for the Western market is the government's ability to hold down the wages of Soviet workers. This means that the Zhigulis produced in Togliatti cost far less in Western Europe than the Fiats produced in Torino. It means that with unionized crew members, many Western shipping lines cannot afford to keep their big passenger ships afloat, but that Soviet vessels, manned at Soviet union rates, cross the Atlantic and cruise the Mediterranean at a profit.

But the low-paid workers in the factories do not seem to be able to turn out much that would sell in the West. One suggestion has been to set up a special kind of factory to produce high-quality goods for export only. Optical goods and furs were among the suggested products. Nothing has been heard of the plan, which had high-level backing but might have created the same kind of problems the dollar stores in Soviet tourist areas do. Soviet consumers would wonder why they were only able to buy the second best.

Most Soviet-American trade is not at the fur coat or camera level. It usually involves large amounts of industrial equipment and technology in one direction and raw materials, for the most part, in the other. Most of the partners are the big companies. Soviet trade officials like to deal with presidents and vice presidents and like companies to have offices in Moscow. But the Russians do not seem to be able to provide adequate facilities, and this, too, is an impediment to the development of trade.

Many Westerners complete their 3-year tours of duty in Moscow without ever moving out of their hotel rooms and into permanent quarters. Only the office managers are granted multiple entry and exit visas; the rest of the staff must fill out forms and wait every time they want to leave the country. The strains of living in Moscow are great enough in normal times, but when one part of the government chooses to make an example of someone invited there by another part, in this case the KGB and the Ministry of Foreign Trade and International Harvester representative Jay Crawford, morale sinks, business suffers, and businessmen leave.

Crawford was arrested in 1978 on patently false currency-speculation charges. He was clearly the victim of a Soviet reprisal for the arrest of two Soviet spies in Woodbridge, New Jersey. Crawford was able to refute most of the evidence against him and win release—but not acquittal—after some weeks of jail and rough handling. Two Moscow-based companies lost their managers through sudden transfer requests as an apparent result of the Crawford case. The Soviet trading officials who deal with the Americans made no attempt to apologize or smooth things over, an American familiar with the case said: "Not by as much as a raised eyebrow or a nuance in conversation was it ever intimated how unfortunate the Crawford case was for business, or that it was in any way connected with the Woodbridge spy case. The line was that a crook was caught and dealt with under Soviet law. They aren't flexible enough to permit anything else; there isn't that kind of give and take between partners in Moscow. If one of them dared to try to communicate something human, he might lose his job."

The expense, the morale problems, and the red tape tend to drive out small and medium-sized companies and leave most of the business to the big companies. The exceptions are smaller companies with a product or process the Russians would like very much to acquire. In such cases, somehow, the deal is speeded up.

Dealing with the big corporations also opens up the possibility of two kinds of business undertakings dear to the hearts of Soviet planners. One is long-term, the other compensation. They are often combined, but not always. Japan's coal project in Siberia is a good example of both. The Japanese need assured, long-term supplies of coking coal and have the technology to offer to extract and process it, for Soviet benefit as well. Payment is in coal, not yen.

It's another pair of shoes, as the Russians say, when the trading partner is offered raw material or manufactured goods he doesn't want or need. A large German concern was asked to build a nylon fiber plant in the Soviet Union.

Agreed. Then payment was offered in nylon fiber. Not agreed. The German fiber industry at that time was working at only 60 percent of capacity; the Russian goods would have gone to an already saturated market, with no chance of sale.

A small Cleveland company, producer of a specialized line of machine tools, was sought out by Soviet trade representatives in the United States and offered a contract. Agreed. One of the terms then offered was half-payment in Soviet machine tools. The Cleveland negotiators protested they didn't need any machine tools. The Soviets repeated their viewpoint, at the same time talking about the need to show maximum flexibility. Finally, in a late-evening session over vodka, one of the Russians asked whether it would be possible for the Clevelanders to take just one of their machines, so that the deal would look better to the Ministry. They reluctantly agreed, and now the Soviet machine stands in a prominent corner of the Cleveland shop, under a dust cover that is whisked off whenever a Soviet visitor is about to arrive.

Compensation dealing got a spectacular assist from OPEC's price increases in 1974 and subsequent years, as did Russia's other exports of raw materials, although to a lesser degree. Western oil technology increased in price a little, but the oil that paid for it quadrupled in price. Through compensation and straight sales deals, the Soviet Union was able to reduce its trading deficit with the West from 3 billion rubles to 1 billion in a single year, 1977, only by being able to sell a little more oil at a much higher price.

The best compensation arrangements are those sought by Western or Japanese companies to take care of a need, rather than those devised by the Soviets to ease payment problems. Such an undertaking is the giant Kursk iron and steel combine. It produces iron ore pellets, rather than the bulky unrefined ore, for shipment to Germany. Japan and Germany are ideal partners, not only because of their technology, but because they are close to Soviet raw materials on the east and the west.

But what these foreign partners really would like the Soviet Union is as yet unwilling to grant: partnerships on an equal basis, with Western technology combining with Soviet materials and workers to produce goods that could be sold on the domestic market or anywhere else in the world. China offers such partnerships, including plans to make tape recorders of Japanese design to sell in the United States. Poland pays for part of its Polski Fiat plant by making extra engines to sell in Italy.

One hindrance, Westerners say, is that a roughly equivalent level of technical development is required, and that is sometimes hard to find among Soviet industrial partners. Another is the grip that state planning has on the Soviet economy. How could Western comanagers' plans fit into 5-year plans?

A final reason for the lack of such projects in Soviet foreign trade is Russia's refusal to permit joint ventures. Some high trade officials have hinted from time to time that limited experiments might be tried with joint ventures, although there is strong opposition in the Party to anything that would reintroduce a foreign capitalist presence in the internal workings of the Soviet economy, in contrast to the build-and-leave system followed to date. It is possible, however, that the Chinese example may provide impetus for change.

Westerners who deal with the Soviet trade establishment do not see much hope of flexibility in the current ranks. They say that even high-level officials do not seem to understand the workings of a market economy, and that they think that Western entrepreneurs can be ordered around as Soviet state industry managers are and that consumers in Paris and Manchester can be forced to buy felt boots and wooden dolls because it improves the political climate.

These Westerners see hope, however, in the younger Soviet bureaucrats they meet on trade missions and in the regular meetings of the joint councils the Soviets have set up with Western partners. "They are not capitalist by any means," one of their German opposite numbers said. "They are planners who want to make the plan work better. They know that we plan, too, for regional development and economic growth, and they study our planning process to see how we keep it from freezing out initiative."

Soviet trade with the West and Japan has every natural advantage that an economics textbook could envision, if the politicians would keep out of the way. Assured supplies of raw materials are what Japan and the West, particularly Europe, need, now more than ever. The technology to modernize is what the Soviet Union needs. One complements the other, pays for the other.

If such conditions are present for a growth of trade, will this trade eventually reach the level of interdependence? Interdependence, it is argued, has its good and bad sides. In one way, it makes it easier for one side to engage in pressures, turning off the Soviet oil valve or the Western electronics switch if the partner's political actions are not deemed suitable. In another, it would lead to moderation as more attention is paid to the arguments of the technocrats on both sides and less to those of the military. Nations with a thickening network of trade are less likely to go to war—or are they? History provides examples on both sides of the argument; the worst war it has recorded was that between the trading partners Russia and Germany.

For better or worse, the movement in Soviet foreign trade is so slow, and the economies involved on both sides are so large, that there is little likelihood of trade's becoming a real issue for many decades. Neither side, moreover, seems to want it. The Germans, for example, who increased their Soviet trade eightfold in the seventies, make sure their other foreign trade is spread around to partners all over the world. Ordinary commercial practices are not the only reason; political dependence on one market, east or west, is what they want to avoid. Germany's huge volume of trade with Russia still amounts to only about 5 percent of its foreign trade total. Imports of raw material pose no danger of a Soviet hand on the valve: they amount to 15 percent of the natural gas and 5 percent of the oil. Other Western nations' degree of dependence on Soviet supplies is even smaller. The United States imports no oil at all from the Russians. Western European customers would, in fact, like to get more but have found the Russians unable to supply them.

Unless the Soviet Union can sell more raw materials and manufactured goods, it will continue to be limited in what it can buy, and the web of interdependence will remain thin. Soviet officials from Brezhnev down talk about the need for trade, stress that present rates are only a beginning, and talk of projects stretching well beyond the year 2000 and involving tens of billions of dollars. They often point to the spectacular rise in trade in the early seventies, particularly with Germany, as a sign for the future.

But in the view of Western businessmen and trade officials, that great leap was a phenomenon that cannot be easily repeated. The main reason is Soviet inability to pay. Sometimes accounts can be squared with raw material exports. But usually a drastic cutback in imports is also taken, and that means fewer machine tools, computers, and licenses to help Soviet industry produce more saleable products for the next round in the market. Or they borrow. There was no Soviet-bloc debt in the West at all in the sixties; by 1974 it added up to $13 billion, and by the end of the decade it totaled $40 billion. More than $12 billion of that is owed by the Soviet Union. No one in the West worries about repayment, since the credit of all the bloc countries is excellent, but hard currency used for debt service cuts further into the funds available for purchases. In the Soviet Union, 28 percent of the hard-currency earnings from exports goes for debt interest.

As the Soviet Union enters the next decade of foreign trade activity, it is in a holding position rather than being poised for any great leap forward. It is retrenching in its own west, Eastern Europe, where terms of trade can be determined to Soviet advantage and hard currency is no problem. Eastern European technology falls short of world levels in most cases, but often, as the variety of Eastern European goods on the Soviet domestic market shows, it is as good or better than the Soviet. While Western trade with the Soviet Union grows only slowly, there is a constant increase in Russia's volume with Comecon, much of it in joint ventures that involve no capitalists.

There are cures for these Soviet shortcomings, but they run up against Party resistance. One cure would be to give the managers of the Soviet economy more scope and initiative, to make it more profitable for them and their organizations to show a profit, as the Hungarians have done so successfully. There are repeated reforms, but in the words of a Western official who regularly deals with the Soviet state industry, "The technicians are overruled every time, by the political factors, and the result is that they change the faces of managers, they centralize and they decentralize, but nothing really changes in the direction it must: toward convertibility of their currency, decision making in the hands of the managers, not the Party, striving for efficiency and exacting penalties for not attaining it."

Party controls limit economic performance, in short, and that limits prospects of trade with the West. Interdependence seems far away. Soviet officials view this with equanimity. They do not wish to have a controlling role in Western economies, even in the supply of a single commodity, they say. And they do not wish to become entangled in the web of trade with the West. The Party, it seems, has discovered a self-regulating mechanism to perpetuate its economic role.

But all this is a matter of degree, not absolutes. If there are no more Afghanistans for a while, it is likely that East and West will become marginally more dependent on each other's trade, and that this—marginally—will bring about some moderation of behavior, tendencies of cooperation rather than of confrontation. The European Community may not like Italy's fiscal policies, but it regularly bails out the Italians with loans to protect its other members. Such a development might occur in a small way in the greater East-West economic community, even though its aims and methods are far from common as yet. Marginal effects and advantages, degrees of change—all are, after all, net gains from the days not long ago when there was no trade relationship of consequence at all, and no possibility of benefit to either side.

9

Arms Control

THE WARRING SEVENTIES came to an end with a war pitting Soviet divisions against Afghan guerrilla bands—tanks and helicopter gunships against ancient rifles. The Afghan fighting shared the characteristics of the other conflicts of the decade, from Jordan to Northern Ireland, in that it was limited, both in area and in choice of weapons, below the nuclear threshold. But unlike most of the other wars of the seventies, this last one had the potential of increasing to the danger level—a world nuclear conflagration. The threat did not stem so much from the chances of escalation in Afghanistan and neighboring areas as from the damage done to détente and the limitation of strategic nuclear arsenals.

The invasion of Afghanistan caused President Carter to withdraw the SALT II treaty from the Senate ratification process so that, as the President put it, "Congress and I can assess Soviet actions." He stressed that his administration continued to believe that the treaty is in the best interests of the United States, but many in that same administration were calling SALT II dead, not simply delayed.

The death, and even the delay, of the agreement negotiated over 4 years and approved by both heads of state went against the proclaimed interests of two of the three parties involved, the White House and the Kremlin, and against a majority (but perhaps not two-thirds) of the third party, the U.S. Senate.

Why, then, was SALT II put on the shelf? And what are the likely consequences, to the Russians, the Americans, and to the important nuclear arms decisions Western Europe must make?

The main reason the Russians let Afghanistan kill or wound SALT II seems to be that they considered it already dead in the Senate and, as discussed earlier, believed the consequences of a successful Moslem defiance of Communist rule in Afghanistan far more serious a threat to their domestic stability in the Moslem republics than the threat of no new SALT treaty.

The Soviet leadership also felt it had lost a round in Europe, after NATO approved the stationing in Western Europe of 572 new American Pershing II and ground-launched Tomahawk cruise missiles, both capable of striking targets in the USSR. NATO's decision had been coupled with an offer of arms reduction talks with the Warsaw Pact, it is true, but the alliance had spurned an earlier Soviet offer that had been made contingent on first refusing the American weaponry.

The Americans withdrew SALT from debate because, the White House felt, the Soviet buildup in tactical weapons (which had caused NATO's concern) as well as in strategic weapons not covered by SALT, coupled with Soviet expansion into the Third World, made the Russians such an unreliable partner in arms control that Senate approval of the treaty was unlikely. Afghanistan provided a glaring example both of growing Soviet armed might and expansionist tendencies. It also provided a graceful way out for the Carter administration. Other factors in the decision included the national anger and uncertainty over the holding of the 50

American hostages in Iran, which was seen as a sign of the loss of the United States' power in the world, although it had nothing at all to do with SALT or, as far as was known, with the Russians, and the fact that President Carter was facing a tough contest for re-election.

The consequences for both adversaries, and for Europe, seem likely to be increased cost and insecurity—whether it is the budget drain of the $33 billion MX missile system (permitted under SALT II but unlikely to have been built in a period of warmer relations) or the perceived need to counter Soviet adventurism with some kind of American counter-adventure force for the Third World. In Europe, the debates that led to the reluctant acceptance of the new NATO nuclear weapons were begun afresh, since rearming NATO was contingent on controlling the level of strategic systems the United States and the Soviet Union are permitted. With less restraint between the big powers, Europe's middle powers returned to their arguments about the wisdom of trying to compete at all.

The dangers and costs of this Soviet-American missile matching game began to be apparent soon after the treaty was withdrawn from the Senate, when even SALT II opponents conceded that without its limitations, the MX system might offer the United States no protection against a Soviet first strike. The MX system, with 200 missiles moving among 4,600 underground launch sites, was designed with SALT in mind: both to permit easy Soviet verification under future treaties and to take advantage of the restrictions on the Russians in SALT II.

Under the limits on land-based missiles accepted by the Russians, no first strike could have knocked out all the MX missiles. But with the treaty out of force, there would be no such restrictions, and the Soviet Union could easily produce enough warheads to make MX obsolete before it was even built.

In response to the new situation, the United States considered building even more MX sites and reviving the enormously costly anti-missile missile projects both sides had forsworn in SALT I. Although both these plans seemed to provide temporary security against a Soviet buildup, they were also perfect examples of what SALT II had been designed to prevent: expensive, uncertain steps in an arms race that would be quickly countered by similar action from the other side.

These concerns about the costs to a world without SALT II, however, could very well turn out to be the best argument for supporting a resumption of strategic arms negotiations, at both the intercontinental and European theater levels, when an improved East-West climate again permits it.

If there was a reason to negotiate SALT I in the sixties, despite Vietnam and Czechoslovakia, and SALT II in the seventies, despite the Carter human rights campaign and Soviet-Cuban Third World incursions, that reason was mutual benefit: a world a little less edgy about nuclear destruction, and a little less economically burdened by the need to match the latest weapons developments of the other side.

It is thus just possible that even SALT's opponents will be able to see, during the cooling-off period caused by Afghanistan, that a bad or imperfect treaty is, after all, preferable to no treaty at all.

Missile and bomber gaps, Soviet threats, and American threats are juggled by political and military leaders in both nations, particularly the United States, around budget time. Ordinary citizens must grope through mazes of acronyms like MIRVs and ALCMs to try to find the truth. Most of the groping takes place on the American side; Soviet military and strategic information is so closely restricted that Moscow officials habitually quote American figures when discussing their own as well as the adversary forces.

And yet, trying to understand the arms race and arms limitation is important, not only for the obvious reason of survival in a nuclear age, but for assessing the impact of politics on arms, and arms on politics, in a variety of international situations that affect the Soviet-American strategic relationship, the most important of which are those in China and Western Europe.

Understanding means going back to the beginning of strategic arms talks, to Helsinki in November 1969. The SALT I talks began in a glow of East-West understanding, fed by the Finns, who had their entire foreign policy and independence at stake in promoting this understanding. The United States delegation included negotiators who later took opposite sides on SALT II: Harold Brown, at that time on leave as president of Caltech, later to become Secretary of Defense, and Paul Nitze, later to become the leading voice of the Committee on the Present Danger, the anti-SALT II lobby.

SALT I, which moved from Helsinki to Vienna, set an important precedent just by taking place. The Russians had come to the West over the years with disarmament and arms control proposals that ranged from Khrushchev's repeated calls for "general and complete disarmament" to nuclear test bans. None, however, had contained verification provisions the West considered adequate. Agreement was reached on nuclear test prohibition only because nuclear tests were clearly detectable in the atmosphere, and later, with the development of better techniques, underground, without the need for verification procedures on Soviet soil.

SALT I's basis was verifiable arms controls. Two developments brought about this change from previous Soviet stances: satellite technology had advanced so much since the first Soviet sputnik that neither side could hide strategic secrets with much assurance of success. And a whole series of political and economic factors in the Soviet Union made meeting the Americans halfway seem a prudent course. It could be argued, as Brezhnev maintained in a 1973 speech explaining SALT and détente to a Soviet audience, that Soviet strength made both possible. "The power and influence of the Soviet Union, of the entire socialist commonwealth, has grown," he said. "Détente is being furthered and security is growing, too. That permits the Soviet Union to concentrate in increasing measure on the solution of peaceful and creative tasks."

But it also could be argued that Soviet weakness brought the Russians to the SALT negotiating table: the recognition that their economy could not stand the strains of the arms race, the push for consumer goods, and the threat from China.

Responding to a threat of war by agreeing to limit strategic missiles and bombers may seem unusual, but when the two achievements of SALT I are assessed, the Soviet position becomes understandable. In addition to a modest beginning of mutual limitation of offensive weapons, the main achievement was to call off, before it really got started, the race to develop a defense system against enemy missiles (the so-called antimissile missiles) in both the Soviet Union and the United States. In a field where billions of dollars are tossed around like poker chips, the antiballistic missile's/ABM/cost, estimated at $22 billion on both sides, stood out. Had the systems been developed, they would have touched off another round of specialized development for offensive missiles designed to penetrate the defenses. And they would have made the deterrent—and thus peace-keeping—capability of existing stockpiles of offensive missiles on both sides questionable, destabilizing the balance of terror that had held for more than 2 decades. A final argument for the Russians was that the ABM system wasn't necessary to protect the Soviet Union from the threat, current or in the foreseeable future, of China's weak and primitive nuclear arsenal.

When Brezhnev and Nixon signed SALT I in Moscow in 1972, they were signing an ABM ban agreement (actually,

SALT I permits each side two ABM deployment sites, later reduced to one each). But the United States insisted that the limitation of offensive weapons be linked with the ABM treaty, and the result was an interim agreement freezing the deployment of fixed-site and submarine-launched intercontinental missiles for 5 years, and covering those under construction as well as deployed.

The United States considered limiting offensive as well as defensive missiles a major advantage, since no United States deployment was underway at the time, but the Soviet Union was embarked on a large-scale program of deployment. The freeze, however, turned out to be the main target of attack by the anti-SALT faction in the United States, and the rallying point, in fact, for future criticism, all of it based on the contention that the Soviet Union benefited from the freeze at the United States' expense.

The freeze did leave missile stockpiles out of balance: The Soviets had about 2,400, the Americans 1,700. The Russians, moreover, launched an ambitious program of MIRVing—converting their older missiles to multiple warheads. This was not breaking the rules of the game, but it made the critics even more concerned, notwithstanding the fact that the Americans, too, were MIRVing missiles.

The two other concerns of the critics were that the Russians would cheat on even this very favorable agreement, and that the limits set on missiles were so high as to be meaningless. SALT I provided for "national technical means" of verification to check on compliance by both sides. For the United States, this meant the "Big Bird" and other satellites, equipped with infrared sensing techniques able to penetrate most known systems of camouflage. Big Bird caught the Russians trying to conceal work at missile sites and submarine bases—not evidence of violating the arms limitation section of SALT, but a violation in itself of the agreement not to resort to deliberate concealment to impede verification.

Questions of compliance—which need not necessarily be charges of violation—are brought before a consultative commission. Both sides have raised questions since the first SALT signing. In each case raised by the United States, the Soviet side stopped the activity being questioned or produced additional information to explain it satisfactorily. In short, no real violations was the experience of SALT I.

The Vladivostok meeting between Presidents Ford and Brezhnev at the end of 1974 brought an answer to the critics of the high numbers involved in the earlier agreement. An aide memoire spelled out the limits to be sought in the SALT II talks. Instead of the uneven missile freeze, it provided for "aggregate limits" on each side of 2,400 strategic nuclear delivery vehicles: land- and submarine-launched missiles, and bombers as well. Similar aggregate limits were put on multiple warhead (MIRV) systems at 1,320 each. Earlier ambiguities on what constituted light and heavy missiles were taken care of in an agreement to ban conversion of launchers from light to heavy missiles, and new fixed-launcher construction was also banned. The aide memoire also agreed to limit the deployment of new types of strategic arms, and finally it continued the verification provisions of the interim agreement, which meant that satellites and neighboring ground monitoring stations would be able to check on compliance.

The stage was set for the long and difficult negotiations of SALT II, against a political background that went far beyond questions of throw-weight and multiple targeted warheads. Between the start of the negotiations shortly after the Ford-Brezhnev meeting, at the beginning of 1975, and their conclusion in 1979, the two sides had to deal with the Soviet moves in Portugal, Angola, and the Horn of Africa, not to mention the Southeast Asian turmoil. The Russians had to deal with the uncertainty of primary campaigns and the 1976 election, and then with the human rights offensive that the new administration brought in.

Both sides say that linking outside events and policies to

the SALT progress is wrong, since the limitation of strategic arms is important for world survival, as well as being beneficial to each of the partners in the talks. But both have departed from this principle many times.

Soviet Foreign Minister Andrei Gromyko, for example, in commenting on the early actions of the Carter administration, said, "Everything that has been said recently in the United States about human rights certainly poisons the atmosphere" in the arms talks, although he stopped short of making progress in SALT dependent on what the Soviet Union would consider progress—silence—in human rights.

On the American side, despite repeated assurances by Secretary of State Vance that the administration did not link Soviet behavior outside the arms talks to their success or failure (and a lot of hair-splitting about Vance's opposing linkage and Brzezinski's favoring it), the division of power in the United States system made a kind of linkage inevitable. The United States Senate had to approve SALT, and the United States Senate was not only free of White House restraints but also at one of its periodic high points of independence from the White House. It was also exceedingly sensitive to the vote-getting value of calling attention to the Soviet threat, whether in securing re-election or in trying for higher office.

The negotiators concerned themselves with three main issues as the talks continued and the months and years passed: to provide for equal numbers of delivery vehicles for both sides, to begin the process of reduction in these numbers, and to restrain technical improvements that would make these other limits meaningless.

In addition, the Soviet Union threw in an issue (as it had in SALT I) that will keep coming up in the future: the inclusion of the NATO weapons that, although not strategic, are capable of reaching Soviet targets. "Whether an American missile is aimed at us from a silo in North Dakota or from a base in Germany is of no consequence to the people in the target area," a Soviet official said in explaining the wish for inclusion of these tactical nuclear forces. The United States prevailed in SALT II in its wish not to include these forces, but statements including them in the overall balance of East-West power, and indications that a major part of future SALT negotiations will be devoted to them, make it certain the issue will remain alive.

Vladivostok provided a framework of agreement that brought a spurt of progress to the SALT negotiators in Geneva, and Secretary of State Henry Kissinger's prediction of a treaty within months seemed justified. A joint draft was agreed to. But the difficult issue of the middle-distance weapons emerged again, in the form of United States objections to the Soviet Tupelov 22M bomber, code-named the Backfire by the Americans, and the United States' new cruise missile systems, which the Russians said ought to be limited by SALT.

The Backfire is a medium-range bomber able to strike at targets in the United States with refueling in the air on a one-way mission. Because of its basic nonstrategic function, the Russians contended it had no place in the SALT limit of 2,400 strategic delivery vehicles. Inclusion of the Backfire, of course, would have meant a commensurate reduction in the number of other bombers or missiles permitted the Soviet Union.

Cruise missiles have been in arsenals in the East and the West since the forties, but recent improvements in miniaturization and electronic guidance changed them into formidable means of penetrating air defenses. Launched from the ground or planes outside the defense perimeter, they approach targets close to the ground, where they are hard to knock out. The Soviets consider cruise missiles with a range greater than 600 kilometers (about 375 miles) strategic weapons, when launched from the air. They sought to have all cruise missiles of over that range included in the strategic delivery vehicle limit of 2,400 and, in addition, wanted a ban on the further development of such missiles for ground and sea launching.

With cruise missiles and the Backfire still unresolved, Carter took office determined to give the arms limitation negotiations a new direction—that of adding significant reductions in strategic nuclear arsenals, along with further technological limits. These two steps, the new administration believed, would answer criticism (including its own in the campaign) that the high numerical limits were in themselves an advantage to the Soviet Union.

Vance proposed cuts amounting to a third of the strategic arms on both sides on his first visit to Moscow in March 1977. The Soviet Union held to the Vladivostok agreement and rejected the cuts, although in the final days of the Ford administration, it had agreed to a reduction to 2,250 from the original 2,400 ceiling on missiles and bombers.

SALT II negotiations wound up in May 1979 with a treaty composed of nineteen articles and dozens of "agreed statements" and "common understandings," footnotes to the articles designed to prevent differing interpretations as to what the treaty provisions mean. In addition, there is a protocol and various supplemental statements of further clarification and future aims.

The treaty's main provisions are these:

—An aggregate limit of 2,400 bombers, air-to-surface ballistic missiles, and submarine and ground-launched intercontinental ballistic missiles, with the number for each side to be lowered later to 2,250.

—A limit of 1,320 on the total number of missiles that may have multiple warheads, or on bombers carrying long-range cruise missiles.

—A limit of 820 on launchers of multiple-warhead missiles.

In addition to these numerical limits, which permit each side to mix bombers and different kinds of missiles in the proportions they wish, as well as to decide the mix of cruise and MIRVed missiles, several other bans and agreements are included in SALT II.

Neither side is permitted to build any more fixed launchers for strategic missiles, nor can they test more than one new type of light strategic missile in that treaty period. There is a ban on increasing the numbers of warheads on existing missiles, and a limit of ten warheads on one new missile type each.

There are also ceilings on launch and throw weights, limits on the number of cruise missiles each plane may carry, bans on the spread of ballistic missiles to surface ships and the sea bed, and provisions for better verification. Both sides agreed to use their own "national technical means" of checking on compliance, and not to interfere with this process by scrambling or encoding the telemetric signals used from missile to ground station during testing.

Since MIRVing missiles has the effect of multiplying them, special agreements were made to control the installation of multiple warheads. Once a missile has been tested with MIRVs, all missiles of that type will be counted as being MIRVed, even if they have also been tested with single warheads.

The similarity of some missiles causes confusion in counting, and the Soviet Union agreed for this reason to discontinue deployment of its new SS-16 strategic missile. The SS-16 shares components with the intermediate-range SS-20, not covered by SALT, and if the program had continued, distinguishing between the two would have been difficult.

SALT II was intended to last through 1985, but the inability to agree on some issues caused the need for a protocol, which was to have expired at the end of 1981, to cover them. These issues involve mobile missile launchers like the

American MX, which was not to be flight-tested during the protocol period, and long-range cruise missiles, for which testing but not deployment was permitted.

In the joint statement of principles appended to the treaty, both nations agreed to continue the negotiations with the aim of reducing and limiting strategic weapons, including those temporarily restrained in the protocol. It also left open the possibility of introducing the nuclear arms in Europe in future SALT negotiations. Finally, a "Backfire Statement" pledged the Soviet Union not to give the bomber intercontinental capability or to increase its production.

To comply with SALT II, the Russians would have to dismantle 250 to 300 presently deployed strategic offensive systems. The Americans have to make no such cuts, although older systems have to be phased out when the deployment of new Trident submarines gains momentum.

United States officials called SALT II a good treaty for the United States and for the Soviet Union and pointed to the complexity and difficulty of the negotiations to date, but also to their gains: the ABM race that never took place, and the freeze and then the cautious cuts in the competing strategic systems, as well as the limits on improvements. The final benefit of the SALT process, they say, is that it is a continuing treaty, barring legislative vetoes.

SALT's American critics gather in two groups, one opposing the treaty because it does not go far enough in limiting arms and because its many loopholes permit new buildups, the other opposing it because it goes too far in giving the Soviet Union the advantage.

No such division, of course, is apparent in the Soviet Union, where defense budgets are a matter for neither public debate nor approval.

Both sides looked forward optimistically to SALT III, agreeing to begin negotiations on it as soon as its predecessor went into force upon Senate ratification. With the setback dealt by Afghanistan, however, it appears likely that the next time the negotiators sit down, it will be to renegotiate parts of SALT II in tandem with breaking new ground on SALT III—what some observers have called SALT two and one-half. This means further negotiations on limitation and reduction of strategic arms, and further technical limitation on them. With verification, methods that involve cooperation and go beyond national technical methods will be sought. The United States and the Soviet Union also left the door open to any other steps to ensure strategic stability, and any other measures to reduce the risk of nuclear war.

Neither Europe nor China was mentioned anywhere in the treaty or the accompanying statements, but both will figure prominently in the talks that lie ahead, Europe directly and China in the background.

China is involved because of the nuclear threat it poses to the Soviet Union from the east and the south, with no hint of a treaty to limit its admittedly feeble capacity. As long as this threat remains, Soviet negotiators are going to be reluctant to make the "significant and substantial reductions in the numbers of strategic offensive arms (and) qualitative limitations on strategic offensive arms, including restrictions on the development, testing, and deployment of new types of . . . arms and the modernization of existing" ones, as they have agreed to do in the guidelines for the subsequent negotiations. In this sense, SALT III shares with every other major Soviet-American issue the complication of the triangle.

Russia cannot negotiate arms control with only a single adversary in mind, although the United States can, since its fears of China as a strategic threat, never very great, have all but disappeared because of the new relationship with Peking.

"They [the Russians] have a two-front situation to worry about, and we have, in effect, a one-front," an American SALT source said. "It isn't entirely clear whether they consider China their number one enemy and us their number two; we have heard it both ways. Let us say that they look on us as a greater potential threat because of our strength, and the Chinese as a greater actual threat because of their posture.

"But in any case, their worries about the Chinese sharply limited their willingness to engage in any real cuts in their strategic arsenal. The reductions they did agree to do not mean much when compared to the enormous size of the arsenals of nuclear weapons remaining on both sides. But it does give them a relative sense of security *vis-à-vis* the Chinese."

The lack of major reductions, however, is one of the main points of contention of the one faction of American critics of SALT II. The rejection by the Soviets of the Vance plan for a one-third cut and Russia's subsequent refusal to consider larger cutbacks during the regular negotiating sessions, they say, has left the arms race all but unchecked.

There seems to be no way to resolve this conflict as long as Soviet-Chinese relations remain hostile, and as long as it remains impossible to distinguish an SS-19 missile produced as protection against a threat from China from one intended to deter, or attack, the West.

Europe has a prominent place in the future of strategic arms negotiations because of the unresolved issues of the tactical weapons on both sides, because of the Soviet buildup in Central Europe, and because since the beginning of SALT, the Soviet Union has been trying to include the NATO forces capable of striking the Soviet heartland with nuclear warheads from Western European bases.

Europe's own defense posture is complicated not only by its relationship to the Soviet Union, its adversary, and to the United States, its protector, but by constantly changing relationships among its nations. At different times and in different capitals the idea of an independent European defense force is revived and rejected. Its advantages are the reintegration of France's military and the possibility of Europe's playing a separate role in the East-West dialogue. Its disadvantages are the cost, economic and political, of getting replacements for the manpower and weaponry that the United States provides for Europe.

But the main problem for European defense in the eighties—and for the Soviet-American relationship to Europe—will be the question of whether negotiations can reduce the threat of nuclear war in Europe, even marginally, as earlier negotiations have marginally reduced the threat of nuclear war between the great powers.

The issue seems to have about equal chances of strengthening Europe's political cohesion, and its links to the United States, or of dividing the European nations from each other and from the United States. And this is likely to be true whether the two sides decide to limit arms in Europe or add to them. The Soviet Union, always eager to find means of weakening and dividing the Western partnership, will have a rare opportunity to do so as an unexpected side effect of the debate on nuclear security.

Britain and France developed their own nuclear weapons after World War II, but the nuclear controversy began to affect Europe only after NATO decided in 1956 to accept United States nuclear weapons for its forces facing the Soviet army. The decision, long the subject of debates, protest marches, and propaganda from the East, was made a month after Soviet troops crushed the Hungarian revolution, one of the recurring spurs to NATO unity the Russians have been providing in the course of carrying out their own objectives.

Since that time, Soviet energies have been directed toward removing the Western European nuclear threat, through encouraging the peace and antinuclear movements in the West and through diplomatic initiatives, in and outside the SALT framework.

The Russians' great success in this effort of more than 2 decades has been in preventing the deployment of the enhanced radiation weapon or neutron bomb in Europe. The weapon is best known as the one that destroys people but leaves their homes and factories intact for the conqueror. But its utility for NATO is as a counter to the overwhelming superiority of Soviet tank forces in Central Europe. The neutron weapon could wipe out these tank columns by destroying their crews. Until a defense could be found against it, the weapon would be worth thousands of tanks to the West's defense planners—or to the East's; Brezhnev told a group of visiting American congressmen that the Soviet Union had developed and tested a neutron weapon but had decided not to use it. There is no reliable information as to whether the neutron bomb is in fact in the Soviet arsenal. But none of this was mentioned, in any case, in the Soviet campaign against the deployment of the weapon in the West.

The campaign succeeded because the United States mishandled the issue, because the bomb itself was a good and new illustration of the horrors of nuclear war, because the European left and other political forces are easy to rally on any nuclear issue, and because the Russians used good tactics.

"The Soviet ambassador to the Netherlands got the order of Lenin as thanks for his services," a NATO official said, "but mostly it was the mistakes of the United States and NATO." NATO sources admit that they knew nothing about the controversy until reading about it in the American press, and that they had to keep up on developments in the same way. When it became public, the handling was no better. The United States got the West Germans to give reluctant approval to stationing the neutron weapon on their territory, which exposed Chancellor Schmidt to great political crossfire from the left of the Social Democrats. Then President Carter suddenly announced his decision to suspend development of the weapon.

NATO was left with the Dutch opposed to the bomb and the Germans angry at the sequence of events that left them open to criticism at home and abroad. As a result, Schmidt promised parliament that there would be no further defensive political steps of that kind: "The responsibility and the risk involved in dealing with this situation must be borne by the Allies jointly."

But dividing NATO on an important issue was not the sole success of the Russians in the neutron weapon controversy, or even the important one. Here is the view of a NATO official on what was lost: "For the first time in the West-East confrontation, the decision to halt the neutron weapon—and it is going to have to be a final one, hard to climb back from—was made because of the Soviet Union's views on that weapon. Now a precedent has been set, and it will be very difficult, if not impossible, for the West to adopt a new weapon, as contrasted to evolutionary development, without subjecting its decision to this Soviet veto. This is a situation that doesn't exist at all in the other direction, in Western ability to veto what the Russians want to do."

What the Russians are doing is building up forces, particularly the intermediate-range SS-20, a mobile, land-based missile that can hit targets 4,000 miles away (ample for any corner of Western Europe), and the Backfire bomber. And they are building these forces in the middle of Europe. At the time of SALT II, there were 100 of each threatening Europe, and even under the agreed limitations, the number of Backfires was being increased by a third every year. The SS-20s, of course, faced no limitation at all.

The one salutary effect of the Soviet building, NATO and other Western defense officials say, is that it might just succeed in frightening Western Europe enough to cancel out the newly won veto power the Russians seem to be enjoying over the introduction of Western weaponry to restore the balance.

They view these "gray zone" weapons—so-called because they are not covered by SALT—in two ways. In the first place, the West should be able to pose a credible deterrent to the forces the East has deployed, in terms of weapons actually in place in Western Europe for use in the event of war. In the second, it should have sufficient weapons, in place or in the process of deployment, to use as the bargaining chips needed in the mutual reduction of forces. To persuade the Soviet Union to put a cap on its SS-20 deployment or to reduce it, the West must be able to offer concessions of equal weight.

But, as the eighties began, European defense analysts contend, it had neither.

The West's gray zone weapons, fighter bombers stationed in Britain and on the Continent, could reach the SS-20 sites in Western Russia, but their reaction time is a great deal longer than that of a missile, and there are satisfactory ways of shooting down planes, but not missiles. Compared to 100 SS-20s—in effect 300, since each is equipped with three independent re-entry warheads—or to the Soviet Backfire bombers, they are not much of an asset for the West, either in case of war or at the conference table, these analysts say. The Europeans, who have shown they can get together on civilian aircraft projects like the Airbus to outperform the Russians, can build their own tactical missiles and aircraft. Chinese interest attests to European prowess in missiles and control systems (although not in anything like the size and range of the SS-20s). But all this takes time; even a crash development program would require some years, and during that period there is very little with which to bargain with the Russians, leaving a very nervous Western Europe under the shadow of the SS-20s.

The United States does have interim weapons, the Pershing II, a more powerful and longer-range version of an older missile long stationed in Europe as part of NATO's tactical forces, and the Tomahawk cruise missile. Both have the range to permit them to reach the SS-20s, and both would be able to react faster than the fighter-bombers hampered by air defenses. Once the United States stationed them in Europe it could also take them away, in exchange for concessions on the other side of the border.

But the trouble with the cruise missile and Pershing II was that these threatened Western Europeans were falling over each other trying not to have them stationed in their particular countries. The Germans were willing to accept Pershings but did not want to be the only nation so doing—Moscow would be certain to consider such a decision proof of a revival of militarism, and the other Western European nations might also be worried about too great a surge of German military power. The Netherlands and Belgium would be logical SS-20 targets in case of war because of their ports at Rotterdam—the largest in the world—and Antwerp. But their governments displayed great reluctance to have missiles stationed on their territory, particularly the big and complex Pershings. When they joined NATO, Denmark and Norway made voluntary pledges not to have foreign bases or nuclear weapons on their soil. The Soviet Union, instead of being grateful for this pledge, uses it as an excuse to watch over Danish and Norwegian defense policy and protest what it considers infractions of the agreement. When Norway agreed to store some bulldozers and other equipment for British and Canadian troops planning Arctic maneuvers, for example, the Russians protested and said the real aim of the warehousing was to store nuclear material. Scandinavia, then, is hardly welcome ground for Pershings, and, for a variety of political reasons, neither are NATO's southern flank members, Italy, Portugal, and Turkey, although the cruise missiles, which can be positioned unobtrusively in any military base, are less of a problem.

Above all, the United States was wary about pushing its allies too hard, causing another neutron bomb affair. But despite initial agreement on a new arms program for NATO, there are still concerns in Western Europe that this is exactly what will happen. "We are all too likely to take the dangerous technological way of replying to the Russian buildup," a British defense analyst said. "It is exactly the reaction they wanted when they stepped up their SS-20 and tank deployment. It has all the potential of splitting the alliance. If the United States moves in with the Pershings, the Russians will react with a propaganda campaign that will make the neutron debate seem like a poetry reading. The Dutch and Belgians will take the French route out of NATO, and they will be quite right."

Other analysts disagree with this interpretation of the aim of the Soviet buildup. In the view of a NATO specialist in the East-West balance, the Russians have been surprised at NATO's unity since the buildup began, above all in the West's increasing defense budgets and building up of conventional forces. In this view, the Russians miscalculated badly by believing their own propaganda about the softness and disunity of Europe and then found themselves saddled with the problems of a more resolute NATO, willing to increase defense budgets by an annual 3 percent, and finally, with many misgivings and fail-safe clauses, to accept the Pershing IIs and cruises.

Without even the impetus of the invasion of Afghanistan, which took place later the same month of December 1979, the alliance agreed to have the cruise missiles based in the future in the Netherlands, Belgium, Britain, Italy, and West Germany, and to have 108 Pershings stationed in West Germany. There were many conditions and hesitations; the smaller nations won grace periods before making a final decision, and all agreed to couple the buildup with offers of arms reduction talks with the East, as well as with the removal of 1,000 of the 6,800 American nuclear warheads stationed in Europe. The decision could be delayed because the cruise missile was not expected to complete development and testing before 1983.

Why did the Soviet Union decide to risk this reaction by increasing the power and efficiency of its forces? There are two Soviet buildups to discuss in this case. One was the general program of modernization that began in 1955, as the post-Stalin leadership realized that, 10 years after the end of the Second World War, it was counting on wartime arms and equipment to defend the nation. Within that general buildup, which has continued, was a spurt that started in 1970 or 1971, mostly in modernization and concentration of firepower.

Those were the military decisions. That they were taken at unfortunate times for the political climate did not seem to matter. The Soviet Union expects the imperialists to mistrust them and arm to the teeth; it apparently does not calculate the cost to itself of responding to this response, or the cost to SALT's support in the United States when, after each agreement, an ambitious new program of missile development begins.

The Soviet Union certainly does not build up its forces in order to split Europe, but for good and sufficient reasons of its own that will be discussed later. That its buildup has the potential to divide Europe, along with the countereffect of helping NATO's cohesion in other respects, is a welcome dividend to Russia. The same is true of the other side of the issue—limitation and reduction of arms. Russia seeks agreement on this, as does the United States, for its own reasons. New divisions in Europe's alliances, if they happen, would be a bonus.

The potential for misunderstanding and acrimony between the United States and its European allies is much greater in future than it was in the previous SALT negotiations, because the Europeans are much more directly affected by many of the issues. Europeans complained that they were informed, not really consulted, in the earlier SALT rounds; the Americans responded that only a tiny part of SALT I and II concerned them.

Europeans reading the State Department's 5,000-word background briefing paper on SALT II would find only a single, short paragraph referring to them: "Allied security will also be preserved and enhanced by the Salt II agreement. The U.S. has consulted closely with its NATO allies throughout the course of the negotiations, and has taken into account allied security concerns in its negotiating positions."

If consulting closely means informing one's partners what one has just agreed to with the Soviet Union, a German defense analyst said, then the United States has done that. But as far as getting together beforehand to work out what the United States would offer the Russians, and what changes it might accept to its proposals, the analyst continued, that simply did not happen. United States officials disagree vigorously with this view.

But future SALT talks, it is agreed, are different: "Whether it wants to or not, NATO is going to be involved in the talks," a NATO official said. "How to do it is difficult. Too many voices would make negotiation impossible—even those who worry about the Russians and Americans making decisions over their heads agree to that. But too much is at stake in terms of the weapons these countries count on for their defense, as opposed to the distant nuclear arsenals of Moscow and Washington, for them not to have a role."

Europe figures in future Soviet-American arms limitation talks for three basic reasons: the gray zone weapons, the system of forward basing, and conventional weapons problems.

A forward based system (FBS) consists of medium-range United States aircraft, at European land bases or on carriers, that can strike targets in the Soviet Union with nuclear warheads.

FBS is a device to keep tactical aircraft dual-based, with a home in the United States and duty in Europe. The system means extra planes can be flown to Europe quickly in times of crisis. As with similar plans for army units, it prevents foreign balance of payments drains for the United States and eases manpower and community relations problems. Carrying FBS to its ultimate point would mean having all tactical planes in United States bases except in times of trouble. But that, too, would have its problems, including the maintenance of adequate facilities in Europe and the crisis-escalating effect that the despatch of FBS aircraft to Europe would have—which might be so great that it acts as a deterrent against their use.

Western analysts think the Soviet Union would like to bargain for the complete removal of FBS from Europe. In SALT I, the Soviet side not only brought up the removal of FBS but also demanded the destruction of European FBS bases so that planes could not be flown to the European theater from the United States. Just to make sure, Russia also called for a ban on the use of carrier basing. At that time, the United States refused. But an agreement that would provide for keeping the bases intact would be an easy bargaining chip for the United States to push across the table in return for a lessening of the dimensions of the Eastern missile and bomber fleets that make Europeans feel so uneasy. After all, the United States could be back in Europe in a few hours, if the need arose.

There has already been one American withdrawal from Europe, in exchange for nothing from the Soviet side, and Russian negotiators have not forgotten this. Until the sixties, American Thor and Jupiter missiles were stationed in Britain, Italy, and Turkey. United States basing was found to be better for political reasons, and improving technology made the longer reach possible. But when the missiles went home, nothing was dismantled on the other side. If the Russians remember this, so do the Europeans, and they worry about the United States agreeing to go home again without much effort to ensure security from the East.

They worry, too, about NATO's conventional arms arsenal. NATO forces are equipped with weapons, both land and airborne, that can fire nonnuclear as well as nuclear warheads. The Soviet Union's larger hardware does not have this flexibility. But any mutual cuts in the weapons based in Europe could wipe out conventional as well as nuclear capability for NATO and greatly reduce its ability to respond flexibly to a crisis.

With all these problems and complexities, NATO sources say, the alliance is in one of its frequent states of disarray, and, as one official admitted, "The Russians are catching up, and we are giving them the breathing space to do so. We are not leading the way ourselves in arms limitation, but in the best case, letting the Russians and Americans do it, and in the worst, the Russians alone."

Is the huge Soviet military establishment proof of the expansionist aims of the leadership, or is it essentially defensive? If that question could be answered satisfactorily, a great deal of national budget money could go from missiles to medical centers, and many young men could go home. A straight answer seems impossible to obtain at the official level in the Soviet Union; the usual response is a repetition of statements that deny there is any great arms buildup and then justify it on the grounds that the West is doing it, too.

A rough theory might be put forward, however, on the basis of past Soviet actions as well as statements that would say yes, the Soviet Union's buildup is essentially defensive, but defensive of past expansionist gains. That theory, if correct, is a better guide to contemporary Soviet behavior than it is a tool for predicting the future; nations that were once expansionist sometimes continue to be and sometimes do not.

It could be argued that the Soviet advisers in South Yemen, Ethiopia, Angola, and Southeast Asia are there to achieve expansionist aims, but these examples, and even the occupation contingent in Afghanistan, are not a massive commitment of military power the way the buildup on the Soviet territory is. Citizens of Berlin or Amsterdam do not think that the Vietnamese or Ethiopians are going to roll their tanks through their streets someday, but some of those citizens think the Soviets just might.

The Russians scoff at such Western topics as debates on how long it would take their tanks to get to the Rhine, and they always put quotation marks around Soviet threat. It is indeed hard to imagine the presence of tanks and young infantrymen with shaved heads on the boulevards of Western cities. It is equally hard to imagine such scenes on the boulevards of Prague or Budapest, but they did take place. But this, of course, is in the Soviet sphere of influence. Maintaining that sphere, it could be argued, is the main reason for the drain on the economy, manpower, and international reputation that the massive Russian military machine represents. Those strains, it will be argued further, are the world's best guarantee that in the long run the Russians will not be able to add very much, if anything, to their empire and indeed will be hard pressed to maintain what they have.

The Soviet Union is the only major country in the world with unresolved territorial problems requiring it to remain on a virtual war footing, decade after decade. There is controversy over territory all over the world, and much time can be spent discussing who really ought to have the right to Belfast, Hawaii, or Vladivostok. Most of these disputes do not require an enormous war machine to keep them settled. In some cases, such as Somalia's claims on Kenya and Ethiopia, there is no possibility of redress because of the claimant's weakness. The Soviet Union is not weak militarily, however, because it chooses to direct its resources that way, and its system prevents people from standing up and objecting.

The Soviet government is only following priorities established in the first years of Bolshevik power, when War Communism became the order of the day and the first territory was won back from the Whites. That territory has been defended zealously ever since against any conceivable attempt to capture it—not from abroad, but from within, and not by armed force, but by actions as minor as printing a handbill critical of the Politburo.

From this need to defend the interior of the country from its own people, the Soviet regime's defensive imperative moves outward to the republics where, but for the power of the central authorities, the various Soviet nationalities might be tempted to seek real autonomy or independence. Some of them were able to do so when czarism was abolished and the Empire crumbled, but as soon as Moscow's authority had regained enough strength, they were brought back. The Baltic nations were able to hold out the longest, until 1940.

From 1944 to 1948, the Russians chopped off bits of territory, large and small, from Eastern Europe to keep as their own and then, in effect, annexed the whole area. This, it was said at the time, brought "secure borders" to the region for the first time in centuries and thus served the cause of peace.

It served instead the cause of insecurity and the arms race. However justified the Soviet Union felt in gaining territory to compensate for its terrible losses in World War II, however valid the historical claims to some of them are, however legal the treaties with Germany renouncing the use of force to reclaim them, the fact remains that the Soviet Union and its dependencies are sitting on 40,000 square miles of former German territory, and that the Soviet leadership believes that unless much of this territory and its hinterland is studded with SS-20 emplacements and thousands of tanks, it just might change hands again.

Western Europe suffered, too, in the war, but when the war was over not a square mile of territory had changed hands against the will of its inhabitants. The Western powers apparently were paying attention to their own histories, particularly those of Germany and France, which taught them that territorial seizures lay the groundwork for the next war. The Soviet Union may have reasoned that these rules did not apply to it. Until an honest history book is written in the USSR, or scholars are permitted access to documents, we will not know.

Compared to the territory the Communists took from the Germans, what the czars took from the Chinese is enormous. And unlike the Germans, who have renounced any intention of changing the borders back by war, the Chinese are not renouncing anything, although they are realistic about their chances of enforcing any change in borders. Should the Russians believe the Chinese and not the Germans, or believe the Germans and not the Chinese, or distrust, or believe, both? Their answer can be seen in the patterns of deployment of men and war machinery in the West, South, and East.

10

Conclusion

IS IT POSSIBLE to maintain an empire in the era of anti-colonialism? The Soviet Union has demonstrated that it is possible, but costly, in terms of manpower, drains on the economy, and damage to its reputation in the world. If it is agreed in East and West that the vast resources of the United States are not up to all the demands of a world role, and if all earlier colonial powers—Britain, France, the Netherlands, Spain, and Portugal—have had to leave the scene, how do the Russians differ?

They do not, and therein lies the world's hope. On one hand, nationalism, separatism, and the search for roots and identity are more at work in the world than ever before; on the other, the national needs of the USSR make it increasingly less attractive for Russia to squander money abroad.

The Soviet Union simply started too late; all the other former colonial powers are beginning to enjoy some of the benefits of their decisions, reluctant or otherwise, to leave, to learn that it is possible to continue to have investment and trade without all the burdens of a huge colonial bureaucracy and military establishment.

But the Soviet Union is a nation that has this same kind of apparatus for its own people—hundreds of thousands of officials, for example, whose only task it is to keep peasants from owning too many cows or tilling too much acreage privately—and thus does not feel the strain a democracy would in the additional task of watching over the loyalty of Pole, Uzbek, and South Yemeni. If this burden were ever removed, the effect would be noticed, but such an eventuality may have to await changes in the Soviet Union that at the same time would remove the domestic system of overseers.

Soviet officials say that they really have no choice in a policy of expansionism, because the rest of the world wants to become Communist. This modern version of the white man's burden rationale for colonialism is firmly anchored in the doctrine of the inevitable progress of men and women and nations toward the higher forms of social relationship that Marx foresaw. It is therefore seriously offered in conversations: "The ideological struggle must continue. There would be no way to stop it, even if we wanted to. In the first place, history shows that there is a logical progression from slavery through feudalism and bourgeois democracy to socialism. These laws are working. Not only do we not want to impose socialism on other countries, including the United States, but we do not believe it will be necessary, because people will choose it themselves. The Americans already have the Soviet revolution to thank for their health and welfare and worker benefits, which would otherwise have been much more slow in coming. Our job is to make our example so attractive that it stands for all the world as an irresistible model."

And thus, with this reasoning, it is possible to argue that expansion into other nations and continents does not harm détente, since the Russians, the Cubans, and the East Germans are only giving historical forces a little help. When the United States, however, offers China Most Favored Nation

status and does not offer it to the Soviet Union, that is harmful to détente, as the same official argued. The current Chinese leadership has taken the nation away from the Marxist
path by increasing its differences with the Soviet Union; the
United States' position in the historical lineup is, of course,
that of a capitalist power with whom it is possible for the
Russians to make temporary accommodations, under the
tenets of Lenin's peaceful coexistence, but that will always
ultimately be an adversary.

Leninism, when applied to the Third World, also teaches
that the "natural ally" of former colonial peoples is the Soviet Union, and this is why there are 20,000 Cuban soldiers
and 3,000 Cuban civilians in Angola, and 11,000 Cuban soldiers and 2,000 Russian advisers in Ethiopia, and 85,000 Soviet troops in Afghanistan.

Soviet design for the Third World can best be seen in the
list of nations that were not Communist-ruled at the end of
the fifties but are Communist-ruled, if sometimes tenuously,
at the end of the seventies: Afghanistan, Cuba, Vietnam,
Laos, Cambodia, and Ethiopia.

But, as the Americans and other Western nations found,
foreign adventures are costly and often unrewarding. Cuban
deaths in the African fighting have been estimated at 1,500.*
An estimated 1,000 Russians were killed or wounded in the
first two weeks of the Afghan fighting alone, U.S. sources
said. Cuba's economy as well as its bereaved families pay for
Africa, too; in the third decade of Fidel Castro's revolution,
coffee and cooking oil are still rationed and meat appears on
tables once a week. And Russians pay for Cuba. The $8
million daily subsidy that is often cited in the West as the
Cuban price tag for Russian help is cited, privately, in the
East as well.

_____

* Which, in proportion to the population, would represent a loss of 34,000
men to the United States.

There is damage, too, to the Soviet reputation in world affairs when too many other nations fail to see anything very progressive in having the Soviet military machine on their continent, even if it is with proxy troops. When the capitalists from the rich nations raise these objections, that is to be expected, but when the poor and the non-aligned do, that causes difficulties. It was the poor and non-aligned who sponsored and supported the U.N. resolutions condemning the invasion of Afghanistan. And China is always there to remind Third World nations just exactly what Soviet aims are for their neighbors or perhaps for themselves.

All these drawbacks can be cited for successful colonial ventures, but they apply even more to the rare but occasional unsuccessful one. When a large part of the nation is in disagreement with the changes the Soviet advisers helped bring about, and when tribal loyalties, fighting traditions, and terrain make opposition feasible, there is always the possibility that the men, money, and propaganda losses might be wasted entirely, or the conflict prolonged, like Vietnam, for years of costly demands on the foreign power's economy and social stability. Afghanistan is a shorter way of describing such a situation.

These costs are only those of the current phase of attempting to expand the empire. Those of holding on to what has already been acquired are the really important ones. They begin with keeping the Soviet Union on a footing not very much different from the War Communism introduced by Lenin and Trotsky when the government was in the hands of a few beleaguered and untested revolutionaries, which means Communist Party interference in everything public and in much of what ought to be private. Costs of expansion continue with the influence of the military in political and economic life, whether it is the generals' insistence on having a standing army so large that the needs of industry and public works are shorted, or their right of first call on the researchers and engineers whose talents are so much needed in the civilian sector. Compared to these sacrifices borne for decades by the Soviet nation, the loss of soldiers in Afghanistan or Angola, however tragic to their families, is minor indeed.

Seen in this light, the monolithic Party organization and the rows of armored divisions and ranks of missiles are really a burden on the Soviet Union, one the nation would benefit from reducing or getting rid of.

There is tacit acceptance of this view from time to time in the Soviet Union in its efforts to control arms or to give more decision-making power to the managers of the state economy. But all such attempts run into the danger of tampering with the status quo. "It's not very efficient, but it's safe," is not the kind of banner one would expect to see in a May Day parade, but it is, in effect, what the Russians march behind most of the time.

This conservatism makes détente a very appealing concept to the Soviet leadership, because, as defined in Moscow, it means keeping what is theirs, getting the United States to agree to exchanges largely beneficial to the Soviet economy and technological capabilities, and being able, at least to their own satisfaction, of making up the rules.

The main rule is that détente does not eliminate the continuation of the ideological struggle—as explained, this is something beyond anyone's power to call off. But what cannot be called off can at least be channeled into certain areas where the risk of conflict is the smallest. Here is the caution working again, and also a certain realism. Soviet doctrine is not for everybody (not right now, the ideologists in Moscow would quickly add). And the Soviet Union isn't strong enough, right now, to project it everywhere, particularly into the sphere of influence it recognizes as the West's.

Whether there is military parity or slight superiority from time to time in either camp or in specific weapons systems, both sides have the power to destroy the other, and both sides, too, have the power to tailor their politics so that the risk of setting off such a nuclear war is unlikely.

Both sides have weaknesses that can be exploited by the other without too great a fear of setting off the nuclear trip-wire. The Soviet Union (and China before it) found these American weaknesses to be in the Middle East and Africa, in particular around United States oil supplies. The part of the Third World closest to the United States, Latin America, is another matter and receives special handling.

The United States, for its part, hits closer to home, exploiting the weaknesses around the Soviet border and in the heartland itself: China, Eastern Europe, the Soviet nationalities, and the dissident intellectuals, to describe a series of circles that gets closer and closer to Moscow.

Both sides, it should be stressed, are able to justify their policies as natural extensions of the ideologies that serve their societies: Human rights, it can be claimed, is a basic concern of the United States—not, or not only, a way of pointing out shortcomings in the Soviet Union. Helping the oppressed peoples of the world is a Communist aim in itself, not just a means of overthrowing dictators friendly to the United States. Both sets of justifications fail in some measure; the Americans admit this and the Russians do not.

Russia would like to come to the help of the oppressed people in the United States, it says, but its previous attempts to solve American domestic problems have ended in failure. The Communist Party of the United States has been a joke for decades. It could not organize any kind of respectable following even in the depression, and black Americans have paid little attention to its solutions to their plight, such as Stalin's plan for a black republic on the model of the Soviet nationality enclaves.

Unemployment, inflation, women's rights—the Communist Party of the United States has mobilized vigorous campaigns to fight for or against them, as the case may be, but unless one is a regular listener to Radio Moscow, one is unlikely to be aware of any of them.

But those who live in Central America or Africa and wish to blame their troubles on the Americans or the local dictator are likely to listen. The organizers of revolutionary or liberation movements in those places do not have to have orders from Moscow. Their own condition is sufficient to get them started. Offers of help from any quarter are then appreciated and accepted. The offers do not often come from the West; it is far likelier that the West is supplying the regular forces the insurgents are fighting. Those able to look to the period beyond liberation might see another form of dictatorship emerging from the teams of advisers and strong military establishment needed for victory. But in such struggles for survival, few leaders are able to see that far ahead.

The United States has the choice of answering these Soviet probes in a number of ways: by trying to do something about the cause of the distress, by shoring up the dictators to keep things quiet, or by trying to get the Soviet Union not to interfere in such situations.

And what if the Russians reply that they were invited, along with Cubans and Eastern Europeans, by the people in charge of the country or the liberation movement? It is probably pointless to use the parallel of South Vietnam. What ought to be effective and what, according to some evidence, has been effective is to make Soviet behavior the condition for American behavior elsewhere.

The United States needs some semblance of good relations with the Russians because of the threat of nuclear war. Short of that, its needs are not pressing. The Russians have the same primary and fundamental need of wishing to avoid the holocaust, but a great many other needs in addition: for technology to help their economy function better and develop their resources, above all, but also for recognition as one of the two arbiters of world politics.

This advantage the United States has enjoyed for a decade, ever since the Ussuri fighting pushed both Communist great powers into the position of competing for American favor, political and economic.

And yet the course of events in that decade has made it appear almost as though the situation were reversed, with the United States needing the Soviet Union. The Russians were able to accept the label of détente and then define it so narrowly as to exclude almost all elements of good relations, leaving only the barest exclusion of bad ones. The Soviet side can, and does, point to what the Americans did after agreeing to détente: it tied increased trade to performance on human rights; it made deals with China; it strengthened NATO. To the United States, all these actions are consistent with the prerogatives of sovereign states and are, in any case, only responses to actions of the Soviet Union.

The United States then points to what the Soviet Union did after agreeing to détente: it embarked on a massive arms buildup; it sent expeditionary forces to Angola, Ethiopia, and South Yemen; it tried a coup in Portugal, cracked down on dissidents and American correspondents, plunged Southeast Asia into a new series of wars and devastation through its Vietnamese allies, and then turned on its own neutral neighbor, Afghanistan.

If the record of the two sides shows anything, it is that détente, as practiced to date by the two great powers, is a narrow concept indeed. But the record also seems to show that the Soviet Union has been more successful than the United States in avoiding any constraints on its behavior.

Despite UN resolutions, Soviet troops remain in Afghanistan and Soviet advisers run the Kabul government. And even the advocates of embargo in Washington admit privately that grain and electronic equipment will flow again to the Soviet Union, either through third parties or relaxed U.S. regulations.

There are, however, many measures of success. The ability

to add unstable and distant states to one's sphere of influence is certainly one of them. But the kind of sincere and deep cooperation with the West that the Soviet Union could benefit from if the other conditions were better would seem to be even more attractive to a vast nation in great need of modernization and development.

This second kind of success seems to be the aim of China in its relationship with the United States. The Chinese invasion of Vietnam showed that not only Russia seems to need adventures outside its borders. But before and after that ill-advised act, the Chinese were demonstrating far greater skill in taking advantage of the opening to the West than the Russians, with their head start, had done. The label applied to this policy is a pretty good one: pragmatism, doing what works. The Chinese seem to be able to apply it, and the Russians do not, because of an ingredient missing in the present Chinese outlook—rivalry with the United States. Perhaps the Chinese are content with one big rivalry, that with the Soviet Union, or perhaps they have chosen to gain strength first before testing the United States.

If the Soviet Union can be said to have missed the first opportunity that détente offered, by seeking to maximize its benefits while minimizing its concessions to the West, there seems little likelihood that the next stage—in which China will be competing for Western favor—will bring any change in Soviet policy.

But also in the next stage, the abilities of the West to hit at Soviet weak spots appear as great as, or greater than, the Soviet abilities to do harm to the West. An important decision for the West, however, is whether to make use of these opportunities in the way that, as past practice shows, the Soviet Union would do if it had the chance.

Clearly the Soviet leadership expects the West to act in this way, and little wonder. Each member of the leadership circle got to the top through a form of political struggle that makes Western electoral politics seem like the affairs of coin-collecting clubs. In the Stalinist days, when these leaders were making their marks, the losing side frequently ended up in prison or executed as purge victims. Now that these men are in the Politburo, they would be unusual indeed if they saw the West in any other way than as a mirror-image of themselves.

(Were not the pragmatic Chinese leaders products of the same system, with the terror and factional infighting that brought them to the top much more recent? They were, of course; it is possible that the explanation for their different kind of conduct toward the United States can be found in the differences of power that make it unrealistic for them to try a head-to-head rivalry with the United States as the Soviet Union does.)

In any case, the position of the Soviet leadership leaves the United States the option of a hard line—the kind of policy Russia may expect and certainly would understand—or a softer one—the kind of policy that was followed until the invasion of Afghanistan, somewhat to the surprise of the Russians, as they have let it be known, and certainly to their puzzlement. A hard line would say things such as: "The question of who rules Eritrea is of some concern to the United States, but the question of who rules the Ukraine ought to be of primary concern to the USSR." This is only another way of saying that the United States has a great many more levers of pressure, below the threshold of a nu-clear conflict, than the Soviet Union does. But it is also a way of acting as the Russians would, if they were in a position to do so. Whether the West should become more like the East, or work to have the East become more like it, is a matter that policymakers must determine. In any case, the Western side has a broad range of issues that can be used to support either strategy.

Human rights is the first such issue. The human rights

debate goes to the heart of the system of governance in the Soviet Union, since it is a system based on the denial of individual freedom. The defenders of the system contend that people have given up certain rights in order to be able to enjoy the larger goals of Soviet society, full employment and freedom from want. And yet, that society continues to disappoint all but the most modest of these aspirations, and, after all, its leaders have signed a document, the Helsinki Final Act, that commits them to a respect for the rights of the individual on a basis whose roots clearly are the Western doctrines of the Enlightenment. If the issue did not generate its own momentum—and despite arrests and persecution, it does—there is the added factor of a Slavic pope dedicated not only to the rights of men and women to be free, but also to the rights of nations to be free.

The nationalities problem in the Soviet Union has a potential that makes the United States' unsolved minority problems seem of quite manageable dimension. This is true in part because of the size of the Soviet minorities, which collectively may be a majority of the Union population, with the Russians being the real minority. (Official census figures are vague on the point.) It is also due to the fact that where American administrations have made some hesitant progress toward equality for minority citizens, the Soviet Union's system has permitted its leaders to solve all nationality problems by ignoring or suppressing them. But, as leaderships from London to Tehran have found, minorities have a way of presenting the bill, sooner or later.

The economy is a perennial weakness of the Soviet system, one that has been tinkered with in the past but never really reformed, because a succession of thinkers in the nineteenth and early twentieth centuries said that society's miseries were caused by private ownership of the means of production and the resultant exploitation of man by man. What this means in practical terms is that huge factories produce only large-size nails, although small ones are also needed, because the plan calls for a certain weight of nails and large ones are easier to make. This example, cited by a former factory manager, stands for hundreds of thousands of others, and not only in industry. Private farming plots account for nearly a third of the nation's food production, and yet successive governments, fearful of encouraging rural capitalism, have wavered between rules designed to restrict them, and—when food shortages get too severe—concessions designed to encourage them.

And finally, to conclude a short list, there is China, the gravest problem in Soviet foreign policy and a not inconsiderable one in Soviet domestic policy, when the cost of the border army and backup missile systems is counted.

How the United States reacts to all these problem areas for the Soviet leadership—and the counterreaction of the Soviet Union—will do much to determine whether the jittery climate of the postwar world continues or abates. All factors are important, but China is the key.

Playing the China card. The term originated in Moscow, not Washington, but the definition of what it constitutes is remarkably similar in both places. Said one Soviet official: "We think that the triangle and the China card are potential threats, but it depends entirely on what is done with the arrangements. It's not wrong to have relations among these three countries. But it depends on what these relations are used *for*. If they become an anti-Soviet force, that is our legitimate concern." Said an American diplomat in Moscow: "The China card is wholly a matter of intention. The Soviet perception of our intentions has to be the ruling factor. The United States must be careful not to play the China card too obviously; the Soviets are suspicious, but we must do all we can to convince them that it is in the world's interest to help China return to the family of nations, to responsibility."

Both these are definitions of the soft way of playing the

card. The hard line is best described by recollecting what the Soviet Union did when it held the card. If it did not actually order the Chinese "volunteers" to go into battle against the Americans in Korea, it is plain that under the political conditions in the Communist bloc in that period, no Chinese gun could have been raised if the Soviet Union had not desired it.

An American military alliance with the Chinese would have adverse effects on the whole network of American relations with Russia, and there are drawbacks to every other kind of hard line. Human rights can end in personal misery and prison sentences for the dissidents. If pressed too hard, it can also cause the vast majority of Soviet citizens who are untouched by dissidence to support the more repressive features of their government, since it is relatively easy for Moscow to link dissent with foreign influence and therefore with treason.

Western interference in the Soviet nationalities problem could easily have a similar effect for the European part of the population, and decolonization would be set back rather than helped. Economic pressures are difficult to use because of the diversity of Soviet trade ties in the West and in Japan.

The greatest potential for backfiring is the China relationship. It could lead to war, probably not against the stronger partner but against the weaker. Diplomats in Moscow consider there to be a three-in-ten chance of a Russian preemptive attack on China, but, as one of them with experience of the other situation noted, that was the same figure being cited for the chances of the Russians invading Czechoslovakia.

Short of an attack, it is certain that following the hard line on China would strengthen all the forces in the Soviet Union that the United States should not want to strengthen: the military and the armaments drain on the economy, above all, but also the power of the police and the Party. The siege mentality and paranoia about China, already a strong factor in the way the country is run, would be paramount.

"This is an argument," a Chinese diplomat said, "that could have been used with equal force in saying that nothing should have been done to oppose Hitler, because it would have only made him angry and a tougher enemy."

Or, as an American diplomat in Moscow put it, the United States cannot let the Soviet Union define what its relationship with China ought to be. In supplying technology, for example, the Russians have complained about America's policy of even-handedness: "Trying to treat them equally, they say, really favors China, since it hasn't reached the stage of development to be entitled to the same high level of technology the Russians get. By being even-handed, they say, we are helping the Chinese to leapfrog some earlier stages."

The Soviet Union has limits, too, in what it can do in exploiting the weaknesses of the United States. They mostly concern arousing public opinion about a Soviet threat, this one without the quotation marks used by Moscow.

The Soviet Union may have succeeded in plucking Ethiopia from American influence and making of it its first African satellite, or in encouraging its Southeast Asian ally to mount the barely disguised invasion of a neighboring nation. Russian leaders may believe their own propaganda about American and Pakistani aggression being the cause of the invasion of Afghanistan, or at least hope that the rest of the world, in time, will come to accept this justification. Russia may consider that the long-term benefits of these achievements of expansionism outweigh any short-term propaganda losses. But such short-term losses become cumulative.

Much of the rest of the world is unable to understand why ten divisions of Russians occupy Afghanistan, or why two divisions of Cubans are active in Africa. Admirers of the Cubans who are also admirers of the Eritrean rebels find this particularly difficult, since the former Cuban advisers to the Eritreans were forced to turn against them. If one wins battles but loses confidence, perhaps it is time to win fewer battles. In places like Scandinavia, where the Russians had enjoyed some sympathy and the Americans very little, the effect of the latest wave of Soviet colonizing was to reverse this order of things in public opinion, even in the left. The American villain in Vietnam was replaced by the Vietnamese and the Russian; no amount of labeling the boat people as drug pushers and prostitutes, as the Communist press attempted to do, was of much help. The United States' human rights policy helped this opinion shift as much as Russia's foreign moves did.

A final factor in probing the weaknesses of one's adversary is that, for such a probe to be effective, there must be a genuine issue, not a propaganda one, to exploit. The Third World people who seek Soviet aid are truly oppressed, not just dissatisfied troublemakers. The Soviet Union chooses its targets in the Third World not only because governments or factions ask for help, not only because they are desperately poor and faced by many enemies, but because a good case can be made against Western failures or excesses in the past that helped bring about that state of affairs. Similarly, the West does not pick out the Soviet electrical power system, whose record is pretty good, but the Soviet system of human rights guarantees, whose record is abysmal.

The main rule of this diplomatic game, however, is to keep it a game, not turn it into a war. It is known that the American specialists of the Soviet government were called in for meeting after meeting before the decision was taken to aid Ethiopia against Somalia, and it can be assumed that the same procedure preceded Afghanistan. The leadership wants to be as sure as it can of the American reaction to new adventures. Only when the experts reassured the policymakers that the United States would not react beyond verbal protests, in the case of Ethiopia, was the go-ahead given.

In the case of Afghanistan, it is likely that the stronger American reaction was anticipated, but that the Soviet leadership calculated that it had little to lose: SALT seemed dead in the Senate, NATO had approved a new round of nuclear modernization for Europe, and, in an election year, fears of the Soviet threat were likely to be played up rather than down by the administration in Washington.

Nevertheless, in Soviet eyes, the Afghan incursion was not a bold move into the United States' sphere of influence. For more than a century, Afghanistan had been contested for by Britain and the czars, and when the Americans replaced the British, the contest continued. But even at the height of the U.S. global role, the United States never made a real Cold War issue of influence over Kabul. The stakes were not really high enough, and the Russians had all the advantages of geography.

Until the texts of those Politburo meetings at the end of 1979 are made public, the world will not know how seriously the Russians considered an American military move as a response to their invasion. It is likely that they counted, as do the Americans, on the nuclear balance of terror to be the final limiting factor in international behavior. When viewed in this light, even the adventure in Afghanistan seems consistent with past Soviet caution and conservatism.

This same caution is an important ingredient of United States—and Western European and Japanese—policy toward China. Use the China card as pressure on the Soviet Union by all means, this thinking goes, but not as the direct and tough pressure that some quarters, including the Chinese, say they would like: a military arrangement, if not an alliance, and supplies of arms that go far beyond the carefully considered defensive weapons offered thus far. The Russians were able to do this with impunity in the fifties, of course, but the Russians now say that if the Americans do it, what is left of détente will be finished. Whether this should be the determining factor in Western policy or not is one thing. A more important point, American diplomats in Moscow stress, is that the United States should wish to sell arms to

China as little as it wishes to sell them to the Soviet Union, and for the same reason. Neither is an ally, and neither is the kind of regime that America ought to want to arm.

British and French reasoning is different. With stronger defense capabilities comes increased confidence, and with confidence might come more stable international behavior, including agreement to participate in arms limitation and control negotiations. The United States does not object to this policy (it would do it little good to object in any case), and it certainly shares the Western European goal of aiding the liberal and stable forces in China.

The logical consequence of this American-European-Japanese policy toward furthering a responsible China is the eventual healing of the Chinese-Soviet division; détente, in other words, between Moscow and Peking. An American diplomat with long experience in negotiations with both the Chinese and the Russians expressed a view shared by the great majority of those Westerners questioned on the subject: "Nothing is permanent in politics or diplomacy, but the rift is so deep as to approach permanence. It is based mostly on the Soviet insistence that they must be in charge, that they are the founders of modern Communism, and that the Chinese threaten all of this. The guardians of the faith cannot permit rivalry."

The diplomat, and others, conceded that there could be the possibility of improved government-to-government relations, as distinct from ideological peace. It was noted that this governmental rapprochement was the first step in patching relations with Yugoslavia on the part of both Moscow and Peking.

Should the West want and work for friendly relations between the two Communist giants? Is not Western and Japanese security far better served when they are quarreling?

The war-scare headlines that accompanied the Afghan, Vietnamese-Cambodian, and Chinese-Vietnamese fighting is one answer. As long as the two great Communist powers are on a war footing, even if they choose to do their fighting in part by proxy, the rest of the world will be less secure.

Détente with China would encourage those same forces in the Soviet Union that are encouraged by détente with the West, which is to say there would be a rise in the influence of those wishing foreign contacts and domestic liberalization, and a decline in the influence of the military-security apparatus.

There is, of course, the possibility that newly reconciled China and Russia would reverse the triangle and form a new version of the alliance the West faced in the fifties. This would have to be preceded, in all probability, by a solution to the ideological differences, and that, in turn, would depend on the (unlikely) acceptance by one nation of the other's authority in matters of doctrine.

If rapprochement comes about through the emergence of liberal groups in both Communist nations, and Western policy has had a role in their emergence, then there should be no reversal of the triangular relationship, only its evening out to include all three sides on a basis, more or less, of amity.

Liberal groups are more easily identifiable in China, where the official line is to admit backwardness and the need for American help—and even that the West does some things better than the Chinese have been doing.

No such admission has ever been made by Soviet officialdom; indeed, the rhetoric is of quite another kind. Is it possible to deal sweetly and reasonably with a nation whose spokesmen proclaim it to be on the side of history, predestined to lead the tide of change sweeping the world? Do the capitalists have anything at all to offer a nation whose leaders depict them as fighting a desperate last-ditch stand against the three irresistible forces in the contemporary world, "world socialism, the international working class movement, and national liberation movements," by which is

meant Communist-ruled countries, large Communist Parties
in the industrial nations of the West, and the have-nots of the
Third World?

The Western diplomats who deal with Soviet officials have
learned to handle the inevitable-wave theory of international
relations by not paying very much attention to it, paying
attention instead to what the Soviet Union does. This means
negotiations for mutual advantage, if possible, with SALT
the best example, ignoring both the threats and the lofty but
empty agreements the Soviets like to conclude, and that
Westerners call "froth and mirrors."

One example of the differences between Soviet rhetoric
and actual performance, these diplomats say, was the situation in Africa during the final months of negotiation of
SALT II. Westerners in constant contact with the Russians
during the period are convinced that there was, quite delib-
erately, a much lower level of Soviet and Cuban activity in
Ethiopia. All this was coupled with strong statements about
the African liberation struggle's continuing and the rejection
of any form of linkage. But the Russians wanted SALT, and
the Russians knew that negotiations might be impaired, and
ratification certainly affected, by their actions in other foreign policy spheres. It was thus possible to hold back the
inevitable tide of history for a time.

The circumstances were different when the decision to
hold Afghanistan had to be taken. Not only did the Soviet
Union have little to lose in Washington by bending détente
to the breaking point, but also it had a great deal to lose
among its own restive Moslem population if the Moslem re-
bellion in Afghanistan were permitted to continue unchal-
lenged. If SALT had been accorded better chances in the
Senate, or if NATO were still vacillating over accepting new
American arms, the decision might have been different. It
might have been considered sufficient to send massive rein-
forcements of Soviet advisers across the border to help fight

the rebels, which would not have upset a status quo the United States did not like but had accepted since 1978. But an invasion force was sent instead, and Soviet-American relations plummeted, just as they had after the previous invasions the Soviet Union feels necessary to stage about once a decade. Just as they improved after the 1956 Hungarian and the 1968 Czechoslovak fighting receded a bit from memory, so will they improve after Afghanistan. Unless there is an absolute reversal of Soviet policies, however, akin to the 1978 switch of the Chinese, spectacular improvement of relations is unlikely.

The entire history of Russia's relations with the outside world has been one of little steps toward reconciliation and acceptance, and sometimes, in Lenin's phrase about a different situation, one step forward and two steps back. When one stands back and measures the incremental progress of a decade or two, however, it is sometimes quite considerable.

Those who carry on the daily work of these relations believe that the West must continue to seek modest but solid gains, hoping for a change for the better in the Soviet Union but not seeking to influence that change in the Western or any other particular direction. This does not rule out encouraging the modernizers by choices of policy, but it does rule out trying to influence the direction of modernization. The West cannot do this and should not try to, no matter how tempting it might be or how much the Soviet Union attempts to interfere in the domestic course of the rest of the world.

There are internal factors that will influence the Soviet Union's course, however. Slowly but certainly, the Soviet people are becoming more important in the considerations of the leadership. Public opinion doesn't count for very much, but it counts for more than it used to. Russians worry about their image in the world, and the leadership, although insulated from much of this concern, has begun to notice these worries. And finally, the standard of living is slowly improving, setting off the familiar cycle of rising expectations. These trends have always been present in Soviet society, but they were so minuscule in previous periods—the fifties, for example—that their growth represents an entirely new stage entering the eighties.

The best chance for the West, however, is the existence of the Soviet triangle. American politicians can follow the example of American businessmen in Moscow: If the climate isn't favorable, go south to China, where American technical help and trade are paid for, not only in dollars and raw materials, but in behavior that more nearly conforms to the idea of détente than what the Soviet Union has been practicing. In the broad range of relations—academic exchanges, business and equipment deals, joint exploitation of resources, arguing for the independence of small nations, treatment of resident Westerners, even level of espionage activity—the Chinese seem easier and better to deal with. This doesn't mean that the West should abandon the Russians: Russia is far too important, particularly for the Europeans, and its isolation would be as dangerous and touchy as its presence in world councils. But the triangle can be used as a constant reminder in dealing with the Soviet Union that there is, in fact, a competitor to think about. That is pressure, it is true, but it is pressure of a far gentler kind than contributing to an armed confrontation, and perhaps as effective.

The one place where this use of the alternative partner will not work for the United States is in strategic security affairs.

Eventually, the Americans must deal with the Russians, and the Russians with the Americans, in SALT. But even in the arms limitation talks that lie ahead, there is a place for the triangle. China can serve as an example to the Soviet Union of how détente could work, if behavior in other areas of foreign policy were more reasonable. The Russians can call this linkage, if they wish, but they may wish to respond by working for stability in parts of the world that, because of their influence, are not very stable now, and to see the results for mutual security at the negotiating table and in the ratification process in the United States Senate.

The invasion of Afghanistan seemed to sweep all these considerations aside. When the Red Army moved across the border, détente was as much a victim as the Afghan people. Linkage was restored; after years of denying that such a policy existed, the Carter administration withdrew the SALT II treaty from Senate consideration. The Olympic games were threatened, and as many of the benefits of détente as could be were revoked, from extra wheat sales, technology transfers, and scientific exchanges to fishing rights.

These actions were based on Washington's contention that the Soviet Union had brought about the greatest threat to peace since World War II. The United States' allies as well as its adversaries took issue with this claim; Vietnam, Korea, and the various Mideast conflicts were cited as greater dangers, on the one hand, and on the other, the Carter administration was widely accused of overreacting in an election year in which a main issue was lack of presidential leadership.

But the Soviet invasion did seem to go against every rule of restraint in the unwritten code of détente that the Soviet Union had been following. The West, of course, had long argued that the Soviet-backed incursions into South Yemen, Ethiopia, and Angola had badly bent if not broken the rules. Afghanistan removed any question. For one thing, it was worse even than the earlier invasions of Hungary and Czechoslovakia, because it extended Soviet rule into an area previously nonaligned. Of equal importance seemed to be the cumulative effect of Soviet Third World actions, not only on Washington, but also on American public opinion. Americans and others in the West spoke of a red tide, moving

from country to country, and both they and their governments had the added anxiety of seeing the wave approaching
the oil supplies of the West and Japan in the Persian Gulf.

The United States-led reaction did not succeed in rolling
back the Russians, nor was it realistically intended to. But it
did hurt, in soft and hard ways, as Communist officials concede. The 104 votes in the General Assembly against the
Soviet position, the condemnation of the Islamic nations,
and the dampening of the Olympic celebration in Moscow,
they say, all have been registered in Soviet public opinion,
and despite widespread public support of the government's
explanations for the move into Afghanistan, some questions
are being asked. Soviet officials dismiss all of these moves as
American-led hysteria. But Soviet citizens may ask themselves why it is that the Americans are so powerful that they
can line up 103 nations with them, including many the Russians thought were their friends. Other effects will be slower
in coming: resentment among the Soviet Moslem population—some of whose relatives moved into Afghanistan to escape Stalin's policies decades ago—and the cuts in consumer
goods supplies that will result from the grain and technology
boycotts.

Endangering relations with the United States and com-
plicating the already difficult domestic situation are effects
that the Soviet leadership must have measured and not dismissed lightly. Why, then, did they order the armies across
the border? Intended and unintended consequences must be
considered.

As far as snubbing the Americans and being snubbed by
them goes, certainly there are elements in the Soviet leadership just as happy to have a period of national unity and
belt-tightening to counteract the creeping consumerism of
recent years. Soviet officials have privately expressed yearn-
ings for the safe old years when blue jeans and jazz were
banned as Western decadence on the orders of Stalin, the

same safe leader who knew how to rally Russians behind national goals. Others believe that the easy dependence on American grain to cover the problems of Soviet agriculture was a bad thing, too. Management people admired and appreciated the American, Japanese, and German technology they were being supplied, but worried that it made it too easy to neglect Soviet research in some fields. In any case, past experience has demonstrated that technology boycotts are neither airtight nor of long duration. But when all of these measures from the outside are added up, they amount to a reinforcement of the Russian siege mentality, the way of thinking that has limited international contacts, domestic economic development, and political liberalization since the time of the czars.

This mentality played an important part in the decision to move into Afghanistan, Communist officials say—if not the most important part. A resurgence of the old fears of encirclement, with China and the United States profiting from the unrest in the Islamic world to hit at the USSR through turbulent Afghanistan, is the justification given for the invasion. The officials add to this threat another one from the West: a dangerous West Germany newly armed with American nuclear missiles.

Here is where the intended—or unavoidable but acceptable—consequences come in. Russian officials say the American reaction surprised them, but only in its degree. They expected, and were quite willing to accept, some kind of response because the alternatives, in their view, would have been far worse. To let the Moslem uprising in Afghanistan continue at a time of high volatility in Iran and other neighboring Moslem nations was a far greater danger, in this view, than any worsening of the already low level of relations with the Americans.

Any talk of pushing through Pakistan toward the oft-mentioned warm water ports is conspicuously missing from such explanations. As with the China hysteria that always emerges in conversations with Soviet and other Communist officials, care must be taken to distinguish between the real and the propaganda promotion. There are times in Soviet politics when a line is put forward, and everyone, from teacher and artist to press spokesman, echoes it, at official functions and social occasions. That is the danger with the encirclement-defensive argument about Afghanistan. After the invasion, it was being stressed not only in private conversations with trusted sources, but in Op Ed pieces written for the West by Soviet journalists, the dispatches of Western correspondents in Moscow, and even in paid advertisements.

But the argument has internal consistency, and it conforms to past actions of the Soviet Union: hitting at weak links, not challenging the United States directly, and above all, acting with the other elements of the triangle in mind. The Soviet Union, this view says, is certainly stronger than either China or Germany, but it has reason to be wary of them, particularly when it considers their potential strength if the United States comes to their aid.

Direct conflict with the United States had been successfully avoided, and the unwillingness of the United States to be drawn into such conflicts after Vietnam encouraged the Soviet Union to take bolder actions in the Third World.

Yet, in this Communist view, the Americans were working indirectly against Soviet interests during this period, and particularly from 1978 on. They arranged for ground radar stations for the Chinese and otherwise strengthened China's armed forces, whether it was by training scientists or by building up industry. On the other side of the Soviet borders, the Americans were busily persuading the Germans, Italians, British, and other NATO members to accept missiles that could reach far into the Soviet Union, creating an entirely new situation in Central Europe.

In such accounts, the terms of NATO and facts like the reservations of some of the NATO members about the cruise and Pershing missiles are swept aside, and the old and feared German enemy remains. With China, the defensive nature of the American arms technology is ignored.

A Soviet dissident social scientist now in the West had measured public opinion during the Russians' previous invasion, that of Czechoslovakia, and found that citizens supported their government by an overwhelming majority. They did not fear the Czechs and Slovaks. They feared the Germans and thought that loosening Communist Party control, as the Czechoslovak reformers had done, left Czechoslovakia, and hence the Soviet Union, open to the German threat.

The social scientist left before the Afghan crisis, but from his sources in Moscow he was able to report that fear of China played an equally large part in the equally widespread acceptance of that invasion.

There are facts and explanations to counter these fears and anxieties, but the Soviet people do not hear them. The United States urged the Germans to accept a new generation of missiles, and the Germans did accept them, because of a prior Soviet move in aiming new SS-20 missiles at Western Europe. The average Russian has never heard of these SS-20s. But he or she has heard of the 20 million dead the Germans inflicted on Russia in World War II. Little has appeared in the Soviet press about the new moderate policies of the Chinese leaders. What does appear is relentless propaganda about their plans to wage war.

The Soviet Union sought to explain the battlefield reverses of its Afghan clients as early as 1978 with the charge that the Chinese, who have a short border with Afghanistan, and the Pakistanis, with American help, were aiding the Moslem rebels. American reports that such arming took place only after the invasion—as an effect, not a cause—are not reported accurately in the Soviet Union.

When the United States' role in making the Russians feel threatened from the West and South is coupled with the actions of the Americans in bilateral relations with Russia, it is easy, in the Soviet view, to conclude that not very much is at stake if one displeases the Americans. From the time of Watergate, when the best President and Secretary of State the Russians could imagine working with were pushed from power, Moscow has seen less and less advantage in détente and more and more in stretching détente to the limit. Human rights, defense budget increases, the strengthening of NATO, and above all, the switch to China—all made the United States an unattractive partner. Suggestions that Soviet actions played a role in American reactions are dismissed.

With nothing to lose by offending the United States, but a great deal to lose by doing nothing, in the Soviet view, the decision was clear: send in the troops, install a Janos Kadar, and clean up a situation that the Soviet Union may not have caused and certainly could not continue to tolerate. According to some officials, the first Afghan coup of 1978 was supported, but not engineered, from the Soviet Union, and the real trouble began when the Russians locked themselves into a friendship and aid treaty with that shaky first regime of Mohammed Nur Taraki. In any case, it took some time to get a Moscow-approved leader installed. Like Hungary's Kadar, the puppet Babrak Karmal was detested by most of his countrymen. But there is a certain parallel in the first actions of both men: placate nationalism and religious feeling, stop the worst excesses of their predecessors, and try to build a consensus on a base of accepting the inevitability of the Soviet occupation.

The neutrality for Afghanistan, suggested as a compromise solution by the West European nations to preserve Afghan sovereignty and Soviet security, has as little a role in such a plan as did the neutrality the Hungarians wanted. Imre Nagy, the Hungarian premier who made the plea, was kidnapped from his embassy sanctuary and executed.

Soviet security needs, as seen from Moscow, are best served by Soviet troops. This is why the Red Army is still encamped at its line of furthest advance in World War II, in East Germany, and why even loyal Communist allies have to put up with Soviet garrisons for decades. Can any invasion be defensive? The Soviets (and the Chinese a year before them, in Vietnam) argue that it can: not defensive against the Afghans, who were threatening no one, but against the other elements of the triangle.

Implicit in this version is, of course, the thought that the Soviet Union has no intention of following up with a move into the next country, whether Iran or Pakistan, and a push toward the Gulf and Western oil lines. It is stressed that this is not because the hasty formation of an American firemen's force will deter them; the Russians may be only on a par with the Americans in strategic arms and tactical weapons, but in their part of the world they are far ahead in the ability to move troops and supply them.

Many reasons are cited for the lack of further aggressive plans on the part of the Russians: the possibility of escalation to the nuclear level; the fact that there is trouble enough trying to tame a small Moslem nation, in terms of loss of face in the Third World; losses of sons for Soviet families, the pall over the Olympic games, and the strain on the economy caused by the Western embargo and the priorities of the military; the lack of real oil needs; and the eventual hope of restoring détente.

Soviet officials dispute the CIA claim that their country will become a net importer of oil sometime in the mid-eighties and contend they have neither the wish nor the need to seek new sources abroad. It is true that the rate of increase in production is declining. But new methods of raising oil from old fields are being tried and, although costly, are effective. Certainly they are far less costly than trying to seize the oil of another Moslem nation. It is akin to the argument used by Americans opposing the establishment of bases and an emergency force to fight for Persian Gulf oil: take the money and explore for more at home.

As regards détente, the final reason for moderating Soviet behavior, it is noteworthy that both the Soviet and American leadership were careful not to pronounce its death sentence or announce the rebirth of the Cold War in the angry exchanges that followed Afghanistan. President Carter would frequently refer to the continuing need for a SALT agreement in his speeches condemning the invasion. President Brezhnev, dealing with what the Soviets considered irrational American behavior, nevertheless kept to the theme that détente was still there, to be salvaged, and if not by the Americans, by the French or the Germans.

They were both recognizing the advantages of détente to both sides, whether in trade and grain sales or slowing the arms race. This recognition is shared by the Europeans, both Eastern and Western. The former benefit by a more liberal atmosphere that permits looser domestic rule and contacts with the West; the latter by doing more business and having to spend less on their armies.

But it can be argued convincingly that the Soviet Union has violated every facet of détente, in the process reviving the Cold War all by itself. Certainly a large part of the outside world believes this to be true. The Soviets disagree. Everything that happened in Afghanistan, they say, was within the rules of international relations as they interpret them. Afghanistan did not fall within the limits of the Brezhnev Doctrine, which proclaims the right of interference in the affairs of any member of the Soviet Bloc. It was covered, instead, by a doctrine that provides military help as "internationalist duty" to any revolutionary regime. Once this duty is performed, of course, the nation becomes a member of the Soviet Bloc and subject to permanent guardianship.

These justifications aside, the invasion did have the important effect of defining détente—for the United States, for the Soviet Union, and for the world.

Afghanistan left the line clearly drawn, as it had been drawn between the Soviet Bloc and Greece and Turkey by the Truman Doctrine of the 1940s. If you cross the line, you lose détente. With that loss, you lose many things that are more important to Russia than to America, and one thing equally important to both: the nuclear balance. If there is a lesson here for the Soviet Union, so is there, too, for the United States. As long as it considers actions in the Third World, through covert means or strike forces, it risks the danger of a countermove by the Russians.

But the main message is for the Soviet leaders of the eighties, who now know that they cannot hope to build a new colonial empire, or perhaps even to hold on to all of what they already have, if there are liberation movements within it—if they want to maintain détente at the same time.

It will be the role of the American policymakers to decide whether to freeze détente and make it a less desirable alternative, or to enrich it, making it a much better option than trying to add another underdeveloped country to the Soviet empire.

If there is any question about which course is better, it seems likely that China will serve more and more as a model of the advantages cooperation with the United States can bring—without loss of sovereignty, ideology, or freedom of action in world affairs.

If China is not an attractive example for the Soviet leadership, it certainly will have an attraction for those forces in Russia outside the leadership who believe that better relations with the West bring only advantages—for the development of the economy, for an improved standard of living, and for a liberalized cultural life. As the arrest of Andrei Sakharov showed, the climate after Afghanistan weakened these forces. But it is possible that the limits now clearly sketched out will strengthen them once more. The Soviet leadership knows what those limits are. It observed the old ones in Greece and Turkey; no further westward push has taken place in Europe for 30 years because Russia must calculate that America would respond. With no place forward to go, eventually the Russians went back, toward a better relationship with the West. The world of the eighties is a much more complicated place than the Europe of the forties; Southern Africa alone has great potential for East-West conflict, and the rest of the Third World is dotted with trouble spots where lines will be hard to draw. But, as Afghanistan showed the Russians, and Vietnam the United States, such conflicts produce no easy victories but do produce difficulties in world public opinion, in social and economic strains at home. The arguments against them are all the stronger when the alternative is considered: détente, the relaxation of tension between the world's two great powers, with the chance, and hope, that real cooperation will some day develop.

Index